John Wright

Prayers for Priest and People

The parish and the home - a book of services and devotions for clerical and lay

workers

John Wright

Prayers for Priest and People
The parish and the home - a book of services and devotions for clerical and lay workers

ISBN/EAN: 9783337117955

Printed in Europe, USA, Canada, Australia, Japan

Cover: Foto ©Lupo / pixelio.de

More available books at **www.hansebooks.com**

Prayers

for

Priest and People

the

Parish and the Home

*A Book of Services and Devotions
for Clerical and Lay Workers*

EDITED BY

REV. JOHN WRIGHT, D.D.

*Author of "Early Bibles of America" and "Early
Prayer Books of America"*

St. Paul, Minn.
THE WRIGHT PUBLISHING COMPANY
1898

Copyright, 1898,
BY JOHN WRIGHT.

PRESS OF EVANS & COMPANY,
ST. PAUL, MINN.

PREFACE.

The material of this book has been accumulating for several years, chiefly through the contributions of representative Church clergymen. Widely known men, who have given their best energies to special lines of thought and work, were invited to formulate certain prayers. A response in nearly every case was promptly given. One, who has long been interested in explorations in Egypt, contributed the "Prayers for the Harmony of Revelation and Science." Another, who has frequently written and spoken on the subject of Christian Socialism, penned the "Prayers for the Employer and the Employed." A third, associated with work among youth, wrote several prayers for Sunday Schools, and a fourth, through long years a worker among young men, is responsible for several of the devotions that relate to this class. Under the headings, "Prayers for a Vestry Meeting," "Prayers for Graces and Virtues," "Family Prayers," and in various other places in the book, may be found forms of devotion that appear for the first time. The new prayers are over one hundred in number. The writers, with a few exceptions, made it a condition that their names should not be mentioned, and this condition will be sacredly observed.

Bishops Huntington, Gillespie and Quintard, and the late Bishops Brown, Paddock and Coxe, permitted the introduction of prayers they had prepared for use in their own dioceses. Bishop Coxe especially desired a place in the book for the hymn entitled, "Gloria Christi." This has been published before, but the Bishop enlarged and revised it as it now appears. In his last letter concerning it he wrote, "Every line of it is a blow aimed at Socinianism." The hymn has been placed among the offices for the sick, for the reason that "Gloria Christi," with its many titles of our Lord, should be especially comforting to the sick and the afflicted.

An effort has been made to accentuate the teachings of the Christian year, by printing under the collect for each Sunday other prayers, selected adapted or contributed.

In making selections of prayers, the Latin, Greek, German and other rituals, both ancient and modern, have been consulted. A generous use has been made of the Mozarabic rite, from recent translations.

The book, while constructed upon Catholic lines, has not been prepared for any one school of thought in the Church, but is intended to represent a breadth of views. To this end, under each heading may be found a variety of prayers, so that a selection can be made according to the preference of the person using the manual.

Aside from the offices for the clergy, are many forms and devotions that should render the book useful to the laity. Subjects that pertain to the religion of every-day life have been expressly amplified.

J. W.

St. Paul, Minn., Epiphany, 1898.

CONTENTS.

	PAGE
THE RITES OF THE CHURCH	1
OCCASIONAL OFFICES	94
MISSIONARY PRAYERS	104
PRAYERS FOR THE CHURCH AND THE CLERGY	113
PRAYERS FOR THE PARISH AND PARISH ORGANIZATIONS	118
PRAYERS FOR THE HOME	135
PRAYERS FOR THE STATE AND NATION	153
PRAYERS FOR COLLEGES, SCHOOLS AND CHARITABLE INSTITUTIONS	156
PRAYERS RELATING TO SOCIAL SUBJECTS	160
PRAYERS FOR THE HARMONY OF REVELATION AND SCIENCE	161
PRAYERS FOR GRACES AND VIRTUES	162
SPECIAL THANKSGIVINGS	165
PRAYERS FOR THE BEGINNING AND THE ENDING OF THE YEAR	168
COLLECTS OF THE CHRISTIAN YEAR	170
OTHER COLLECTS FROM THE BOOK OF COMMON PRAYER	206
LENTEN PRAYERS	208
VARIOUS PRAYERS	210

The Apostles' Creed.

I BELIEVE in God the Father Almighty, Maker of heaven and earth:
And in Jesus Christ his only Son our Lord: Who was conceived by the Holy Ghost, Born of the Virgin Mary: Suffered under Pontius Pilate, Was crucified, dead, and buried: He descended into hell; The third day he rose again from the dead: He ascended into heaven, And sitteth on the right hand of God the Father Almighty: From thence he shall come to judge the quick and the dead.
I believe in the Holy Ghost: The holy Catholic Church; The Communion of Saints: The Forgiveness of sins: The Resurrection of the body: And the Life everlasting. Amen.

The Nicene Creed.

I BELIEVE in one God the Father Almighty, Maker of heaven and earth, And of all things visible and invisible:
And in one Lord Jesus Christ, the only-begotten Son of God; Begotten of his Father before all worlds, God of God, Light of Light, Very God of very God; Begotten, not made; Being of one substance with the Father; By whom all things were made: Who for us men and for our salvation came down from heaven, And was incarnate by the Holy Ghost of the Virgin Mary, And was made man: And was crucified also for us under Pontius Pilate; He suffered and was buried: And the third day he rose again according to the Scriptures: And ascended into heaven, And sitteth on the right hand of the Father: And he shall come again, with glory, to judge both the quick and the dead; Whose kingdom shall have no end.
And I believe in the Holy Ghost, The Lord and Giver of Life, Who proceedeth from the Father and the Son; Who with the Father and the Son together is worshipped and glorified; Who spake by the Prophets: And I believe one Catholic and Apostolic Church: I acknowledge one Baptism for the remission of sins: And I look for the Resurrection of the dead, And the Life of the world to come. Amen.

The Rites of the Church.

✣

THE MINISTRATION OF PUBLIC BAPTISM OF INFANTS, TO BE USED IN THE CHURCH.

- *The People are to be admonished, that it is most convenient that Baptism should not be administered but upon Sundays and other Holy-days, or Prayer-days. Nevertheless, (if necessity so require,) Baptism may be administered upon any other day.*

- *There shall be for every Male-child to be baptized, when they can be had, two Godfathers and one Godmother; and for every Female, one Godfather and two Godmothers; and Parents shall be admitted as Sponsors, if it be desired.*

- *When there are children to be baptized, the Parents or Sponsors shall give knowledge thereof, before the beginning of Morning Prayer, to the Minister. And then the Godfathers and Godmothers, and the People with the Children, must be ready at the Font, either immediately after the last Lesson at Morning Prayer, or else immediately after the last Lesson at Evening Prayer, as the Minister by his discretion shall appoint. And the Minister coming to the Font, (which is then to be filled with pure Water,) and standing there, shall say,*

Hath this Child already been baptized, or no?

¶ *If they answer, No: then shall the Minister proceed as followeth, the people all standing until the Lord's Prayer.*

Dearly beloved, forasmuch as all men are conceived and born in sin; and our Saviour Christ saith, None can enter into the kingdom of God, except he be regenerate and born anew of Water and of the Holy Ghost; I beseech you to call upon God the Father, through our Lord Jesus Christ, that of his bounteous mercy he will grant to *this Child* that which by nature *he* cannot have; that *he* may be baptized with Water and the Holy Ghost, and received into Christ's holy Church, and be made *a* living *member* of the same.

¶ *Then shall the Minister say.*

Let us pray.

Almighty and everlasting God, who of thy great mercy didst save Noah and his family in the ark from perishing by water; and also didst safely lead the children of Israel thy people through the Red Sea, figuring thereby thy holy Baptism; and by the baptism of thy well-beloved Son Jesus Christ in the river Jordan, didst sanctify Water to the mystical washing away of sin; We beseech thee, for thine infinite mercies, that thou wilt mercifully look upon *this Child;* wash *him* and sanctify *him* with the Holy Ghost; that *he*, being delivered from thy wrath, may be received into the ark of Christ's Church; and being stedfast in faith, joyful through hope, and rooted in charity, may so pass the waves of this troublesome world, that finally *he* may come to the land of everlasting life, there to reign with thee, world without end; through Jesus Christ our Lord. *Amen.*

¶ *Or this.*

Almighty and immortal God, the aid of all who need, the helper of all who flee to thee for succour, the life of those who believe, and the resurrection of the dead; We call upon thee for *this Infant*, that *he*, coming to thy holy Baptism, may receive remission of sin, by spiritual regeneration. Receive *him*, O Lord, as thou hast promised by thy well-beloved Son, saying, Ask, and ye shall have; seek, and ye shall find; knock, and it shall be opened unto you. So give now unto us who ask; let us who seek, find; open the gate unto us who knock; that *this Infant* may enjoy the everlasting benediction of thy heavenly washing, and may come to the eternal kingdom which thou hast promised by Christ our Lord. *Amen.*

¶ *Then the Minister shall say as followeth; or else shall pass immediately to the Questions addressed to the*

Sponsors. But Note, *That in every church the intermediate parts of the Service shall be used, once at least in every month, (if there be a baptism,) for the better instructing of the People in the grounds of Infant Baptism.*

Hear the words of the Gospel, written by St. *Mark*, in the tenth Chapter, at the thirteenth Verse.

They brought young children to Christ, that he should touch them : and his disciples rebuked those that brought them. But when Jesus saw it, he was much displeased, and said unto them, Suffer the little children to come unto me, and forbid them not : for of such is the kingdom of God. Verily I say unto you, Whosoever shall not receive the kingdom of God as a little child, he shall not enter therein. And he took them up in his arms, put his hands upon them, and blessed them.

¶ *After the Gospel is read, the Minister shall make this brief* Exhortation *upon the words of the Gospel.*

Beloved, ye hear in this Gospel the words of our Saviour Christ, that he commanded the children to be brought unto him; how he blamed those who would have kept them from him; how he exhorteth all men to follow their innocency. Ye perceive how, by his outward gesture and deed, he declared his good will toward them; for he embraced them in his arms, he laid his hands upon them, and blessed them. Doubt ye not, therefore, but earnestly believe, that he will likewise favourably receive *this* present *Infant;* that he will embrace *him* with the arms of his mercy; that he will give unto *him* the blessing of eternal life, and make *him partaker* of his everlasting kingdom.

Wherefore, we being thus persuaded of the good will of our heavenly Father towards *this Infant*, declared by his Son Jesus Christ; and nothing doubting but that he favourably alloweth this charitable work of ours in bringing *this Infant* to his holy Baptism; let us faithfully and devoutly give thanks unto him, and say,

Almighty and everlasting God, heavenly Father, We give thee humble thanks, That thou hast vouchsafed to call us to the knowledge of thy grace, and faith in thee: Increase this knowledge, And confirm this faith in us evermore. Give thy Holy Spirit to *this Infant*, That *he* may be born again, And be made *an heir* of everlasting salvation; Through our Lord Jesus Christ, Who liveth and reigneth with thee and the Holy Spirit, Now and forever. Amen.

¶ *Then shall the Minister speak unto the Godfathers and Godmothers on this wise.*

Dearly beloved, ye have brought *this Child* here to be baptized; ye have prayed that our Lord Jesus Christ would vouchsafe to receive *him*, to release *him* from sin, to sanctify *him* with the Holy Ghost, to give *him* the kingdom of heaven, and everlasting life. Ye have heard also that our Lord Jesus Christ hath promised in his Gospel to grant all these things that ye have prayed for: which promise he, for his part, will most surely keep and perform.

Wherefore, after this promise made by Christ, *this Infant* must also faithfully, for *his* part, promise by you that are *his* sureties, (until *he* come of age to take it upon *himself*,) that *he* will renounce the devil and all his works, and constantly believe God's holy Word, and obediently keep his commandments.

¶ *The Minister shall then demand of the Sponsors as followeth; the Questions being considered as addressed to them severally, and the Answers to be made accordingly.*

I demand therefore,

Dost thou, in the name of this Child, renounce the devil and all his works, the vain pomp and glory of the world, with all covetous desires of the same, and the sinful desires of the flesh, so that thou wilt not follow, nor be led by them?

Answer. I renounce them all; and, by God's help, will endeavour not to follow, nor be led by them.

Minister. Dost thou believe all the Articles of the Christian Faith, as contained in the Apostles' Creed?

Answer. I do.

Minister. Wilt thou be baptized in this Faith?

Answer. That is my desire.

Minister. Wilt thou then obediently keep God's holy will and commandments, and walk in the same all the days of thy life?

Answer. I will, by God's help.

¶ *Then shall the Minister say.*

O merciful God, grant that the old Adam in *this Child* may be so buried, that the new man may be raised up in *him*. *Amen.*

Grant that all sinful affections may die in *him*, and that all things belonging to the Spirit may live and grow in *him*. *Amen.*

Grant that *he* may have power and strength to have victory, and to triumph, against the devil, the world, and the flesh. *Amen.*

Grant that whosoever is here dedicated to thee by our office and ministry, may also be endued with heavenly virtues, and everlastingly rewarded, through thy mercy, O blessed Lord God, who dost live, and govern all things, world without end. *Amen.*

Almighty, everliving God, whose most dearly beloved Son Jesus Christ, for the forgiveness of our sins, did shed out of his most precious side both water and blood; and gave commandment to his disciples, that they should go teach all nations, and baptize them In the Name of the Father, and of the Son, and of the

Holy Ghost; Regard, we beseech thee, the supplications of thy congregation; sanctify this Water to the mystical washing away of sin; and grant that *this Child*, now to be baptized therein, may receive the fulness of thy grace, and ever remain in the number of thy faithful children; through Jesus Christ our Lord. *Amen.*

¶ *Then the Minister shall take the Child into his hands, and shall say to the Godfathers and Godmothers,*

Name this Child.

¶ *And then, naming it after them, he shall dip it in the Water discreetly, or shall pour Water upon it, saying,*

N. I baptize thee In the Name of the Father, and of the Son, and of the Holy Ghost. Amen.

¶ *Then the Minister shall say,*

We receive this Child into the congregation of Christ's flock, and do *sign *him* with the sign of the Cross, in token that hereafter *he* shall not be ashamed to confess the faith of Christ crucified, and manfully to fight under his banner, against sin, the world, and the devil; and to continue Christ's faithful soldier and servant unto *his* life's end. Amen.

*Here the Minister shall make a Cross upon the Child's forehead.

¶ *If those who present the Infant shall desire the sign of the Cross to be omitted, although the Church knoweth no worthy cause of scruple concerning the same, yet in that case, the Minister may omit that part of the above which followeth the Immersion, or the pouring of Water on the Infant.*

¶ *Then shall the Minister say,*

Seeing now, dearly beloved brethren, that *this Child* is regenerate, and grafted into the body of Christ's Church, let us give thanks unto Almighty God for these benefits; and with one accord make our prayers unto him, that *this Child* may lead the rest of *his* life according to this beginning.

¶ *Then shall be said, all kneeling.*

Our Father, who art in heaven, Hallowed be thy Name. Thy kingdom come. Thy will be done on earth, As it is in heaven. Give us this day our daily bread. And forgive us our trespasses, as we forgive those who trespass against us. And lead us not into temptation; But deliver us from evil. Amen.

¶ *Then shall the Minister say.*

We yield thee hearty thanks, most merciful Father, that it hath pleased thee to regenerate *this Infant* with thy Holy Spirit, to receive *him* for thine own *Child* by adoption, and to incorporate *him* into thy holy Church. And humbly we beseech thee to grant, that *he*, being dead unto sin, and living unto righteousness, and being buried with Christ in his death, may crucify the old man, and utterly abolish the whole body of sin; and that, as *he is* made *partaker* of the death of thy Son, he may also be *partaker* of his resurrection; so that finally, with the residue of thy holy Church, *he* may be *an inheritor* of thine everlasting kingdom; through Christ our Lord. *Amen.*

¶ *Then, all standing up, the Minister shall say to the Godfathers and Godmothers this* Exhortation *following.*

Forasmuch as *this Child hath* promised by you *his* sureties to renounce the devil and all his works, to believe in God, and to serve *him*; ye must remember, that it is your parts and duties to see that *this Infant* be taught, so soon as *he* shall be able to learn, what a solemn vow, promise, and profession, *he hath* here made by you. And that *he* may know these things the better, ye shall call upon *him* to hear Sermons; and chiefly ye shall provide, that *he* may learn the Creed, the Lord's Prayer, and the Ten Commandments, and all other things which a Christian ought to know and believe to his soul's health; and that *this Child* may be virtuously brought up lead a godly and a Christian life; remembering always, that Baptism doth represent unto us our profession; which is, to follow the example of our Saviour Christ, and to be made like unto him; that, as he died, and rose again for us, so should we, who are baptized, die from sin, and rise again unto righteousness; continually mortifying all our evil and corrupt affections, and daily proceeding in all virtue and godliness of living.

¶ *Then shall he add, and say,*

Ye are to take care that *this Child* be brought to the Bishop to be confirmed by him, so soon as *he* can say the Creed, the Lord's Prayer, and the Ten Commandments, and *is* sufficiently instructed in the other parts of the Church-Catechism set forth for that purpose.

The Ministration of Private Baptism of Children in Houses.

¶ *The Minister of every Parish shall often admonish the People, that they defer not the Baptism of their Children longer than the first or second Sunday after their birth, or other Holy-day falling between, unless upon a great and reasonable cause.*

¶ *And also he shall warn them, that without like great cause and necessity, they procure not their Children to be baptized at home in their houses. But when need shall compel them so to do, then Baptism shall be administered as followeth.*

¶ *First, let the Minister of the Parish (or in his absence, any other lawful Minister that can be procured) with those who are present, call upon God, and say the Lord's Prayer, and so many of the Collects appointed to be said before in the Form of Public Baptism, as the time and present exigence will suffer. And then, the Child being named by some one who is present, the Minister shall pour Water upon it, saying these words:*

N. I baptize thee In the Name of the Father, and of the Son, and of the Holy Ghost. Amen.

¶ *Then the Minister shall give thanks unto God, and say,*

We yield thee hearty thanks, most merciful Father, that it hath pleased thee to regenerate *this Infant* with thy Holy Spirit, to receive *him* for thine own *Child* by adoption, and to incorporate *him* into thy holy Church. And humbly we beseech thee to grant, that *he*, being dead unto sin, and living unto righteousness, and being buried with Christ in his death, may crucify the old man, and utterly abolish the whole body of sin; and that, as *he is* made *partaker* of the death of thy Son, *he* may also be *partaker* of his resurrection; so that finally, with the residue of thy holy Church, *he* may be *an inheritor* of thine everlasting kingdom; through Christ our Lord. *Amen.*

¶ *And let them not doubt, but that the Child so baptized is lawfully and sufficiently baptized, and ought not to be baptized again. Yet nevertheless, if the Child, which is after this sort baptized, do afterward live, it is expedient that it be brought into the Church, to the intent that if the Minister of the same Parish did himself baptize that Child, the Congregation may be certified of the true Form of Baptism, by him privately before used: In which case, all standing, he shall say thus:*

I certify you, that according to the due and prescribed Order of the Church *at such a time*, and *at such a place*, before divers witnesses, I baptized *this Child;* who *is* now by Baptism incorporated into the Christian Church: for our Lord Jesus Christ doth not deny his grace and mercy unto such Infants, but most lovingly doth call them unto him, as the holy Gospel doth witness to our comfort.

¶ *But if the Child were baptized by any other lawful Minister, then the Minister of the Parish where the Child was born or christened, shall examine whether the same hath been lawfully done. And if the*

Minister shall find, by the answers of such as bring the Child, that all things were done as they ought to be; then shall he not christen the Child again, but shall receive him as one of the flock of true Christian People, saying thus:

I certify you, that in this case all is well done, and according unto due order, concerning the baptizing of *this Child;* who *is* now by Baptism incorporated into the Christian Church: for our Lord Jesus Christ doth not deny his grace and mercy unto such Infants, but most lovingly doth call them unto him, as the holy Gospel doth witness to our comfort.

¶ *Then the Minister shall say as followeth.*

Hear the words of the Gospel, written by St. *Mark*, in the tenth Chapter, at the thirteenth Verse.

They brought young children to Christ, that he should touch them; and his disciples rebuked those that brought them. But when Jesus saw it, he was much displeased, and said unto them, Suffer the little children to come unto me, and forbid them not: for of such is the kingdom of God. Verily I say unto you, Whosoever shall not receive the kingdom of God as a little child, he shall not enter therein. And he took them up in his arms, put his hands upon them, and blessed them.

¶ *After the Gospel is read, the Minister shall make this brief* Exhortation *upon the words of the Gospel.*

Beloved, ye hear in this Gospel the words of our Saviour Christ, that he commanded the children to be brought unto him; how he blamed those who would have kept them from him; how he exhorteth all men to follow their innocency. Ye perceive how, by his outward gesture and deed, he declared his good will toward them; for he embraced them in his arms, he laid his hands upon them, and blessed them.

Doubt ye not therefore, but earnestly believe, that he hath likewise favourably received *this* present *Infant;* that he hath embraced *him* with the arms of his mercy; and, as he hath promised in his holy Word, will give unto *him* the blessing of eternal life, and make *him partaker* of his everlasting kingdom.

Wherefore, we being thus persuaded of the good will of our heavenly Father, declared by his Son Jesus Christ, towards *this Infant*, let us faithfully and devoutly give thanks unto him, and say the Prayer which the Lord himself taught us.

Our Father, who art in heaven, Hallowed be thy Name. Thy kingdom come. Thy will be done on earth, As it is in heaven. Give us this day our daily bread. And forgive us our trespasses, As we forgive those who trespass against us. And lead us not into temptation; but deliver us from evil. Amen.

¶ *Then shall the Minister demand the name of the Child; which being by the Godfathers and Godmothers pronounced, the Minister shall say as followeth.*

Dost thou, in the name of this Child, renounce the devil and all his works, the vain pomp and glory of the world, with all covetous desires of the same, and the sinful desires of the flesh, so that thou wilt not follow, nor be led by them?

Answer. I renounce them all; and, by God's help, will endeavour not to follow, nor be led by them.

Minister. Dost thou believe all the Articles of the Christian Faith, as contained in the Apostles' Creed?

Answer. I do.

Minister. Wilt thou then obediently keep God's holy will and commandments, and walk in the same all the days of thy life?

Answer. I will, by God's help.

¶ *Then the Minister shall say.*

We receive this Child into the congregation of Christ's flock; and do *sign *him* with the sign of the Cross, in token that hereafter *he* shall not be ashamed to confess the faith of Christ crucified, and manfully to fight under his banner, against sin, the world, and the devil; and to continue Christ's faithful soldier and servant unto *his* life's end. Amen.

Here the Minister shall make a Cross upon the Child's forehead.

¶ *The same rule is to be observed here, as to the omission of the sign of the Cross, as in the Public Baptism of Infants.*

¶ *Then shall the Minister say,*

Seeing now, dearly beloved brethren, that *this Child is* regenerate, and grafted into the body of Christ's Church, let us give thanks unto Almighty God for these benefits; and with one accord make our prayers unto him, that *this Child* may lead the rest of *his* life according to this beginning.

¶ *Then shall be said, all kneeling.*

We yield thee hearty thanks, most merciful Father, that it hath pleased thee to regenerate *this Infant* with thy Holy Spirit, to receive *him* for thine own *Child* by adoption, and to incorporate *him* into thy holy Church. And humbly we beseech thee to grant, that *he*, being dead unto sin, and living unto righteousness, and being buried with Christ in his death, may crucify the old man, and utterly abolish the whole body of sin; and that, as *he is* made *partaker* of the death of thy Son, *he* may also be *partaker* of his resurrection; so that finally, with the residue of thy holy Church, *he* may be *an inheritor* of thine everlasting kingdom; through Christ our Lord. *Amen.*

¶ *Then, all standing up, the Minister shall say to the Godfathers and Godmothers this* Exhortation *following.*

Forasmuch as *this Child hath* promised by you *his* sureties to renounce the devil and all his works, to believe in God, and to serve him; ye must remember, that it is your parts and duties to see that *this Infant* be taught, so soon as *he* shall be able to learn, what a solemn vow, promise, and profession, *he hath* here made by you. And that *he* may know these things the better, ye shall call upon *him* to hear Sermons; and chiefly ye shall provide, that *he* may learn the Creed, the Lord's Prayer, and the Ten Commandments, and all other things which a Christian ought to know and believe to his soul's health; and that *this Child* may be virtuously brought up to lead a godly and a Christian life; remembering always, that Baptism doth represent unto us our profession; which is, to follow the example of our Saviour Christ, and to be made like unto him; that, as he died, and rose again for us, so should we, who are baptized, die from sin, and rise again unto righteousness; continually mortifying all our evil and corrupt affections, and daily proceeding in all virtue and godliness of living.

¶ *Then shall he add, and say,*

Ye are to take care that *this Child* be brought to the Bishop to be confirmed by him, so soon as *he* can say the Creed, the Lord's Prayer, and the Ten Commandments, and *is* sufficiently instructed in the other parts of the Church-Catechism set forth for that purpose.

¶ *But if they who bring the Infant to the Church do make such uncertain answers to the Minister's questions, as that it cannot appear that the Child was baptized with water,* In the Name of the Father, and of the Son, and of the Holy Ghost, *(which are essential parts of Baptism,) then let the Minister baptize it in the Form before appointed for Public Baptism of Infants; saving that at the dipping of the Child in the Font, he shall use this Form of words:*

If thou art not already baptized, *N.*, I baptize thee In the Name of the Father, and of the Son, and of the Holy Ghost. Amen.

¶ *If Infant Baptism, and the receiving of Infants baptized in private, are to be at the same time, the Minister may make the Questions to the Sponsors, and the succeeding Prayers, serve for both. And again, after the Immersion, or the pouring of Water, and the receiving into the Church, the Minister may use the remainder of the Service for both.*

THE MINISTRATION OF BAPTISM TO SUCH AS ARE OF RIPER YEARS, AND ABLE TO ANSWER FOR THEMSELVES.

¶ *When any such Persons as are of riper years are to be baptized, timely notice shall be given to the Minister; that so due care may be taken for their examination, whether they be sufficiently instructed in the Principles of the Christian Religion; and that they may be exhorted to prepare themselves, with Prayers and Fasting, for the receiving of this holy Sacrament.*

¶ *And if they shall be found fit, then the Godfathers and Godmothers (the People being assembled upon the Sunday, Holy-day or Prayer-day appointed) shall be ready to present them at the Font, immediately after the second Lesson, either at Morning or Evening Prayer, as the Minister, in his discretion, shall think fit. And standing there, the Minister shall say,*

Hath this Person been already baptized, or no?

¶ *If they answer,* No: *then shall the Minister (the People all standing until the Lord's Prayer) proceed as followeth.*

Dearly beloved, forasmuch as all men are conceived and born in sin, (and that which is born of the flesh is flesh,) and they who are in the flesh cannot please God, but live in sin, committing many actual transgressions; and our Saviour Christ saith, None can enter into the kingdom of God, except he be regenerate and born anew of water and of the Holy Ghost; I beseech you to call upon God the Father, through our Lord Jesus Christ, that of his bounteous goodness he will grant to *these Persons* that which by nature *they* cannot have; that *they* may be baptized with Water and the Holy Ghost, and received into Christ's holy Church, and be made lively *members* of the same.

¶ *Then shall the Minister say.*

Let us pray.

Almighty and everlasting God, who of thy great mercy didst save Noah and his family in the ark from perishing by water; and also didst safely lead the children of Israel thy people through the Red Sea, figuring thereby thy holy Baptism; and by the Baptism of thy well-beloved Son Jesus Christ in the river Jordan, didst sanctify the element of Water to the mystical washing away of sin; We beseech thee, for thine infinite mercies, that thou wilt mercifully look upon *these* thy *Servants;* wash *them* and sanctify *them* with the Holy Ghost; that *they*, being delivered from thy wrath, may be received into the ark of Christ's Church; and being stedfast in faith, joyful through hope, and rooted in charity, may so pass the waves of this troublesome world, that finally *they* may come to the land of everlasting life, there to reign with thee, world without end; through Jesus Christ our Lord. *Amen.*

¶ *Or this.*

Almighty and immortal God, the aid of all who need, the helper of all who flee to thee for succour, the life of those who believe, and the resurrection of the dead; We call upon thee for *these* thy *Servants*, that *they*, coming to thy holy Baptism, may receive remission of *their* sins, by spiritual regeneration. Receive *them*, O Lord, as thou hast promised by thy well-beloved Son, saying, Ask, and ye shall receive; seek, and ye shall find; knock, and it shall be opened unto you. So give now unto us who ask; let us who seek, find; open the gate unto us who knock; that *these* thy *Servants* may enjoy the everlasting benediction of thy heavenly washing, and may come to the eternal kingdom which thou hast promised by Christ our Lord. *Amen*.

* *Then the Minister shall say,*

Hear the words of the Gospel, written by St. *John*, in the third Chapter, beginning at the first Verse.

There was a man of the Pharisees, named Nicodemus, a ruler of the Jews: the same came to Jesus by night, and said unto him, Rabbi, we know that thou art a teacher come from God: for no man can do these miracles that thou doest, except God be with him. Jesus answered and said unto him, Verily, verily, I say unto thee, Except a man be born again, he cannot see the kingdom of God. Nicodemus saith unto him, How can a man be born when he is old? can he enter the second time into his mother's womb, and be born? Jesus answered, Verily, verily, I say unto thee, Except a man be born of water and of the Spirit, he cannot enter into the kingdom of God. That which is born of the flesh is flesh; and that which is born of the Spirit is spirit. Marvel not that I said unto thee, Ye must be born again. The wind bloweth where it listeth, and thou hearest the sound thereof, but canst not tell whence it cometh, and whither it goeth: so is every one that is born of the Spirit.

* *After which he shall say this* Exhortation *following*

Beloved, ye hear in this Gospel the express words of our Saviour Christ, that except a man be born of water and of the Spirit, he cannot enter into the kingdom of God. Whereby ye may perceive the great necessity of this Sacrament, where it may be had. Likewise, immediately before his ascension into heaven, (as we read in the last Chapter of Saint Mark's Gospel,) he gave command to his disciples, saying, Go ye into all the world, and preach the Gospel to every creature. He that believeth and is baptized shall be saved; but he that believeth not shall be damned. Which also showeth unto us the great benefit we reap thereby. For which cause Saint Peter the Apostle, when upon his first preaching of the Gospel many were pricked at the heart, and said to him and the rest of the Apostles, Men and brethren, what shall we do? replied and said unto them, Repent, and be baptized every one of you for the remission of sins, and ye shall receive the gift of the Holy Ghost. For the promise is to you and your children, and to all that are afar off, even as many as the Lord our God shall call. And with many other words exhorted he them, saying, Save yourselves from this untoward generation. For (as the same Apostle testifieth in another place) even Baptism doth also now save us, (not the putting away of the filth of the flesh, but the answer of a good conscience towards God,) by the resurrection of Jesus Christ. Doubt ye not therefore, but earnestly believe, that he will favourably receive *these* present *Persons*, truly repenting, and coming unto him by faith; that he will grant *them* remission of *their* sins, and bestow upon *them* the Holy Ghost; that he will give *them* the blessing of eternal life, and make *them partakers* of his everlasting kingdom.

Wherefore, we being thus persuaded of the good will of our heavenly Father toward *these Persons*, declared by his Son Jesus Christ; let us faithfully and devoutly give thanks to him, and say,

Almighty and everlasting God, heavenly Father, We give thee humble thanks, For that thou hast vouchsafed to call us to the knowledge of thy grace, and faith in thee: Increase this knowledge, And confirm this faith in us evermore. Give thy Holy Spirit to *these* thy *Servants*, That *they* may be born again, And be made *heirs* of everlasting salvation; Through our Lord Jesus Christ, Who liveth and reigneth with thee and the Holy Spirit, Now and for ever. Amen.

¶ *Then the Minister shall speak to the* Persons *to be baptized on this wise.*

Well-beloved, who are come hither desiring to receive holy Baptism, *ye* have heard how the congregation hath prayed, that our Lord Jesus Christ would vouchsafe to receive you and bless you, to release you of your sins, to give you the kingdom of heaven, and everlasting life. *Ye* have heard also, that our Lord Jesus Christ hath promised in his holy Word to grant all those things that we have prayed for; which promise he, for his part, will most surely keep and perform.

Wherefore, after this promise made by Christ, *ye* must also faithfully, for your part, in the presence of these your Witnesses, and this whole congregation, promise and answer to the following questions.

¶ *The Minister shall then demand of the* Persons *to be baptized as followeth : the Questions being considered as addressed to them severally, and the Answers to be made accordingly.*

Question.

Dost thou renounce the devil and all his works, the vain pomp and glory of the world, with all covetous desires of the same, and the sinful desires of the flesh, so that thou wilt not follow, nor be led by them?

Answer. I renounce them all; and, by God's help, will endeavour not to follow, nor be led by them.

Minister. Dost thou believe all the Articles of the Christian Faith, as contained in the Apostles' Creed?

Answer. I do.

Question. Wilt thou be baptized in this Faith?

Answer. That is my desire.

Question. Wilt thou then obediently keep God's holy will and commandments, and walk in the same all the days of thy life?

Answer. I will, by God's help.

¶ *Then shall the Minister say.*

O Merciful God, grant that the old Adam in *these* thy *Servants* may be so buried, that the new man may be raised up in *them.* Amen.

Grant that all sinful affections may die in *them*, and that all things belonging to the Spirit may live and grow in *them.* Amen.

Grant that *they* may have power and strength to have victory, and to triumph, against the devil, the world, and the flesh. Amen.

Grant that *they*, being here dedicated to thee by our office and ministry, may also be endued with heavenly virtues, and everlastingly rewarded, through thy mercy, O blessed Lord God, who dost live, and govern all things, world without end. *Amen.*

Almighty, everliving God, whose most dearly beloved Son Jesus Christ, for the forgiveness of our sins, did shed out of his most precious side both water and blood; and gave commandment to his disciples, that they should go teach all nations, and baptize them In the Name of the Father, and of the Son, and of the Holy Ghost; Regard, we beseech thee, the supplications of thy congregation; sanctify this Water to the mystical washing away of sin; and grant that *these* thy *Servants*, now to be baptized therein, may receive the fulness of thy grace, and ever remain in the number of thy faithful children; through Jesus Christ our Lord. *Amen.*

¶ *Then shall the Minister take each Person to be baptized by the right hand; and placing him conveniently by the Font, according to his discretion, shall ask the Godfathers and Godmothers the Name; and then shall dip him in the water, or pour water upon him, saying,*

N. I baptize thee In the Name of the Father, and of the Son, and of the Holy Ghost. Amen.

¶ *Then shall the Minister say,*

We receive this Person into the congregation of Christ's flock, and do *sign *him* with the sign of the Cross, in token that hereafter *he* shall not be ashamed to confess the faith of Christ crucified, and manfully to fight under his banner, against sin, the world, and the devil; and to continue Christ's faithful soldier and servant unto *his* life's end. Amen.

**Here the Minister shall make a Cross upon the Person's forehead.*

¶ *The same rule, as to the omission of the sign of the Cross, is to be observed here as in the Baptism of Infants*

¶ *Then shall the Minister say,*

Seeing now, dearly beloved brethren, that *these Persons are* regenerate, and grafted into the body of Christ's Church, let us give thanks unto Almighty God for these benefits; and with one accord make our prayers unto him, that *they* may lead the rest of *their* life according to this beginning.

¶ *Then shall be said the* Lord's Prayer, *all kneeling.*

Our Father, who art in heaven, Hallowed be thy Name. Thy kingdom come. Thy will be done on earth, As it is in heaven. Give us this day our daily bread. And forgive us our trespasses. As we forgive those who trespass against us. And lead us not into temptation; But deliver us from evil. Amen.

We yield thee hearty thanks, most merciful Father, that it hath pleased thee to regenerate *these* thy *Servants* with thy Holy Spirit, to receive *them* for thine own *children* by adoption, and to incorporate *them* into thy holy Church. And humbly we beseech thee to grant, that *they*, being dead unto sin, and living unto righteousness, and being buried with Christ in his death, may crucify the old man, and utterly abolish the whole body of sin; and that, as *they are* made *partakers* of the death of thy Son, *they* may also be *partakers* of his resurrection; so that finally, with the residue of thy holy Church, *they* may be *inheritors* of thine everlasting kingdom; through Christ our Lord. *Amen.*

¶ *Then, all standing up, the Minister shall use this* Exhortation *following; speaking to the Godfathers and Godmothers first.*

Forasmuch as *these Persons have* promised, in your presence, to renounce the devil and all his works, to believe in God, and to serve him; ye must remember, that it is your part and duty to put *them* in mind, what a solemn vow, promise, and profession, *they have* now made before this congregation, and especially before you *their* chosen witnesses. And ye are also to call upon *them* to use all diligence to be rightly instructed in God's holy Word; that so *they* may grow in grace, and in the knowledge of our Lord Jesus Christ, and live godly, righteously, and soberly, in this present world.

¶ *And then, speaking to the baptized* Persons, *he shall proceed and say,*

And as for you, who have now by Baptism put on Christ, it is your part and duty also, being made the *children* of God and of the light, by faith in Jesus

Christ, to walk answerably to your Christian calling, and as becometh the children of light; remembering always, that Baptism doth represent unto us our profession; which is, to follow the example of our Saviour Christ, and to be made like unto him; that, as he died, and rose again for us, so should we, who are baptized, die from sin, and rise again unto righteousness; continually mortifying all our evil and corrupt affections, and daily proceeding in all virtue and godliness of living.

¶ *It is expedient that every Person, thus baptized, should be confirmed by the Bishop, so soon after his Baptism as conveniently may be; that so he may be admitted to the Holy Communion.*

¶ *Whereas necessity may require the baptizing of Adults in private houses, in consideration of extreme sickness; the same is hereby allowed in that case. And a convenient number of persons shall be assembled in the house where the Sacrament is to be administered. And in the exhortation,* Well-beloved, *etc., instead of these words,* come hither desiring, *shall be inserted this word* desirous. *And in case of great necessity, the Minister may begin with the questions addressed to the candidate, and end with the thanksgiving following the baptism.*

¶ *If there be occasion for the Office of Infant Baptism and that of Adults at the same time, the Minister shall use the exhortation and one of the prayers next following in the Office for Adults; only, in the exhortation and prayer, after the words,* these Persons, *and* these thy Servants, *adding,* and these Infants. *Then the Minister shall proceed to the questions to be demanded in the cases respectively. After the immersion, or the pouring of water, the prayer shall be as in this service; only, after the words,* these thy Servants, *shall be added,* and these Infants. *After which the remaining part of each service shall be used; first that for Adults, and lastly that for Infants.*

¶ *If any persons, not baptized in their infancy, shall be brought to be baptized before they come to years of discretion to answer for themselves, it may suffice to use the Office for Public Baptism of Infants; or, in case of extreme danger, the Office for Private Baptism; only changing the word* Infant, *for* Child, *or* Person, *as occasion requireth.*

¶ *If there be reasonable doubt concerning the baptism of any person, such person may be baptized in the manner herein appointed; saving that, at the immersion or the pouring of water, the Minister shall use this form of words:*

If thou art not already baptized, *N.*, I baptize thee In the Name of the Father, and of the Son, and of the Holy Ghost. Amen.

INFANT AND ADULT BAPTISM, COMBINED.

Hath this person been already baptized, or no? Hath this child been already baptized, or no?

¶ *If they answer,* No; *then shall the Minister proceed as followeth.*

Dearly beloved, forasmuch as all men are conceived and born in sin, (and that which is born of the flesh is flesh,) and they who are in the flesh cannot please God, but live in sin, committing many actual transgressions; and our Saviour Christ saith, None can enter into the kingdom of God, except he be regenerate and born anew of water and of the Holy Ghost; I beseech you to call upon God the Father, through our Lord Jesus Christ, that of his bounteous goodness, he will grant to *these Persons and these Infants* that which by nature they cannot have; that they may be baptized with Water and the Holy Ghost, and received into Christ's holy Church, and be made lively members of the same.

¶ *Then shall the Minister say,*

Let us pray.

Almighty and everlasting God, who of thy great mercy didst save Noah and his family in the Ark from perishing by water; and also didst safely lead the children of Israel thy people through the Red Sea, figuring thereby thy holy Baptism; and by the Baptism of thy well-beloved Son Jesus Christ, in the river

Jordan, didst sanctify the element of Water to the mystical washing away of sin; We beseech thee, for thine infinite mercies, that thou wilt mercifully look upon *these* thy *Servants and these Infants;* wash them and sanctify them with the Holy Ghost; that they, being delivered from thy wrath, may be received into the ark of Christ's Church; and being stedfast in faith, joyful through hope, and rooted in charity, may so pass the waves of this troublesome world, that finally they may come to the land of everlasting life, there to reign with thee, world without end; through Jesus Christ our Lord. *Amen.*

* *The Minister shall then demand of the Persons to be baptized as follows: the Questions being considered as addressed to them severally, and the answers to be made accordingly.*

Question.

Dost thou renounce the devil and all his works, the vain pomp and glory of the world, with all covetous desires of the same, and the sinful desires of the flesh, so that thou wilt not follow, nor be led by them?

Answer. I renounce them all; and, by God's help, will endeavour not to follow, nor be led by them.

Question. Dost thou believe all the Articles of the Christian Faith, as contained in the Apostles' Creed.

Answer. I do.

Question. Wilt thou be baptized in this Faith?

Answer. That is my desire.

Question. Wilt thou then obediently keep God's holy will and commandments, and walk in the same all the days of thy life?

Answer. I will, by God's help.

* *The Minister shall then demand of the Sponsors as follows: the questions being considered as addressed to them severally, and the answers to be made accordingly.*

I demand therefore,

Dost thou, in the name of this Child, renounce the devil and all his works, the vain pomp and glory of the world, with all covetous desires of the same, and the sinful desires of the flesh, so that thou wilt not follow, nor be led by them?

Answer. I renounce them all; and, by God's help, will endeavour not to follow, nor be led by them.

Minister. Dost thou believe all the Articles of the Christian Faith, as contained in the Apostles' Creed?

Answer. I do.

Minister. Wilt thou be baptized in this Faith?

Answer. That is my desire.

Minister. Wilt thou then obediently keep God's holy will and commandments, and walk in the same all the days of thy life?

Answer. I will, by God's help.

* *Then shall the Minister say,*

O Merciful God, grant that the old Adam in *these Persons and these Infants* may be so buried, that the new man may be raised up in them. *Amen.*

Grant that all sinful affections may die in them, and that all things belonging to the Spirit may live and grow in them. *Amen.*

Grant that they may have power and strength to have victory, and to triumph against the devil, the world, and the flesh. *Amen.*

Grant that they, being here dedicated to thee by our office and ministry, may also be endued with heavenly virtues, and everlastingly rewarded, through thy mercy, O blessed Lord God, who dost live and govern all things, world without end. *Amen.*

Almighty, everliving God, whose most dearly beloved Son Jesus Christ, for the forgiveness of our sins, did shed out of his most precious side both water and blood; and gave commandment to his disciples, that they should go teach all nations, and baptize them In the Name of the Father, and of the Son, and of the Holy Ghost; Regard, we beseech thee, the supplications of thy congregation; sanctify this Water to the mystical washing away of sin; and grant that *these Persons and these Infants* now to be baptized therein, may receive the fulness of thy grace, and ever remain in the number of thy faithful children; through Jesus Christ our Lord. *Amen.*

* *Then shall the Minister take each Person to be baptized by the right hand; and placing him conveniently by the Font, according to his discretion, shall ask the Godfathers and Godmothers the Name; and then shall dip* him *in the water or pour water upon* him, *saying.*

N. I baptize thee In the Name of the Father, and of the Son, and of the Holy Ghost. Amen.

¶ *Then shall the Minister say,*

We receive this Person into the congregation of Christ's flock; and do *sign *him* with the sign of the Cross, in token that hereafter *he* shall not be ashamed to confess the faith of Christ crucified, and manfully to fight under his banner, against sin, the world, and the devil; and to continue Christ's faithful soldier and servant unto *his* life's end. Amen.

**Here the Minister shall make a Cross upon the Person's forehead.*

¶ *Then the Minister shall take the Child into his hands, and shall say to the Godfathers and Godmothers,*

Name this Child.

¶ *And then, naming it after them, he shall dip it in the water discreetly, or shall pour water upon it, saying.*

N. I baptize thee In the Name of the Father, and of the Son, and of the Holy Ghost. Amen.

¶ Then shall the Minister say,

We receive this Child into the congregation of Christ's flock; and do *sign *him* with the sign of the Cross, in token that hereafter *he* shall not be ashamed to confess the faith of Christ crucified, and manfully to fight under his banner, against sin, the world, and the devil; and to continue Christ's faithful soldier and servant unto *his* life's end. Amen.

**Here the Minister shall make a Cross upon the Child's forehead.*

¶ *If those who present the Infant shall desire the sign of the Cross to be omitted, although the Church knoweth no worthy cause of scruple concerning the same, yet in that case, the Minister may omit that part of the above which followeth the Immersion, or the pouring of Water on the Infant.*

¶ *Then shall the Minister say,*

Seeing now, dearly beloved brethren, that *these Persons and these Infants are* regenerate, and grafted into the body of Christ's Church, let us give thanks unto Almighty God for these benefits; and with one accord make our prayers unto him, that they may lead the rest of their life according to this beginning.

¶ *Then shall be said the Lord's Prayer, all kneeling.*

Our Father, who art in heaven, Hallowed be thy Name. Thy kingdom come. Thy will be done on earth, As it is in heaven. Give us this day our daily bread. And forgive us our trespasses, As we forgive those who trespass against us. And lead us not into temptation; But deliver us from evil. Amen.

¶ *Then shall the Minister say,*

We yield thee hearty thanks, most merciful Father, that it hath pleased thee to regenerate *these* thy *Servants* and *these Infants* with thy Holy Spirit, to receive them for thine own children by adoption, and to incorporate them into thy holy Church. And humbly we beseech thee to grant, that they, being dead unto sin, and living unto righteousness, and being buried with Christ in his death, may crucify the old man, and utterly abolish the whole body of sin; and that, as they are made partakers of the death of thy Son, they may also be partakers of his resurrection; so that finally, with the residue of thy holy Church, they may be inheritors of thine everlasting kingdom; through Christ our Lord. *Amen.*

* *Then, all standing up, the Minister shall use this* Exhortation *following; speaking to the Godfathers and Godmothers first.*

Forasmuch as *these Persons have* promised, in your presence, to renounce the devil and all his works, to believe in God, and to serve him; ye must remember, that it is your part and duty to put *them* in mind, what a solemn vow, promise, and profession, *they have* now made before this congregation, and especially before you *their* chosen witnesses. And ye are also to call upon *them* to use all diligence to be rightly instructed in God's holy Word; that so *they* may grow in grace, and in the knowledge of our Lord Jesus Christ; and live godly, righteously, and soberly, in this present world.

* *And then, speaking to the baptized* Persons, *he shall proceed and say,*

And as for you, who have now by Baptism put on Christ, it is your part and duty also, being made the *children* of God and of the light, by faith in Jesus Christ, to walk answerably to your Christian calling, and as becometh the children of light; remembering always, that Baptism representeth unto us our profession; which is, to follow the example of our Saviour Christ, and to be made like unto him; that as he died, and rose again for us, so should we, who are baptized, die from sin, and rise again unto righteousness; continually mortifying all our evil and corrupt affections, and daily proceeding in all virtue and godliness of living.

¶ *Then the Minister shall say to the Godfathers and Godmothers this* Exhortation *following.*

Forasmuch as *this Child hath* promised by you *his* sureties, to renounce the devil and all his works, to believe in God, and to serve him; ye must remember, that it is your parts and duties to see that *this Infant* be taught, so soon as *he* shall be able to learn, what a solemn vow, promise, and profession *he hath* here made by you. And that *he* may know these things the better, ye shall call upon *him* to hear Sermons; and chiefly ye shall provide, that *he* may learn the Creed, the Lord's Prayer, and the Ten Commandments, and all other things which a Christian ought to know and believe to his soul's health; and that *this Child* may be virtuously brought up to lead a godly and a Christian life; remembering always, that Baptism doth represent unto us our profession; which is, to follow the example of our Saviour Christ, and to be made like unto him; that, as he died, and rose again for us, so should we, who are baptized, die from sin, and rise again unto righteousness; continually mortifying all our evil and corrupt affections, and daily proceeding in all virtue and godliness of living.

¶ *Then shall he add, and say,*

Ye are to take care that *this Child* be brought to the Bishop to be confirmed by him, so soon as *he* can say the Creed, the Lord's Prayer, and the Ten Commandments, and *is* sufficiently instructed in the other parts of the Church-Catechism set forth for that purpose.

The Order of Confirmation, or Laying on of Hands Upon Those who are Baptized, and Come to Years of Discretion.

¶ *Upon the day appointed, all that are to be then confirmed, being placed and standing in order before the Bishop, sitting in his chair near to the Holy Table, he, or some other Minister appointed by him, may read this preface following; the People standing until the Lord's Prayer.*

To the end that Confirmation may be ministered to the more edifying of such as shall receive it, the Church hath thought good to order, That none shall be confirmed, but such as can say the Creed, the Lord's Prayer, and the Ten Commandments; and can also answer to such other Questions, as in the short Catechism are contained: which order is very convenient to be observed; to the end that children, being now come to the years of discretion, and having learned what their Godfathers and Godmothers promised for them in Baptism, may themselves, with their own mouth and consent, openly before the Church, ratify and confirm the same; and also promise, that, by the grace of God, they will evermore endeavour themselves faithfully to observe such things, as they, by their own confession, have assented unto.

¶ *Then the Minister shall present unto the Bishop those who are to be confirmed, and shall say,*

Reverend Father in God, I present unto you these children [*or* these persons] to receive the Laying on of Hands.

¶ *Then the Bishop, or some Minister appointed by him, may say,*

Hear the words of the Evangelist Saint *Luke*, in the eighth Chapter of the Book of the *Acts of the Apostles*.

When the apostles which were at Jerusalem heard that Samaria had received the word of God, they sent unto them Peter and John: who, when they were come down, prayed for them, that they might receive the Holy Ghost: (for as yet he was fallen upon none of them: only they were baptized in the name of the Lord Jesus.) Then laid they their hands on them, and they received the Holy Ghost.

¶ *Then shall the Bishop say,*

Do ye here, in the presence of God, and of this congregation, renew the solemn promise and vow that ye made, or that was made in your name, at your Baptism; ratifying and confirming the same; and acknowledging yourselves bound to believe and to do all those things which ye then undertook, or your Sponsors then undertook for you?

¶ *And every one shall audibly answer,*

I do.

Bishop.

Our help is in the Name of the Lord;
Answer. Who hath made heaven and earth.
Bishop. Blessed be the Name of the Lord;
Answer. Henceforth, world without end.
Bishop. Lord, hear our prayer.
Answer. And let our cry come unto thee.
Bishop. Let us pray.

Almighty and everliving God, who hast vouchsafed to regenerate these thy servants by Water and the Holy Ghost, and hast given unto them forgiveness of all their sins; Strengthen them, we beseech thee, O Lord, with the Holy Ghost, the Comforter, and daily increase in them thy manifold gifts of grace: the spirit of wisdom and understanding, the spirit of counsel and ghostly strength, the spirit of knowledge and true godliness; and fill them, O Lord, with the spirit of thy holy fear, now and for ever. *Amen.*

* *Then all of them in order kneeling before the Bishop, he shall lay his hands upon the head of every one severally, saying,*

Defend, O Lord, this thy Child [*or* this thy Servant] with thy heavenly grace; that *he* may continue thine for ever; and daily increase in thy Holy Spirit more and more, until *he* come unto thy everlasting kingdom. Amen.

* *Then shall the Bishop say,*

The Lord be with you.
Answer. And with thy spirit.

* *And all kneeling down, the Bishop shall add,*

Let us pray.

Our Father, who art in heaven, Hallowed be thy Name. Thy kingdom come. Thy will be done on earth, As it is in heaven. Give us this day our daily bread. And forgive us our trespasses, As we forgive those who trespass against us. And lead us not into temptation; But deliver us from evil. Amen.

* *And these Collects.*

Almighty and everliving God, who makest us both to will and to do those things which are good, and acceptable unto thy Divine Majesty; We make our humble supplications unto thee for these thy servants, upon whom, after the example of thy holy Apostles, we have now laid our hands, to certify them, by this sign, of thy favour and gracious goodness towards them. Let thy fatherly hand, we beseech thee, ever be over them; let thy Holy Spirit ever be with them; and so lead them in the knowledge and obedience of thy Word, that in the end they may obtain everlasting life; through our Lord Jesus Christ, who with thee and the Holy Ghost liveth and reigneth ever, one God, world without end. *Amen.*

O Almighty Lord, and everlasting God, vouchsafe, we beseech thee, to direct, sanctify, and govern, both our hearts and bodies, in the ways of thy laws, and in the works of thy commandments; that, through thy most mighty protection, both here and ever, we may be preserved in body and soul; through our Lord and Saviour Jesus Christ. *Amen.*

¶ *Then the Bishop shall bless them, saying thus.*

The Blessing of God Almighty, the Father, the Son, and the Holy Ghost, be upon you, and remain with you for ever. *Amen.*

¶ *And there shall none be admitted to the Holy Communion, until such time as he be confirmed, or be ready and desirous to be confirmed.*

¶ *The Minister shall not omit earnestly to move the Persons confirmed to come, without delay, to the Lord's Supper.*

The Form of Solemnization of Matrimony.

¶ *The laws respecting Matrimony, whether by publishing the Banns in Churches, or by Licence, being different in the several States, every Minister is left to the direction of those laws, in everything that regards the civil contract between the parties.*

¶ *And when the Banns are published, it shall be in the following form:* I publish the Banns of Marriage between *M.* of ——, and *N.* of ——. If any of you know cause, or just impediment, why these two persons should not be joined together in holy Matrimony, ye are to declare it. This is the first [second *or* third] time of asking.

¶ *At the day and time appointed for Solemnization of Matrimony, the Persons to be married shall come into the body of the Church, or shall be ready in some proper house, with their friends and neighbours; and there standing together, the Man on the right hand, and the Woman on the left, the Minister shall say.*

Dearly beloved, we are gathered together here in the sight of God, and in the face of this company, to join together this Man and this Woman in holy Matrimony; which is an honourable estate, instituted of God in the time of man's innocency, signifying unto us the mystical union that is betwixt Christ and his Church: which holy estate Christ adorned and beautified with his presence and first miracle that he wrought in Cana of Galilee, and is commended of Saint Paul to be honourable among all men: and therefore is not by any to be entered into unadvisedly or lightly; but reverently, discreetly, advisedly, soberly, and in the fear of God. Into this holy estate these two persons present come now to be joined. If any man can show just cause, why they may not lawfully be joined together, let him now speak, or else hereafter for ever hold his peace.

¶ *And also speaking unto the Persons who are to be married, he shall say,*

I require and charge you both, as ye will answer at the dreadful day of judgment when the secrets of all hearts shall be disclosed, that if either of you know any impediment, why ye may not be lawfully joined together in Matrimony, ye do now confess it. For be ye well assured, that if any persons are joined together otherwise than as God's Word doth allow, their marriage is not lawful.

¶ *The Minister, if he shall have reason to doubt of the lawfulness of the proposed Marriage, may demand sufficient surety for his indemnification: but if no impediment shall be alleged, or suspected, the Minister shall say to the man,*

M. Wilt thou have this Woman to thy wedded wife, to live together after God's ordinance in the holy estate of Matrimony? Wilt thou love her, comfort her, honour, and keep her in sickness and in health; and, forsaking all others, keep thee only unto her, so long as ye both shall live?

¶ *The Man shall answer,*

I will.

¶ *Then shall the Minister say unto the Woman,*

N. Wilt thou have this Man to thy wedded husband, to live together after God's ordinance in the holy estate of Matrimony? Wilt thou obey him, and serve him, love, honour, and keep him in sickness and in health; and, forsaking all others, keep thee only unto him, so long as ye both shall live?

¶ *The Woman shall answer,*

I will.

¶ *Then shall the Minister say,*

Who giveth this Woman to be married to this Man?

¶ *Then shall they give their troth to each other in this manner. The Minister, receiving the Woman at her father's or friend's hands, shall cause the Man with his right hand to take the Woman by her right hand, and to say after him as followeth.*

I *M.* take thee *N.* to my wedded Wife, to have and to hold from this day forward, for better for worse, for richer for poorer, in sickness and in health, to love and to cherish, till death us do part, according to God's holy ordinance; and thereto I plight thee my troth.

¶ *Then shall they loose their hands; and the Woman with her right hand taking the Man by his right hand, shall likewise say after the Minister.*

I *N.* take thee *M.* to my wedded Husband, to have and to hold from this day forward, for better for worse, for richer for poorer, in sickness and in health, to love, cherish, and to obey, till death us do part, according to God's holy ordinance; and thereto I give thee my troth.

¶ *Then shall they again loose their hands; and the Man shall give unto the Woman a Ring. And the Minister taking the Ring shall deliver it unto the Man, to put it upon the fourth finger of the Woman's left hand. And the Man holding the Ring there, and taught by the Minister, shall say,*

With this Ring I thee wed, and with all my worldly goods I thee endow: In the Name of the Father, and of the Son, and of the Holy Ghost. Amen.

¶ *Then, the Man, leaving the Ring upon the fourth finger of the Woman's left hand, the Minister shall say,*

Let us pray.

Our Father, who art in heaven, Hallowed be thy Name. Thy kingdom come. Thy will be done on earth, As it is in heaven. Give us this day our daily bread. And forgive us our trespasses, As we forgive those who trespass against us. And lead us not into temptation; But deliver us from evil. Amen.

O Eternal God, Creator and Preserver of all mankind, Giver of all spiritual grace, the Author of everlasting life; Send thy blessing upon these thy servants, this man and this woman, whom we bless in thy Name; that, as Isaac and Rebecca lived faithfully together, so these persons may surely perform and keep the vow and covenant betwixt them made, (whereof this Ring given and received is a token and pledge,) and may ever remain in perfect love and peace together, and live according to thy laws; through Jesus Christ our Lord. *Amen.*

¶ *Then shall the Minister join their right hands together, and say,*

Those whom God hath joined together let no man put asunder.

¶ *Then shall the Minister speak unto the company.*

Forasmuch as *M.* and *N.* have consented together in holy wedlock, and have witnessed the same before God and this company, and thereto have given and pledged their troth, each to the other, and have declared the same by giving and receiving a Ring, and by joining hands; I pronounce that they are Man and Wife,

In the Name of the Father, and of the Son, and of the Holy Ghost. Amen.

¶ *And the Minister shall add this Blessing.*

God the Father, God the Son, God the Holy Ghost, bless, preserve, and keep you; the Lord mercifully with his favour look upon you, and fill you with all spiritual benediction and grace; that ye may so live together in this life, that in the world to come ye may have life everlasting. *Amen.*

THE ORDER FOR THE VISITATION OF THE SICK.

¶ *When any person is sick, notice shall be given thereof to the Minister of the Parish; who, coming into the sick person's house, shall say,*

Peace be to this house, and to all that dwell in it.

¶ *When he cometh into the sick man's presence, he shall say, kneeling down,*

Remember not, Lord, our iniquities, nor the iniquities of our forefathers: Spare us, good Lord, spare thy people, whom thou hast redeemed with thy most precious blood, and be not angry with us for ever.

Answer. Spare us, good Lord.

¶ *Then the Minister shall say,*

Let us pray.

Lord, have mercy upon us.
Christ, have mercy upon us.
Lord, have mercy upon us.

Our Father, who art in heaven, Hallowed be thy Name. Thy kingdom come. Thy will be done on earth, As it is in heaven.

Give us this day our daily bread. And forgive us our trespasses, as we forgive those who trespass against us. And lead us not into temptation; But deliver us from evil. Amen.

Minister. O Lord, save thy servant;

Answer. Who putteth *his* trust in thee.

Minister. Send *him* help from thy holy place;

Answer. And evermore mightily defend *him*.

Minister. Let the enemy have no advantage of *him*;

Answer. Nor the wicked approach to hurt *him*.

Minister. Be unto *him*, O Lord, a strong tower;

Answer. From the face of *his* enemy.

Minister. O Lord, hear our prayer.

Answer. And let our cry come unto thee.

Minister.

O Lord, look down from heaven, behold, visit, and relieve this thy servant. Look upon *him* with the eyes of thy mercy, give *him* comfort and sure confidence in thee, defend *him* from the danger of the enemy, and keep *him* in perpetual peace and safety; through Jesus Christ our Lord. *Amen.*

Hear us, Almighty and most merciful God and Saviour; extend thy accustomed goodness to this thy servant, who is grieved with sickness. Sanctify, we beseech thee, this thy fatherly correction to *him*; that the sense of *his* weakness may add strength to *his* faith, and seriousness to *his* repentance; that, if it shall be thy good pleasure to restore *him* to *his* former health, *he* may lead the residue of *his* life in thy fear, and to thy glory; or else, give *him* grace so to take thy visitation, that, after this painful life ended, *he* may dwell with thee in life everlasting; through Jesus Christ our Lord. *Amen.*

¶ *Then shall the Minister exhort the sick Person after this form, or other like.*

Dearly beloved, know this, that Almighty God is the Lord of life and death, and of all things to them pertaining; as youth, strength, health, age, weakness, and sickness. Wherefore, what-soever your sickness be, know you certainly that it is God's visitation. And for what cause soever this sickness be sent unto you; whether it be to try your patience for the example of others, and that your faith may be found, in the day of the Lord, laudable, glorious, and honourable, to the increase of glory and endless felicity; or else it be sent unto you to correct and amend in you whatsoever doth offend the eyes of your heavenly Father; know you certainly, that if you truly repent you of your sins, and bear your sickness patiently, trusting in God's mercy for his dear Son Jesus Christ's sake, and render unto him humble thanks for his fatherly visitation, submitting yourself wholly unto his will, it shall turn to your profit, and help you forward in the right way that leadeth unto everlasting life.

¶ *If the Person visited be very sick, then the Minister may end his Exhortation in this place, or else proceed.*

Take therefore in good part the chastisement of the Lord: for (as Saint Paul saith in the twelfth Chapter to the Hebrews) whom the Lord loveth he chasteneth, and scourgeth every son whom he receiveth. If ye endure chastening, God dealeth with you as with sons; for what son is he whom the father chasteneth not? But if ye be without chastisement, whereof all are partakers, then are ye bastards, and not sons. Furthermore we have had fathers of our flesh which corrected us, and we gave them reverence: shall we not much rather be in subjection unto the Father of spirits, and live? For they verily for a few days chastened us after their own pleasure; but he for our profit, that we might be partakers of his holiness. These words, good *brother*, are written in holy Scripture for our comfort and instruction; that we should patiently, and with thanksgiving, bear our heavenly Father's correction, whensoever, by any manner of adversity, it shall please his gracious goodness to visit us. And there should be no greater comfort to Christian persons, than to be made like unto Christ, by suffering patiently adversities, troubles, and sicknesses. For he himself went not up to joy, but first he suffered pain; he entered not into his glory before he was crucified. So truly our way to eternal joy is to suffer here with Christ; and our door to enter into eternal life is gladly to die with Christ; that we may rise again from death, and dwell with him in everlasting life. Now therefore, taking your sickness, which is thus profitable for you, patiently, I exhort you, in the Name of God, to remember the profession which you made unto God in your Baptism. And forasmuch as after this life there is an account to be given unto the righteous Judge, by whom all must be judged, without respect of persons, I require you to examine yourself and your estate, both toward God and man; so that, accusing and condemning yourself for your own faults, you may find mercy at our heavenly Father's hand for Christ's sake, and not be accused and condemned in that fearful judgment. Therefore I shall rehearse to you the Articles of our Faith; that you may know whether you do believe as a Christian man should, or no.

* *Here the Minister shall rehearse the* Articles of the Faith, *saying thus,*

Dost thou believe in God the Father Almighty, Maker of heaven and earth?

And in Jesus Christ his only-begotten Son our Lord? And that he was conceived by the Holy Ghost, born of the Virgin Mary; that he suffered under Pontius Pilate, was crucified, dead, and buried; that he went down into hell, and also did rise again the third day; that he ascended into heaven, and sitteth on the right hand of God the Father Almighty; and from thence shall come again, at the end of the world, to judge the quick and the dead?

And dost thou believe in the Holy Ghost; the holy Catholic Church; the Communion of Saints; the Remission of sins; the Resurrection of the flesh; and everlasting Life after death?

¶ *The sick person shall answer,*

All this I stedfastly believe.

¶ *Then shall the Minister examine whether he repent him truly of his sins, and be in charity with all the world; exhorting him to forgive, from the bottom of his heart, all persons that have offended him; and if he hath offended any other, to ask them forgiveness; and where he hath done injury or wrong to any man, that he make amends to the uttermost of his power. And if he hath not before disposed of his goods, let him then be admonished to make his Will, and to declare his Debts, what he oweth, and what is owing unto him, for the better discharging of his conscience, and the quietness of his Executors. But men should often be put in remembrance to take order for the settling of their temporal estates, whilst they are in health.*

¶ *The Exhortation before rehearsed, may be said before the Minister begins his Prayer, as he shall see cause.*

¶ *The Minister shall not omit earnestly to move such sick persons as are of ability, to be liberal to the poor.*

¶ *And then the Minister shall say the Collect following.*

Let us pray.

O Most merciful God, who, according to the multitude of thy mercies, dost so put away the sins of those who truly repent, that thou rememberest them no more; Open thine eye of mercy upon this thy servant, who most earnestly desireth pardon and forgiveness. Renew in *him*, most loving Father, whatsoever hath been decayed by the fraud and malice of the devil, or by *his* own carnal will and frailness; preserve and continue this sick member in the unity of the Church; consider *his* contrition, accept *his* tears, assuage *his* pain, as shall seem to thee most expedient for *him*. And forasmuch as *he* putteth *his* full trust only in thy mercy, impute not unto *him his* former sins, but strengthen *him* with thy blessed Spirit; and, when thou art pleased to take *him* hence, take *him* unto thy favour; through the merits of thy most dearly beloved Son, Jesus Christ our Lord. *Amen*.

¶ *Then shall the Minister say this Psalm.*

PSALM 130. *De Profundis.*

Out of the deep have I called unto thee, O Lord : Lord, hear my voice.

O let thine ears consider well : the voice of my complaint.

If thou, Lord, wilt be extreme to mark what is done amiss : O Lord, who may abide it?

For there is mercy with thee : therefore shalt thou be feared.

I look for the Lord; my soul doth wait for him : in his word is my trust.

My soul fleeth unto the Lord : before the morning watch, I say, before the morning watch.

O Israel, trust in the Lord; for with the Lord there is mercy : and with him is plenteous redemption.

And he shall redeem Israel : from all his sins.

¶ *Adding this.*

O Saviour of the world, who by thy Cross and precious Blood hast redeemed us; Save us, and help us, we humbly beseech thee, O Lord.

¶ *Then shall the Minister say.*

The Almighty Lord, who is a most strong tower to all those who put their trust in *him*, to whom all things in heaven, in *earth*, and under the *earth*, do bow and obey, Be now and evermore thy defence; and make thee know and feel, that there is none other Name under heaven given to man, in whom, and through whom, thou mayest receive health and salvation, but only the Name of our Lord Jesus Christ. Amen.

* *Here the Minister may use any part of the service of this Book, which, in his discretion, he shall think convenient to the occasion; and after that shall say,*

Unto God's gracious mercy and protection we commit thee. The Lord bless thee, and keep thee. The Lord make his face to shine upon thee, and be gracious unto thee. The Lord lift up his countenance upon thee, and give thee peace, both now and evermore. *Amen.*

Prayers which may be said with the foregoing Service, or any part thereof, at the discretion of the Minister.

A Prayer for a sick Child.

O Almighty God, and merciful Father, to whom alone belong the issues of life and death; Look down from heaven, we humbly beseech thee, with the eyes of mercy, upon this child now lying upon the bed of sickness: Visit *him*, O Lord, with thy salvation; deliver *him* in thy good appointed time from *his* bodily pain, and save *his* soul for thy mercies' sake: that, if it shall be thy pleasure to prolong *his* days here on earth, *he* may live to thee, and be an instrument of thy glory, by serving thee faithfully, and doing good in *his* generation; or else receive *him* into those heavenly habitations, where the souls of those who sleep in the Lord Jesus enjoy perpetual rest and felicity. Grant this, O Lord, for thy mercies' sake in the same thy Son our Lord Jesus Christ, who liveth and reigneth with thee and the Holy Ghost ever, one God, world without end. *Amen.*

A Prayer for a sick Person, when there appeareth but small hope of recovery.

O Father of mercies, and God of all comfort, our only help in time of need; We fly unto thee for succour in behalf of this thy servant, here lying under thy hand in great weakness of body. Look graciously upon *him*, O Lord; and the more the outward man decayeth, strengthen *him*, we beseech thee, so much the more continually with thy grace and Holy Spirit in the inner man. Give *him* unfeigned repentance for all the errors of *his* life past, and stedfast faith in thy Son Jesus; that *his* sins may be done away by thy mercy, and *his* pardon sealed in heaven, before *he* go hence, and be no more seen. We know, O Lord, that there is no word impossible with thee; and that, if thou wilt, thou canst even yet raise *him* up, and grant *him* a longer continuance amongst us; yet, forasmuch as in all appearance the time of *his* dissolution draweth near, so fit and prepare *him*, we beseech thee, against the hour of death, that after *his* departure hence in peace, and in thy favour, *his* soul may be received into thine everlasting kingdom; through the merits and mediation of Jesus Christ thine only Son, our Lord and Saviour. *Amen.*

A Commendatory Prayer for a sick Person at the point of departure.

O Almighty God, with whom do live the spirits of just men made perfect, after they are delivered from their earthly prisons; We humbly commend the soul of this thy servant, our dear *brother*, into thy hands, as into the hands of a faithful Creator, and most merciful Saviour; most humbly beseeching thee, that it may be precious in thy sight. Wash it, we pray thee, in the blood of that immaculate Lamb, that was slain to take away the sins of the world; that whatsoever defilements it may have contracted in the midst of this miserable and naughty world, through the lusts of the flesh, or the wiles of Satan, being purged and done away, it may be presented pure and without spot before thee; through the merits of Jesus Christ thine only Son our Lord. *Amen.*

A Prayer for Persons troubled in mind or in conscience.

O Blessed Lord, the Father of mercies, and the God of all comfort; We beseech thee, look down in pity and compassion upon this thy afflicted servant. Thou writest bitter things against *him*, and makest *him* to possess *his* former iniquities; thy wrath lieth hard upon *him*, and *his* soul is full of trouble. But, O merciful God, who hast written thy holy Word for our learning, that we, through patience and comfort of thy holy Scriptures, might have hope; give *him* a right understanding of *himself*, and of thy threats and promises; that *he* may neither cast away *his* confidence in thee, nor place it any where but in thee. Give *him* strength against all *his* temptations, and heal all *his* distempers. Break not the bruised reed, nor quench the smoking flax. Shut not up thy tender mercies in displeasure; but make *him* to hear of joy and gladness, that the bones which thou hast broken may rejoice. Deliver *him* from fear of the enemy, and lift up the light of thy countenance upon *him*, and give *him* peace, through the merits and mediation of Jesus Christ our Lord. *Amen.*

A Prayer which may be said by the Minister in behalf of all present at the Visitation.

O God, whose days are without end, and whose mercies cannot be numbered; Make us, we beseech thee, deeply sensible of the shortness and uncertainty of human life; and let thy Holy Spirit lead us through this vale of misery, in holiness and righteousness, all the days of our lives: that, when we shall have served thee in our generation, we may be gathered unto our fathers, having the testimony of a good conscience; in the communion of the catholic Church; in the confidence of a certain faith; in the comfort of a reasonable, religious, and holy hope; in favor with thee our God, and in perfect charity with the world. All which we ask through Jesus Christ our Lord. *Amen.*

A Prayer which may be said in case of sudden surprise and immediate danger.

O most gracious Father, we fly unto thee for mercy in behalf of this thy servant, here lying under the sudden visitation of thine hand. If it be thy will, preserve *his* life, that there may be place for repentance; but if thou hast otherwise appointed, let thy mercy supply to *him* the want of the usual opportunity for the trimming of *his* lamp. Stir up in *him* such sorrow for sin, and such fervent love to thee, as may in a short time do the work of many days: that among the praises which thy saints and holy angels shall sing to the honour of thy mercy through eternal ages, it may be to thy unspeakable glory, that thou hast redeemed the soul of this thy servant from eternal death, and made *him* partaker of the everlasting life, which is through Jesus Christ our Lord. *Amen.*

A Thanksgiving for the beginning of a Recovery.

Great and mighty God, who bringest down to the grave, and bringest up again; We bless thy wonderful goodness, for having turned our heaviness into joy and our mourning into gladness, by restoring this our *brother* to some degree of *his* former health. Blessed be thy Name that thou didst not forsake *him* in *his* sickness; but didst visit *him* with comforts from above; didst support *him* in patience and submission to thy will; and at last didst send *him* seasonable relief. Perfect, we beseech thee, this thy mercy towards *him;* and prosper the means which shall be made use of for *his* cure: that, being restored to health of body, vigour of mind, and cheerfulness of spirit, *he* may be able to go to thine house, to offer thee an oblation with great gladness, and to bless thy holy Name for all thy goodness towards *him;* through Jesus Christ our Saviour, to whom, with thee and the Holy Spirit, be all honour and glory, world without end. *Amen.*

THE COMMUNION OF THE SICK.

* *Forasmuch as all mortal men are subject to many sudden perils, diseases, and sicknesses, and ever uncertain what time they shall depart out of this life; therefore, to the intent they may be always in readiness to die, whensoever it shall please Almighty God to call them, the Ministers shall diligently from time to time (but especially in the time of pestilence, or other infectious sickness) exhort their parishioners to the often receiving of the Holy Communion of the Body and Blood of our Saviour Christ, when it shall be publicly administered in the Church: that so doing, they may, in case of sudden visitation, have the less cause to be disquieted for lack of the same. But if the sick person be not able to come to the Church, and yet is desirous to receive the Communion in his house; then he must give timely notice to the Minister, signifying also how many there are to communicate with him, (which shall be two at the least;) and all things necessary being prepared, the Minister shall there celebrate the Holy Communion, beginning with the Collect, Epistle, and Gospel, here following.*

The Collect.

Almighty, everliving God, Maker of mankind, who dost correct those whom thou dost love, and chastise every one whom thou dost receive: We beseech thee to have mercy upon this thy servant visited with thine hand, and to grant that *he* may take *his* sickness patiently, and recover *his* bodily health, if it be thy gracious will; and that, whensoever *his* soul shall depart from the body, it may be without spot presented unto thee; through Jesus Christ our Lord. *Amen.*

The Epistle. Heb. xii. 5.

My son, despise not thou the chastening of the Lord, nor faint when thou art rebuked of him: for whom the Lord loveth he chasteneth, and scourgeth every son whom he receiveth.

The Gospel. St. John v. 24.

Verily, verily, I say unto you, He that heareth my word, and believeth on him that sent me, hath everlasting life, and shall not come into condemnation; but is passed from death unto life.

¶ *After which the Minister shall proceed according to the form before prescribed for the Holy Communion, beginning at these words,* Ye who do truly, *etc.*

¶ *At the time of the distribution of the holy Sacrament, the Minister shall first receive the Communion himself, and after minister unto those who are appointed to communicate with the sick, and last of all to the sick person.*

¶ *In the times of contagious sickness or disease, or when extreme weakness renders it expedient, the following form shall suffice: The Confession and the Absolution;* Lift up your hearts, *etc., through the* Sanctus: *The Prayer of Consecration, ending with these words,* partakers of his most blessed Body and Blood: *The Communion: The Lord's Prayer: The Blessing.*

¶ *But if a man, either by reason of extremity of sickness, or for want of warning in due time to the Minister, or for lack of company to receive with him, or by any other just impediment, do not receive the Sacrament of Christ's Body and Blood, the Minister shall instruct him, that if he do truly repent him of his sins, and stedfastly believe that Jesus Christ hath suffered death upon the Cross for him, and shed his Blood for his redemption, earnestly remembering the benefits he hath thereby, and giving him hearty thanks therefor, he doth eat and drink the Body and Blood of our Saviour Christ profitably to his soul's health, although he do not receive the Sacrament with his mouth.*

¶ *When the sick person is visited, and receiveth the Holy Communion all at one time, then the Minister, for more expedition, shall cut off the form of the Visitation at the Psalm, and go straight to the Communion.*

¶ *In the times of contagious sickness or disease, when none of the Parish or neighbours can be gotten to communicate with the sick in their houses, for fear of the infection, upon special request of the diseased, the Minister alone may communicate with him.*

¶ *This Office may be used with aged and bed-ridden persons, or such as are not able to attend the public Ministration in Church, substituting the Collect, Epistle, and Gospel for the Day, for those appointed above.*

¶ *Then shall the Priest say to those who come to receive the Holy Communion.*

Ye who do truly and earnestly repent you of your sins, and are in love and charity with your neighbours, and intend to lead a new life, following the commandments of God, and walking from henceforth in his holy ways; Draw near with faith, and take this holy Sacrament to your comfort; and make your humble confession to Almighty God, devoutly kneeling.

¶ *Then shall this* **General Confession** *be made, by the Priest and all those who are minded to receive the Holy Communion, humbly kneeling.*

Almighty God, Father of our Lord Jesus Christ, Maker of all things, Judge of all men; We acknowledge and bewail our manifold sins and wickedness, Which we, from time to time, most grievously have committed, By thought, word, and deed, Against thy Divine Majesty, Provoking most justly thy wrath and indignation against us. We do earnestly repent, And are heartily sorry for these our misdoings; The remembrance of them is grievous unto us; The burden of them is intolerable. Have mercy upon us, Have mercy upon us, most merciful Father; For thy Son our Lord Jesus Christ's sake, Forgive us all that is past; And grant that we may ever hereafter Serve and please thee In newness of life, To the honour and glory of thy Name; Through Jesus Christ our Lord. Amen.

¶ *Then shall the Priest (the Bishop if he be present) stand up, and turning to the People, say,*

Almighty God, our heavenly Father, who of his great mercy hath promised forgiveness of sins to all those who with hearty repentance and true faith turn unto him; Have mercy upon you; pardon and deliver you from all your sins; confirm and strengthen you in all goodness; and bring you to everlasting life; through Jesus Christ our Lord. *Amen.*

¶ *Then shall the Priest say,*

Hear what comfortable words our Saviour Christ saith unto all who truly turn to him.

Come unto me, all ye that travail and are heavy laden, and I will refresh you. *St. Matt.* xi. 28.

So God loved the world, that he gave his only-begotten Son, to the end that all that believe in him should not perish, but have everlasting life. *St. John* iii. 16.

Hear also what Saint Paul saith.

This is a true saying, and worthy of all men to be received, that Christ Jesus came into the world to save sinners. 1 *Tim.* i. 15.

Hear also what Saint John saith.

If any man sin, we have an Advocate with the Father, Jesus Christ the righteous; and he is the Propitiation for our sins. 1 *St. John* ii. 1, 2.

¶ *After which the Priest shall proceed, saying,*

Lift up your hearts.
Answer. We lift them up unto the Lord.
Priest. Let us give thanks unto our Lord God.
Answer. It is meet and right so to do.

¶ *Then shall the Priest turn to the Lord's Table, and say,*

It is very meet, right, and our bounden duty, that we should at all times, and in all places, give thanks unto thee, O Lord, [* Holy Father,] Almighty, Everlasting God.

*These words [Holy Father] must be omitted on Trinity-Sunday.

¶ *Here shall follow the* Proper Preface, *according to the time, if there be any specially appointed: or else immediately shall be said or sung by the Priest.*

Therefore with Angels and Archangels, and with all the company of heaven, we laud and magnify thy glorious Name; evermore praising thee, and saying,

HOLY, HOLY, HOLY, Lord God of hosts, Heaven and earth are full of thy glory: Glory be to thee, O Lord Most High. Amen.

¶ *Priest and People.*

PROPER PREFACES.

Upon Christmas-day, *and seven days after.*

Because thou didst give Jesus Christ, thine only Son, to be born as at this time for us; who, by the operation of the Holy Ghost, was made very man, of the substance of the Virgin Mary his mother; and that without spot of sin, to make us clean from all sin. Therefore with Angels, *etc.*

Upon Easter-day, *and seven days after.*

But chiefly are we bound to praise thee for the glorious Resurrection of thy Son Jesus Christ our Lord: for he is the very Paschal Lamb, which was offered for us, and hath taken away the sin of the world; who by his death hath destroyed death, and by his rising to life again hath restored to us everlasting life. Therefore with Angels, *etc.*

Upon Ascension-day, *and seven days after.*

Through thy most dearly beloved Son Jesus Christ our Lord; who, after his most glorious Resurrection, manifestly appeared to all his Apostles, and in their sight ascended up into heaven, to prepare a place for us; that where he is, thither we might also ascend, and reign with him in glory. Therefore with Angels, *etc.*

Upon Whitsunday, *and six days after.*

Through Jesus Christ our Lord; according to whose most true promise, the Holy Ghost came down as at this time from heaven, with a sudden great sound, as it had been a mighty wind, in the likeness of fiery tongues, lighting upon the Apostles, to teach them, and to lead them to all truth; giving them both the gift of divers languages, and also boldness with fervent zeal constantly to preach the Gospel unto all nations; whereby we have been brought out of darkness and error into the clear light and true knowledge of thee, and of thy Son Jesus Christ. Therefore with Angels, *etc.*

Upon the Feast of Trinity *only, may be said,*

Who art one God, one Lord: not one only Person, but three Persons in one Substance. For that which we believe of the glory of the Father, the same we believe of the Son, and of the Holy Ghost, without any difference or inequality. Therefore with Angels, *etc.*

¶ *Or else this may be said, the words* [Holy Father] *being retained in the introductory address.*

For the precious death and merits of thy Son Jesus Christ our Lord, and for the sending to us of the Holy Ghost, the Comforter; who are one with thee in thy Eternal Godhead. Therefore with Angels, *etc.*

* *Then shall the Priest, kneeling down at the Lord's Table, say, in the name of all those who shall receive the Communion, this Prayer following.*

We do not presume to come to this thy Table, O merciful Lord, trusting in our own righteousness, but in thy manifold and great mercies. We are not worthy so much as to gather up the crumbs under thy Table. But thou art the same Lord, whose property is always to have mercy: Grant us therefore, gracious Lord, so to eat the flesh of thy dear Son Jesus Christ, and to drink his blood, that our sinful bodies may be made clean by his body, and our souls washed through his most precious blood, and that we may evermore dwell in him, and he in us. *Amen.*

¶ *When the Priest, standing before the Table, hath so ordered the Bread and Wine, that he may with the more readiness and decency break the Bread before the People, and take the Cup into his hands, he shall say the* Prayer of Consecration, *as followeth.*

All glory be to thee, Almighty God, our heavenly Father, for that thou, of thy tender mercy, didst give thine only Son Jesus Christ to suffer death upon the Cross for our redemption; who made there (by his one oblation of himself once offered) a full, perfect, and sufficient sacrifice, oblation, and satisfaction, for the sins of the whole world; and did institute, and in his holy Gospel command us to continue, a perpetual memory of that his precious death and sacrifice, until his coming again: For in the night in which he was betrayed, (*a*) he took Bread; and when he had given thanks, (*b*) he brake it, and gave it to his disciples, saying, Take, eat, (*c*) this is my Body, which is given for you; Do this in remembrance of me. Likewise, after supper, (*d*) he took the Cup; and when he had given thanks, he gave it to them, saying, Drink ye all of this; for (*e*) this is my Blood of the New Testament, which is shed for you, and for many, for the remission of sins; Do this, as oft as ye shall drink it, in remembrance of me.

(a) *Here the Priest is to take the Paten into his hands.*
(b) *And here to break the Bread.*
(c) *And here to lay his hand upon all the Bread.*
(d) *Here he is to take the Cup into his hands.*
(e) *And here he is to lay his hand upon every vessel in which there is any Wine to be consecrated.*

Wherefore, O Lord and heavenly Father, according *The Oblation.* to the institution of thy dearly beloved Son our Saviour Jesus Christ, we, thy humble servants, do celebrate and make here before thy Divine Majesty, with these thy holy gifts, which we now offer unto thee, the memorial thy Son hath commanded us to make; having in remembrance his blessed passion and precious death, his mighty resurrection and glorious ascension; rendering unto thee most hearty thanks for the innumerable benefits procured unto us by the same.

And we most humbly beseech thee, O merciful *The Invocation* Father, to hear us; and, of thy almighty goodness, vouchsafe to bless and sanctify, with thy Word and Holy Spirit, these thy gifts and creatures of bread and wine; that we, receiving them according to thy Son our Saviour Jesus Christ's holy institution, in remembrance of his death and passion, may be partakers of his most blessed Body and Blood.

And we earnestly desire thy fatherly goodness, mercifully to accept this our sacrifice of praise and thanksgiving; most humbly beseeching thee to grant that, by the merits and death of thy Son Jesus Christ, and through faith in his blood, we, and all thy whole Church, may obtain remission of our sins, and all other benefits of his passion. And here we offer and present unto thee, O Lord, ourselves, our souls and bodies, to be a reasonable, holy, and living sacrifice unto thee; humbly beseeching thee, that we, and all others who shall be partakers of this Holy Communion, may worthily receive the most precious Body and Blood of thy Son Jesus Christ, be filled with thy grace and heavenly benediction, and made one body with him, that he may dwell in

us, and we in him. And although we are
unworthy, through our manifold sins, to
offer unto thee any sacrifice; yet we beseech thee to accept this our bounden
duty and service; not weighing our merits, but pardoning our offences, through
Jesus Christ our Lord; by whom, and
with whom, in the unity of the Holy
Ghost, all honour and glory be unto thee,
O Father Almighty, world without end.
Amen.

¶ *Here may be sung a Hymn.*

¶ *Then shall the Priest first receive the Holy Communion in both kinds himself, and proceed to deliver
the same to the Bishops, Priests, and Deacons, in like
manner (if any be present), and after that to the
People also in due order, into their hands, all meekly
kneeling. And sufficient opportunity shall be given
to those present to communicate. But when he
delivereth the Bread, he shall say,*

The Body of our Lord Jesus Christ,
which was given for thee, preserve thy
body and soul unto everlasting life. Take
and eat this in remembrance that Christ
died for thee, and feed on him in thy
heart by faith, with thanksgiving.

¶ *And the Minister who delivereth the Cup shall say,*

The Blood of our Lord Jesus Christ,
which was shed for thee, preserve thy
body and soul unto everlasting life.
Drink this in remembrance that Christ's
Blood was shed for thee, and be thankful.

¶ *If the consecrated Bread or Wine be spent before all
have communicated, the Priest is to consecrate more
according to the Form before prescribed; beginning
at, All glory be to thee Almighty God, etc., and
with these words, partakers of his most blessed*
Body and Blood.

¶ *When all have communicated, the Minister shall
return to the Lord's Table, and reverently place
upon it what remaineth of the consecrated Elements,
covering the same with a fair linen cloth.*

¶ *Then shall the Minister say the Lord's Prayer, the
People repeating after him every Petition.*

Our Father, who art in heaven, Hallowed be thy Name. Thy kingdom
come. Thy will be done on earth, As it
is in heaven. Give us this day our daily

bread. And forgive us our trespasses, as we forgive those who trespass against us. And lead us not into temptation; But deliver us from evil: For thine is the kingdom, and the power, and the glory, for ever and ever. Amen.

¶ *After shall be said as followeth.*

Almighty and everliving God, we most heartily thank thee, for that thou dost vouchsafe to feed us who have duly received these holy mysteries, with the spiritual food of the most precious Body and Blood of thy Son our Saviour Jesus Christ; and dost assure us thereby of thy favour and goodness towards us; and that we are very members incorporate in the mystical body of thy Son, which is the blessed company of all faithful people; and are also heirs through hope of thy everlasting kingdom, by the merits of the most precious death and passion of thy dear Son. And we most humbly beseech thee, O heavenly Father, so to assist us with thy grace, that we may continue in that holy fellowship, and do all such good works as thou hast prepared for us to walk in; through Jesus Christ our Lord, to whom, with thee and the Holy Ghost, be all honour and glory, world without end. *Amen.*

¶ *Then shall be said or sung, all standing,* Gloria in excelsis; *or some proper Hymn from the Selection.*

Glory be to God on high, and on earth peace, good will towards men. We praise thee, we bless thee, we worship thee, we glorify thee, we give thanks to thee for thy great glory, O Lord God, heavenly King, God the Father Almighty.

O Lord, the only-begotten Son, Jesus Christ; O Lord God, Lamb of God, Son of the Father, that takest away the sins of the world, have mercy upon us. Thou that takest away the sins of the world, have mercy upon us. Thou that takest away the sins of the world, receive our prayer. Thou that sittest at the right hand of God the Father, have mercy upon us.

For thou only art holy; thou only art the Lord; thou only, O Christ, with the Holy Ghost, art most high in the glory of God the Father. Amen.

¶ *Then the Priest (the Bishop if he be present) shall let them depart with this Blessing.*

The Peace of God, which passeth all understanding, keep your hearts and minds in the knowledge and love of God, and of his Son Jesus Christ our Lord: And the Blessing of God Almighty, the Father, the Son, and the Holy Ghost, be amongst you, and remain with you always. *Amen*

Scripture Readings with the Sick.

Confession of Sin.

Have mercy upon me, O God, after thy great goodness; according to the multitude of thy mercies do away mine offences.

Wash me throughly from my wickedness, and cleanse me from my sin;

For I acknowledge my faults, and my sin is ever before me.

Turn thy face from my sins, and put out all my misdeeds.

Make me a clean heart, O God, and renew a right spirit within me.

Cast me not away from thy presence, and take not thy Holy Spirit from me.

O give me the comfort of thy help again, and stablish me with thy free Spirit.

Try me, O God, and seek the ground of my heart; prove me, and examine my thoughts.

Look well if there be any way of wickedness in me; and lead me in the way everlasting.

I will arise, and go to my father, and will say unto him, Father, I have sinned against heaven, and before thee, and am no more worthy to be called thy son.

The publican, standing afar off, would not lift up so much as *his* eyes unto heaven, but smote upon his breast, saying, God be merciful to me a sinner.

Thanksgiving.

I will alway give thanks unto the Lord; his praise shall ever be in my mouth.

My soul shall make her boast in the Lord; the humble shall hear thereof, and be glad.

O praise the Lord with me, and let us magnify his Name together.

I sought the Lord, and he heard me; yea, he delivered me out of all my fear.

They had an eye unto him, and were lightened; and their faces were not ashamed.

Lo, the poor crieth, and the Lord heareth him; yea, and saveth him out of all his troubles.

The angel of the Lord tarrieth round about them that fear him, and delivereth them.

O taste, and see, how gracious the Lord is: blessed is the man that trusteth in him.

O fear the Lord, ye that are his saints; for they that fear him lack nothing.

The lions do lack, and suffer hunger; but they who seek the Lord shall want no manner of thing that is good.

The Love of God.

I will mention the loving-kindnesses of the Lord, *and* the praises of the Lord, according to all that the Lord hath bestowed on us, and the great goodness toward the house of Israel, which he hath bestowed on them according to the multitude of his loving-kindnesses.

For he said, Surely they *are* my people, children *that* will not lie: so he was their Saviour.

In all their affliction he was afflicted, and the Angel of his presence saved them: in his love and in his pity he redeemed them; and he bare them, and carried them all the days of old.

I love them that love me; and those that seek me early shall find me.

He brought me to the banqueting house, and his banner over me *was* love.

I drew them with cords of a man, with bands of love.

The Lord hath appeared of old unto me, *saying*, Yea, I have loved thee with an everlasting love: therefore with loving-kindness have I drawn thee.

Behold what manner of love the Father hath bestowed upon us, that we should be called the sons of God: therefore the world knoweth us not, because it knew him not.

God so loved the world, that he gave his only-begotten Son, that whosoever believeth in him should not perish, but have everlasting life.

For scarcely for a righteous man will one die: yet peradventure for a good man some would even dare to die.

But God commendeth his love toward us, in that, while we were yet sinners, Christ died for us.

Hereby perceive we the love *of God*, because he laid down his life for us.

Herein is love, not that we loved God, but that he loved us. We have known and believed the love that God hath to us. God is love; and he that dwelleth in love dwelleth in God, and God in him. We love him, because he first loved us.

I am crucified with Christ: nevertheless I live; yet not I, but Christ liveth in me: and the life which I now live in the flesh I live by the faith of the Son of God, who loved me, and gave himself for me.

The Mercy and Forgiveness of God.

I have blotted out, as a thick cloud, thy transgressions, and as a cloud, thy sins: return unto me; for I have redeemed thee.

Come now, and let us reason together, saith the Lord, though your sins be as scarlet, they shall be as white as snow; though they be red like crimson, they shall be as wool.

The Lord *is* merciful and gracious, slow to anger, and plenteous in mercy.

He will not always chide: neither will he keep *his anger* for ever.

He hath not dealt with us after our sins; nor rewarded us according to our iniquities.

For as the heaven is high above the earth, *so* great is his mercy toward them that fear him

As far as the east is from the west, *so* far hath he removed our transgressions from us.

Like as a father pitieth *his* children, *so* the Lord pitieth them that fear him.

As for our transgressions, thou shalt purge them away.

The Lord is long-suffering to us-ward, not willing that any should perish, but that all should come to repentance.

If we confess our sins, he is faithful and just to forgive us our sins, and to cleanse us from all unrighteousness.

Keeping mercy for thousands, forgiving iniquity, and transgression, and sin.

Their sins and iniquities will I remember no more.

Blessed is he whose unrighteousness is forgiven, and whose sin is covered. Blessed is the man unto whom the Lord imputeth no sin, and in whose spirit there is no guile.

He retaineth not his anger for ever,
because he delighteth in mercy. He will
turn again, he will have compassion upon
us; he will subdue our iniquities; and
thou wilt cast all their sins into the depths
of the sea.

Let the wicked forsake his way, and
the unrighteous man his thoughts, and let
him return unto the Lord, and he will
have mercy upon him; and to our God,
for he will abundantly pardon.

Who crowneth thee with loving-kindness and tender mercies.

It is of the Lord's mercies that we are
not consumed, because his compassions
fail not.

They are new every morning: great *is*
thy faithfulness.

The Lord *is* my portion, saith my soul;
therefore will I hope in him.

The Lord *is* good unto them that wait
for him, to the soul *that* seeketh him.

It is good that *a man* should both hope
and quietly wait for the salvation of the
Lord.

The Lord will not cast off for ever:

But though he cause grief, yet will he
have compassion according to the multitude of his mercies.

For he doth not afflict willingly, nor
grieve the children of men.

Salvation through Faith.

Believe on the Lord Jesus Christ, and
thou shalt be saved, and thy house.

Behold, I lay in Sion a stumbling-stone,
and rock of offence; and whosoever believeth on him shall not be ashamed.

I am come a light into the world, that
whosoever believeth on me should not
abide in darkness.

Thy faith hath saved thee, go in peace.

To him give all the prophets witness,
that, through his name, whosoever believeth on him shall receive remission of
sins.

The Scripture hath concluded all under sin, that the promise by faith of Jesus Christ might be given to them that believe.

As Moses lifted up the serpent in the wilderness, even so must the Son of man be lifted up:

That whosoever believeth in him should not perish, but have eternal life.

By grace are ye saved through faith; and that not of yourselves: *it is* the gift of God.

God sent not his Son into the world to condemn the world; but that the world through him might be saved.

He that believeth on him is not condemned: but he that believeth not is condemned already, because he hath not believed in the name of the only begotten Son of God.

Now faith is the substance of things hoped for, the evidence of things not seen.

We trust in the living God, who is the Saviour of all men, especially of those that believe.

Blessed are they that have not seen, and yet have believed.

But without faith *it is* impossible to please *him:* for he that cometh to God must believe that he is, and *that* he is a rewarder of them that diligently seek him.

Now the just shall live by faith: but if *any man* draw back, my soul shall have no pleasure in him.

But we are not of them who draw back unto perdition; but of them that believe to the saving of the soul.

Whatsoever is born of God overcometh the world: and this is the victory that overcometh the world, *even* our faith.

With the heart man believeth unto righteousness; and with the mouth confession is made unto salvation.

For the scripture saith, Whosoever believeth on him shall not be ashamed.

The Faithfulness of God.

Know therefore that the Lord thy God, he *is* God, the faithful God, which keepeth covenant and mercy with them that love him and keep his commandments to a thousand generations.

Behold this day I *am* going the way of all the earth: and ye know in all your hearts and in all your souls, that not one thing hath failed of all the good things which the Lord your God spake concerning you; all are come to pass unto you, *and* not one thing hath failed thereof.

God *is* not a man, that he should lie: neither the son of man, that he should repent: hath he said, and shall he not do *it?* or hath he spoken, and shall he not make it good?

My covenant will I not break, nor alter the thing that is gone out of my lips.

He hath been alway mindful of his covenant and promise, that he made to a thousand generations.

Thy mercy, O Lord, reacheth unto the heavens, and thy faithfulness unto the clouds.

O Lord, thou *art* my God; I will exalt thee, I will praise thy name; for thou hast done wonderful *things; thy* counsels of old *are* faithfulness *and* truth.

He is faithful that promised.

Encouragements to Prayer.

Call upon me in the time of trouble; so will I hear thee, and thou shalt praise me.

The Lord *is* nigh unto all them that call upon him; yea, all such as call upon him faithfully.

He will fulfil the desire of them that fear him; he also will hear their cry, and will help them.

It shall come to pass, that before they call, I will answer; and while they are yet speaking, I will hear.

Then shalt thou call, and the Lord shall answer: thou shalt cry, and he shall say, Here I *am*.

They shall call on my name, and I will hear them: I will say, It is my people; and they shall say the Lord is my God.

Ask, and it shall be given you; seek, and ye shall find; knock, and it shall be opened unto you:

For every one that asketh receiveth; and he that seeketh findeth; and to him that knocketh it shall be opened.

And all things, whatsoever ye shall ask in prayer, believing, ye shall receive.

Whatsoever ye shall ask in my name, that will I do, that the Father may be glorified in the Son.

If ye shall ask any thing in my name, I will do *it*.

If ye abide in me, and my words abide in you, ye shall ask what ye will, and it shall be done unto you.

The effectual fervent prayer of a righteous man availeth much.

Whatsoever we ask, we receive of him, because we keep his commandments, and do those things that are pleasing in his sight.

The Benefits of Affliction.

Happy is the man whom God correcteth; therefore despise not thou the chastening of the Almighty. For he maketh sore, and bindeth up; he woundeth, and his hands make whole.

Blessed is the man whom thou chastenest, O Lord, and teachest him out of thy law; that thou mayest give him rest from the days of adversity, until the pit be digged for the wicked.

Before I was afflicted I went astray; but now have I kept thy word. It is good for me that I have been afflicted, that I might learn thy statutes. I know, O Lord, thy judgments are right, and that thou in faithfulness hast afflicted me.

Whom the Lord loveth he correcteth, even as a father the son in whom he delighteth.

Our light affliction, which is but for a moment, worketh for us a far more exceeding and eternal weight of glory, while we look not at the things which are seen, but at the things which are not seen; for the things which are seen are temporal, but the things which are not seen are eternal.

It is good for me that I have been afflicted; that I might learn thy statutes.

God is our refuge and strength, a very present help in trouble. Therefore will we not fear, though the earth be removed, and though the mountains be carried into the midst of the sea. Though the waters thereof roar, and be troubled; though the mountains shake with the swelling thereof.

Cast thy burden upon the Lord, and he shall sustain thee: he shall never suffer the righteous to be moved.

I will be glad and rejoice in thy mercy: for thou hast considered my trouble; thou hast known my soul in adversities.

Though I walk in the midst of trouble, thou wilt revive me; thou shalt stretch forth thine hand against the wrath of mine enemies, and thy right hand shall save me.

My flesh and heart faileth; but God is the strength of my heart.

The Lord upholdeth all that fall, and raiseth up all that are bowed down.

Thou hast been a strength to the poor, a strength to the needy in his distress, a refuge from the storm, a shadow from the heat, when the blast of the terrible ones is as a storm against the wall.

He will not lay upon man more than is right, that he should enter into judgment with God.

His anger endureth but a moment; in his favor is life: weeping may endure for a night, but joy cometh in the morning.

Many are the afflictions of the righteous; but the Lord delivereth him out of them all.

Patience.

Be patient therefore, brethren, unto the coming of the Lord. Behold, the husbandman waiteth for the precious fruit of the earth, and hath long patience for it, until he receive the early and latter rain.

Be ye also patient; establish your hearts: for the coming of the Lord draweth nigh.

Grudge not one against another, brethren, lest ye be condemned: behold, the judge standeth before the door.

Take, my brethren, the prophets, who have spoken in the name of the Lord, for an example of suffering affliction, and of patience.

Behold, we count them happy which endure. Ye have heard of the patience of Job, and have seen the end of the Lord; that the Lord is very pitiful, and of tender mercy.

Cast not away therefore your confidence, which hath great recompense of reward.

For ye have need of patience, that, after ye have done the will of God, ye might receive the promise.

My brethren, count it all joy when ye fall into divers temptations;

Knowing *this*, that the trying of your faith worketh patience.

But let patience have *her* perfect work, that ye may be perfect and entire, wanting nothing.

Watchfulness.

Let your loins be girded about, and *your* lights burning;

And ye yourselves like unto men that wait for their lord, when he will return from the wedding; that when he cometh and knocketh, they may open unto him immediately.

Blessed *are* those servants, whom the lord when he cometh shall find watching: verily I say unto you, that he shall gird himself, and make them to sit down to meat, and will come forth and serve them.

And if he shall come in the second watch, or come in the third watch, and find *them* so, blessed are those servants.

And this know, that if the good man of the house had known what hour the thief would come, he would have watched, and not have suffered his house to be broken through.

Be ye therefore ready also: for the Son of man cometh at an hour when ye think not.

The Better Life.

Let not your heart be troubled: ye believe in God; believe also in me. In my Father's house are many mansions: if it were not so, I would have told you. I go to prepare a place for you. And if I go to prepare a place for you, I will come again, and receive you unto myself; that where I am, there ye may be also.

Jesus Christ hath abolished death, and hath brought life and immortality to light through the Gospel.

Eye hath not seen, nor ear heard, neither have entered into the heart of man, the things which God hath prepared for them that love him.

We know that if our earthly house of this tabernacle were dissolved, we have a building of God, an house not made with hands, eternal in the heavens.

I know whom I have believed, and am persuaded that he is able to keep that which I have committed unto him against that day.

Henceforth there is laid up for me a crown of righteousness, which the Lord, the righteous Judge, shall give me at that day; and not to me only, but unto all them also that love his appearing.

For this God is our God, for ever and ever: he will be our guide, even unto death.

God will redeem my soul from the power of the grave; for he shall receive me.

My flesh and my heart faileth; but God is the strength of my heart, and my portion for ever.

Into thy hands I commend my spirit: for thou hast redeemed me, O Lord, thou God of truth.

The righteous shall shine forth as the sun in the kingdom of their Father.

They that be wise shall shine as the brightness of the firmament; and they that turn many to righteousness, as the stars for ever and ever.

He is able to present you faultless before the presence of his glory, with exceeding joy.

And I saw no temple therein; for the Lord God Almighty and the Lamb are the temple of it.

And the city had no need of the sun, neither of the moon, to shine in it: for the glory of God did lighten it, and the Lamb is the light thereof.

And God shall wipe away all tears from their eyes; and there shall be no more death, neither sorrow, nor crying, neither shall there be any more pain: for the former things are passed away.

It is your Father's good pleasure to give you the kingdom.

An entrance shall be ministered unto you abundantly into the everlasting kingdom of our Lord and Saviour Jesus Christ.

The Lord will preserve me unto his heavenly kingdom.

The Lord shall be thine everlasting light, and the days of thy mourning shall be ended.

Thou wilt show me the path of life; in thy presence is fulness of joy, at thy right hand there are pleasures for evermore.

As for me, I will behold thy face in righteousness: I shall be satisfied when I awake with thy likeness.

With thee is the fountain of life: in thy light we shall see light.

So shall we be ever with the Lord.

SPECIAL PRAYERS FOR THE SICK.

For Submission.

O God who art a very present help in every time of trouble; Look with pity upon thy servant, visited by thy hand. Sanctify this sickness to *his* good, and help *him* to bear it with such submission, that *he* may be able to say out of a fervent heart, "Thy will be done." Give *him* a deep sense of thy mercy and a strong hold of thy promises. Let no cloud obscure thy peace from *him* and no temptation bring disquietude to *his* soul. This we ask through Jesus Christ our Lord. Amen.

For the Holy Spirit.

Merciful Father, who hast revealed thyself to us through the Holy Spirit; Grant the blessed presence of the divine Comforter to thy sick servant, that *he* may have abundantly joy, peace and heavenly illumination. Enlarge *his* hopes and strengthen *his* faith, and may *his* sickness, through the blessed Spirit, bring *him* into closer communion with thyself, so that *he* may truly feel that it is good for *him* to be afflicted. Grant this, we beseech thee, for the sake of thy Son, our Saviour Jesus Christ. Amen.

For Fellowship with Christ.

Gracious and adorable Saviour, who didst suffer for us, and canst enter into sympathy with us in all our trials and sorrows; Regard thine afflicted servant with the eyes of thy compassion. Draw tenderly near to *him*, that *he* may have fellowship with thee, and be filled with the assurance that thou lovest *him* and carest for *him*. May the thought of thy cross and passion sustain and comfort *him*. Daily may *he* learn of thee and know the preciousness of thy salvation. Be pleased to give *him* thy mind and conform *him* to thine image, that thou mayest dwell in *him* and *he* in thee. These blessings we ask in thy Name, most merciful Saviour, to whom with the Father and the Holy Ghost, be all honor and glory, world without end. Amen.

For Angelic Ministrations.

Almighty and everlasting God, who succourest those that labour under perils and afflictions, we humbly beseech thy Majesty, that it may please thee to send thy holy angel to uphold with thy comfort thy servant who is suffering distress and affliction; that *he* may both receive thy present aid, and attain eternal healing; through Jesus Christ our Lord. Amen.

For Recovery of Health.

Regard, O Lord, thy sick servant with thy favour and compassion. If it be thy holy will speedily restore *him* to health, that *he* may praise thee for thy goodness and devote *himself* to thy service with renewed zeal, and make *his* life more fruitful in all good works to the glory of thy great Name; through Jesus Christ our Lord. Amen.

For the Despondent.

Merciful Father, we pray thee to deliver thy sick servant from all impatience, and repining at thy chastisements, from dejection of spirit, and distrust of thy mercies, from the fear of death, and from such extremity of sickness, anguish, or agony, as may in any way withdraw *his* mind from thee; through Jesus Christ our Lord. Amen.

For one in Great Pain.

O gracious Father, whose dear Son bore for us unspeakable agonies, being scourged, and crowned with thorns, and nailed to the cross; Have mercy on thy servant who is now in great suffering, and grant *him* grace to fix *his* eyes upon the cross, and to find strength there to copy the example of him who, "for the joy that was set before him, endured the cross;" that following *his* divine Master through suffering, *he* may follow him to his eternal glory; through the same thy Son Jesus Christ our Lord. Amen.

In Prolonged Illness.

O God, who dost mercifully accept the offering of our weakness; Give thy servant grace to abide in communion with thee, that the lengthened season of sickness which hinders *his* work in the world may train *him* for the contemplation of thy glory in the life of the blessed; through Jesus Christ our Saviour. Amen.

Before a Surgical Operation.

Grant, we beseech thee, O Lord, that this thy servant may have bodily strength so as not to sink under the pain which thou hast appointed for *him* to undergo, and also grace to receive that blessing which thou intendest by this pain to bestow upon *him;* through Jesus Christ, who suffered for us upon the cross, who now liveth and reigneth with thee and the Holy Ghost, one God, world without end. Amen.

For one about to make a Will.

O Lord, who puttest into our hearts good desires, and hast inclined thy servant to set *his* house in order; grant that *he* may do it with wisdom and piety according to the precepts of our holy religion and the dictates of right reason, that so being freed from all earthly cares and anxieties *he* may be the better able before *he* go hence to set in order the inward house of *his* soul; through Jesus Christ our Lord. Amen.

For a Sick Person about to Communicate.

O Holy Lord, Father Almighty, everlasting God, we entreat thee in faith that our *brother*, receiving the most holy Body and Blood of thy Son our Lord Jesus Christ, may enjoy health both in body and soul; through the same Jesus Christ our Lord. Amen,

Where there is no hope of Recovery.

Almighty God, we beseech thee to look with compassion upon this thy sick servant, and let thy good Spirit work in *him* whatsoever thou seest wanting, to prepare *him* for the time of *his* dissolution. Give *him* sincere and earnest repentance. Separate *his* heart from the world, and all its fading vanities; and may *he* long after those more excellent and durable joys which are at thy right hand for ever. Lord, lift thou up the light of thy countenance upon *him*, and in all the pains of *his* body, and all the agonies of *his* spirit, let thy comforts refresh *his* soul, and enable *him* patiently to wait till *his* change come. Grant, O Lord, that when *his* earthly house of this tabernacle is dissolved, *he* may have a building of God, a house not made with hands, eternal in the heavens; through thy dear Son, Jesus Christ our Lord. Amen.

Gloria Christi.

[Originally draughted by the Rev. Dr. Muhlenberg; enlarged and re-arranged by the late Bishop of Western New York, the Rt. Rev. Arthur C. Coxe, D.D., LL.D.]

Let us adore the Promised Seed, who hath bruised the Serpent's head.

He is the Shepherd, the Stone of Israel:

The Lion of the tribe of Judah, who hath prevailed:

The Alpha and Omega: the First and the Last:

The Author and Finisher of our Faith, the Shepherd and Bishop of our souls:

The Priest of the Most High God, the true Melchizedek:

The Mediator of the New Covenant, the true Moses:

The Captain of our Salvation, the true Joshua:

The Faithful and True Witness, the Amen.

The Rose of Sharon and the Lily of the Valley:

The Crown of Glory, the Diadem of Beauty unto his people.

The Angel of Great Counsel, the Angel of the Covenant, the Ancient of Days:

The Desire of all nations, the Glory of his people Israel:

The Root and the Offspring of David: the Son of Mary, the Bright and the Morning Star:

God manifest in the flesh: the fulness of the Godhead:

The Brightness of his Father's Glory; the express Image of the Father:

The Dayspring from on High: the Sun of Righteousness risen with healing in his wings:

The Only-Begotten of the Father, full of Grace and Truth.

The Wonderful, the Counsellor, the Mighty God, the Everlasting Father, the Prince of Peace:

The Lamb slain from the foundation of the world, the Propitiation for our sins:

The only Name under Heaven, given among men, whereby we must be saved.

The Mediator between God and man, The Messiah:

Our Prophet, Priest and King; the Lord, our Righteousness:

He that hath the keys of Death and of Hell: the Judge of Quick and Dead:

And he shall reign forever and ever: by his name, JAH.

King of Kings, and Lord of Lords: God over all blessed forevermore.

JESUS CHRIST, the same, yesterday, to-day and forever, Hallelujah. Amen.

Prayers for the Dying.

Almighty God, the help of all who trust in thee; We make our supplication in behalf of thy sick servant approaching the close of *his* mortal life. May it please thee to give thy holy angels charge over *him*, to assist *him* in *his* last conflict, and to conduct *his* soul into the blessed society of thy saints in paradise, there to rest in joy and peace, till thou shalt vouchsafe to *his* body a part in the blessed resurrection of the just; through him who died and rose again, thy Son Jesus Christ our Lord. Amen.

* Unto thee, O Lord, we commend the soul of this thy servant, that dying to the world, *he* may live to thee; and whatever sins *he* has committed through the frailty of earthly life, do thou clear away by thy most loving and merciful forgiveness; through Jesus Christ our Lord. Amen.

O Lord God, receive the soul of this thy servant, and enter not into judgment with *him*. Spare *him* whom thou hast redeemed with thy most precious blood. Count not against *him* the errors of *his* youth, nor the sins and shortcomings of *his* after years, but strengthen *him* in *his* agony. Let not *his* faith waver, *his* hope fail, nor *his* love grow cold. Let the enemy have no advantage over *him*, but let *him* die in peace, rest in hope, rise in glory, and dwell in thy presence forever; through Jesus Christ our Lord. Amen.

For a Dying Child.

O Lord Jesus Christ, who didst take little children in thine arms and bless them; Bless, we beseech thee, this child; take *him* into the arms of thine everlasting mercy, keep *him* from all evil, and bring *him* into the company of those who ever behold the face of thy Father which is in heaven; to whom with thee and the blessed Spirit be all the praise for evermore. Amen.

THE ORDER FOR THE BURIAL OF THE DEAD.

¶ *Here is to be noted, that the Office ensuing is not to be used for any unbaptized adults, any who die excommunicate, or who have laid violent hands upon themselves.*

¶ *The Minister, meeting the Corpse at the entrance of the Churchyard, and going before it, either into the Church or towards the Grave, shall say or sing,*

I am the resurrection and the life, saith the Lord: he that believeth in me, though he were dead, yet shall he live: and whosoever liveth and believeth in me, shall never die. *St. John* xi. 25, 26.

I know that my redeemer liveth, and that he shall stand at the latter day upon the earth: and though after my skin worms destroy this body, yet in my flesh, shall I see God: whom I shall see for myself, and mine eyes shall behold, and not another. *Job* xix. 25, 26, 27.

We brought nothing into this world, and it is certain we can carry nothing out. The Lord gave, and the Lord hath taken away; blessed be the name of the Lord. 1 *Tim.* vi. 7. *Job* i. 21.

* *After they are come into the Church, shall be said or sung one or both of the following Selections, taken from the 39th and 90th Psalms.*

Lord, let me know mine end, and the number of my days : that I may be certified how long I have to live.

Behold, thou hast made my days as it were a span long : and mine age is even as nothing in respect of thee; and verily every man living is altogether vanity.

For a man walketh in a vain shadow, and disquieteth himself in vain : he heapeth up riches, and cannot tell who shall gather them.

And now, Lord, what is my hope : truly my hope is even in thee.

Deliver me from all mine offences : and make me not a rebuke unto the foolish.

When thou with rebukes dost chasten man for sin, thou makest his beauty to consume away, like as it were a moth fretting a garment : every man therefore is but vanity.

Hear my prayer, O Lord, and with thine ears consider my calling : hold not thy peace at my tears:

For I am a stranger with thee, and a sojourner : as all my fathers were.

O spare me a little, that I may recover my strength : before I go hence, and be no more seen.

Glory be to the Father, and to the Son : and to the Holy Ghost;

As it was in the beginning, is now, and ever shall be : world without end. Amen.

Lord, thou hast been our refuge : from one generation to another.

Before the mountains were brought forth, or ever the earth and the world were made : thou art God from everlasting, and world without end.

Thou turnest man to destruction : again thou sayest, Come again, ye children of men.

For a thousand years in thy sight are but as yesterday : seeing that is past as a watch in the night.

As soon as thou scatterest them they are even as a sleep : and fade away suddenly like the grass.

In the morning it is green, and groweth up : but in the evening it is cut down, dried up, and withered.

For we consume away in thy displeasure : and are afraid at thy wrathful indignation.

Thou hast set our misdeeds before thee : and our secret sins in the light of thy countenance.

For when thou art angry all our days are gone : we bring our years to an end, as it were a tale that is told.

The days of our age are threescore years and ten; and though men be so strong that they come to fourscore years : yet is their strength then but labour and sorrow; so soon passeth it away, and we are gone.

O teach us to number our days : that we may apply our hearts unto wisdom.

Glory be to the Father, and to the Son : and to the Holy Ghost;

As it was in the beginning, is now, and ever shall be : world without end. Amen.

* *Then shall follow the* Lesson, *taken out of the fifteenth Chapter of the first Epistle of St. Paul to the Corinthians.*

1 *Cor.* xv. 20.

Now is Christ risen from the dead, and become the firstfruits of them that slept. For since by man came death, by man came also the resurrection of the dead. For as in Adam all die, even so in Christ shall all be made alive. But every man in his own order: Christ the firstfruits; afterward they that are Christ's at his coming. Then cometh the end, when he shall have delivered up the kingdom to God, even the Father; when he shall have put down all rule and all authority and power. For he must reign, till he hath put all enemies under his feet. The last enemy that shall be destroyed is death. For he hath put all things under his feet. But when he saith all things are put under him, it is manifest that he is excepted, which did put all things under him. And when all things shall be subdued unto him, then shall the Son also himself be subject unto him that put all things under him, that God may be all in all. Else what shall they do which are baptized for the dead, if the dead rise not at all? why are they then baptized for the dead? and why stand we in jeopardy every hour? I protest by your rejoicing which I have in Christ Jesus our Lord, I die daily. If after the manner of men I have fought with beasts at Ephesus, what advantageth it me, if the dead rise not? let us eat and drink; for tomorrow we die. Be not deceived: evil communications corrupt good manners. Awake to righteousness, and sin not; for some have not the knowledge of God: I speak this to your shame. But some man will say, How are the dead raised up? and with what body do they come? Thou fool, that which thou sowest is not quickened, except it die: and that which thou

sowest, thou sowest not that body that shall
be, but bare grain, it may chance of wheat,
or of some other grain: but God giveth it
a body as it hath pleased him, and to
every seed his own body. All flesh is not
the same flesh: but there is one kind of
flesh of men, another flesh of beasts, another
of fishes, and another of birds.
There are also celestial bodies, and bodies
terrestrial: but the glory of the celestial is
one, and the glory of the terrestrial is another.
There is one glory of the sun,
and another glory of the moon, and another
glory of the stars: for one star
differeth from another star in glory. So
also is the resurrection of the dead. It is
sown in corruption; it is raised in incorruption:
it is sown in dishonour; it is
raised in glory: it is sown in weakness;
it is raised in power: it is sown a natural
body; it is raised a spiritual body. There
is a natural body, and there is a spiritual
body. And so it is written, The first man
Adam was made a living soul; the last
Adam was made a quickening spirit.
Howbeit that was not first which is spiritual,
but that which is natural; and afterward
that which is spiritual. The first
man is of the earth, earthy: the second
man is the Lord from heaven. As is the
earthy, such are they also that are earthy:
and as is the heavenly, such are they also
that are heavenly. And as we have
borne the image of the earthy, we shall
also bear the image of the heavenly.
Now this I say, brethren, that flesh and
blood cannot inherit the kingdom of God;
neither doth corruption inherit incorruption.
Behold, I shew you a mystery;
We shall not all sleep, but we shall all be
changed, in a moment, in the twinkling
of an eye, at the last trump: for the
trumpet shall sound, and the dead shall
be raised incorruptible, and we shall be
changed. For this corruptible must put
on incorruption, and this mortal must put

on immortality. So when this corruptible shall have put on incorruption, and this mortal shall have put on immortality, then shall be brought to pass the saying that is written, Death is swallowed up in victory. O death, where is thy sting? O grave, where is thy victory? The sting of death is sin; and the strength of sin is the law. But thanks be to God, which giveth us the victory through our Lord Jesus Christ. Therefore, my beloved brethren, be ye stedfast, unmovable, always abounding in the work of the Lord, forasmuch as ye know that your labour is not in vain in the Lord.

¶ *Here may be sung a Hymn or an Anthem ; and, at the discretion of the Minister, the* **Creed**, *and such fitting* **Prayers** *as are elsewhere provided in this Book, may be added.*

¶ *When they come to the Grave, while the Corpse is made ready to be laid into the earth, shall be sung or said.*

Man, that is born of a woman, hath but a short time to live, and is full of misery. He cometh up, and is cut down, like a flower; he fleeth as it were a shadow, and never continueth in one stay.

In the midst of life we are in death; of whom may we seek for succour, but of thee, O Lord, who for our sins art justly displeased?

Yet, O Lord God most holy, O Lord most mighty, O holy and most merciful Saviour, deliver us not into the bitter pains of eternal death.

Thou knowest, Lord, the secrets of our hearts; shut not thy merciful ears to our prayer; but spare us, Lord most holy, O God most mighty, O holy and merciful Saviour, thou most worthy Judge eternal, suffer us not, at our last hour, for any pains of death, to fall from thee.

¶ *Then, while the earth shall be cast upon the Body by some standing by, the Minister shall say.*

Forasmuch as it hath pleased Almighty God, in his wise providence, to take out of this world the soul of our deceased *brother*, we therefore commit *his* body to the ground; earth to earth, ashes to ashes, dust to dust; looking for the general Resurrection in the last day, and the life of the world to come, through our Lord Jesus Christ; at whose second coming in glorious majesty to judge the world, the earth and the sea shall give up their dead; and the corruptible bodies of those who sleep in him shall be changed, and made like unto his own glorious body; according to the mighty working whereby he is able to subdue all things unto himself.

¶ *Then shall be said or sung,*

I heard a voice from heaven, saying unto me, Write, From henceforth blessed are the dead who die in the Lord: even so saith the Spirit; for they rest from their labours. *Rev.* xiv. 13.

¶ *Then the Minister shall say,*

Lord, have mercy upon us.
Christ, have mercy upon us.
Lord, have mercy upon us.

Our Father, who art in heaven, Hallowed be thy Name. Thy kingdom come. Thy will be done on earth, As it is in heaven. Give us this day our daily bread. And forgive us our trespasses, As we forgive those who trespass against us. And lead us not into temptation; But deliver us from evil. Amen.

¶ *Then the Minister shall say one or both of the following Prayers, at his discretion.*

Almighty God, with whom do live the spirits of those who depart hence in the Lord, and with whom the souls of the faithful, after they are delivered from the burden of the flesh, are in joy and felicity; We give thee hearty thanks for the good examples of all those thy servants, who, having finished their course in faith, do now rest from their labours. And we beseech thee, that we, with all those who are departed in the true faith of thy holy Name, may have our perfect consummation and bliss, both in body and soul, in thy eternal and everlasting glory; through Jesus Christ our Lord. *Amen.*

O merciful God, the Father of our Lord Jesus Christ, who is the Resurrection and the Life; in whom whosoever believeth, shall live, though he die; and whosoever liveth, and believeth in him, shall not die eternally; who also hath taught us, by his holy Apostle Saint Paul, not to be sorry, as men without hope, for those who sleep in him; We humbly beseech thee, O Father, to raise us from the death of sin unto the life of righteousness; that, when we shall depart this life, we may rest in him; and that, at the general Resurrection in the last day, we may be found acceptable in thy sight; and receive that blessing, which thy well-beloved Son shall pronounce to all who love and fear thee, saying, Come, ye blessed children of my Father, receive the kingdom prepared for you from the beginning of the world. Grant this, we beseech thee, O merciful Father, through Jesus Christ, our Mediator and Redeemer. *Amen.*

The grace of our Lord Jesus Christ, and the love of God, and the fellowship of the Holy Ghost, be with us all evermore. *Amen.*

Additional Prayers.

Most merciful Father, who hast been pleased to take unto thyself the soul of this thy servant [*or* this child]; Grant to us who are still in our pilgrimage, and who walk as yet by faith, that having served thee with constancy on earth, we may be joined hereafter with thy blessed saints in glory everlasting; through Jesus Christ our Lord. *Amen.*

O Lord Jesus Christ, who by thy death didst take away the sting of death; Grant unto us thy servants so to follow in faith where thou hast led the way, that we may at length fall asleep peacefully in thee, and awake up after thy likeness; through thy mercy, who livest with the Father and the Holy Ghost, one God, world without end. *Amen.*

Almighty and everliving God, we yield unto thee most high praise and hearty thanks, for the wonderful grace and virtue declared in all thy saints, who have been the choice vessels of thy grace, and the lights of the world in their several generations; most humbly beseeching thee to give us grace so to follow the example of their stedfastness in thy faith, and obedience to thy holy commandments, that at the day of the general Resurrection, we, with all those who are of the mystical body of thy Son, may be set on his right hand, and hear that his most joyful voice: Come, ye blessed of my Father, inherit the kingdom prepared for you from the foundation of the world. Grant this, O Father, for Jesus Christ's sake, our only Mediator and Advocate. *Amen.*

* *Inasmuch as it may sometimes be expedient to say under shelter of the Church the whole or a part of the service appointed to be said at the Grave, the same is hereby allowed for weighty cause.*

At the Burial of the Dead at Sea.

* *The same office may be used; but in the Sentence of Committal, the Minister shall say,*

We therefore commit *his* body to the deep, looking for the general Resurrection in the last day, and the life of the world to come, through our Lord Jesus Christ; at whose second coming in glorious majesty to judge the world, the sea shall give up her dead; and the corruptible bodies of those who sleep in him shall be changed, and made like unto his glorious body; according to the mighty working whereby he is able to subdue all things unto himself.

SERVICE IN A PRIVATE HOUSE AT THE FUNERAL OF AN ADULT.

Scripture Selections.

Then said Martha unto Jesus, Lord, if thou hadst been here, my brother had not died. But I know, that even now, whatsoever thou wilt ask of God, God will give *it* thee. Jesus saith unto her, Thy brother shall rise again. Martha saith unto him, I know that he shall rise again in the resurrection at the last day. Jesus said unto her, I am the resurrection and the life: he that believeth in me though he were dead, yet shall he live: and whosoever liveth and believeth in me shall never die. Believest thou this? She saith unto him, Yea, Lord: I believe that thou art the Christ, the Son of God, which should come into the world.

I would not have you to be ignorant, brethren, concerning them which are asleep, that ye sorrow not, even as others which have no hope. For if we believe that Jesus died and rose again, even so them also which sleep in Jesus will God bring with him. For this we say unto you by the word of the Lord, that we which are alive *and* remain unto the coming of the Lord shall not prevent them which are asleep. For the Lord himself shall descend from heaven with a shout, with the voice of the archangel, and with the trump of God: and the dead in Christ shall rise first: Then we which are alive *and* remain shall be caught up together with them in the clouds, to meet the Lord in the air: and so shall we ever be with the Lord. Wherefore comfort one another with these words.

And he showed me a pure river of water of life, clear as crystal, proceeding out of the throne of God and of the Lamb. In the midst of the street of it, and on either side of the river, *was there* the tree of life, which bare twelve *manner of* fruits, and yielded her fruit every month: and the leaves of the tree *were* for the healing of the nations. And there shall be no more curse: but the throne of God and of the Lamb shall be in it; and his servants shall serve him: And they shall see his face: and his Name *shall be* in their foreheads. And there shall be no night there; and they need no candle, neither light of the sun; for the Lord God giveth them light: and they shall reign for ever and ever.

The souls of the righteous are in the hand of God, and there shall no torment touch them. In the sight of the unwise they seemed to die; and their departure is taken for misery, and their going from us to be utter destruction: but they are in peace. For though they be punished in the sight of men, yet is their hope full of immortality. And having been a little chastised, they shall be greatly rewarded; for God proved them, and found them worthy for himself. As gold in the furnace hath he tried them, and received them as a burnt-offering.

The righteous live for evermore; and their reward also is with the Lord, and the care of them is with the most High: Therefore shall they receive a glorious kingdom, and a beautiful crown from the Lord's hand: for with his right hand shall he cover them, and with his arm shall he protect them.

For the Afflicted.

O merciful and loving Father, who doest all things well, and of very faithfulness dost cause thy children to be troubled; We acknowledge thine infinite wisdom and all-wise providence in visiting these thy servants with thy heavy hand, and laying upon them this cross. Make them to bow submissively to thy holy will, and give them a calm and lowly resignation. Make the house of mourning to be better to them than a house of feasting. Soften permanently by thy grace the hearts that now bleed, and draw them steadily and strongly to thee. Comfort them with the hope of heavenly things, and make all earthly desires to wither and vanish away from their hearts, that they may put their whole trust and happiness in thee only; through Jesus Christ our Lord. Amen.

O Lord Jesus Christ, we beseech thee to comfort these thy servants in their present sorrow; and as thou didst send the Holy Ghost to be the Comforter of thy people, strengthen them by the manifestation of his gracious indwelling, that they may be enabled to contemplate the joy of that better home where thou art ever seen and worshipped as the light and satisfaction of thine elect, who dwellest with the Father in the unity of the same Spirit, one God, world without end. Amen.

O Almighty and everlasting God, who art the comfort of the sorrowful and the support of those that are burdened; Look in mercy, we pray thee, on all mourners and sufferers in this world of sorrow, that finding thy mercy present with them in their necessities, their sorrow may be turned into joy, and their earthly tribulations be made to them a gate of entrance into everlasting life; through Jesus Christ our Lord. Amen.

O merciful God, and heavenly Father, who hast taught us in thy holy Word that thou dost not willingly afflict or grieve the children of men; Look with pity, we beseech thee, upon the sorrows of thy *servant*, for whom our prayers are desired. In thy wisdom thou hast seen fit to visit *him* with trouble, and to bring distress upon *him*. Remember *him*, O Lord, in mercy; sanctify thy fatherly correction to *him*; endue *his* soul with patience under *his* affliction, and with resignation to thy blessed will; comfort *him* with a sense of thy goodness; lift up thy countenance upon *him*, and give *him* peace; through Jesus Christ our Lord. Amen.

For one deprived of a Husband or a Wife.

O Lord, gracious and merciful; We beseech thee to sustain and comfort thy servant who has been deprived of the companion of *his* life. Draw graciously near to *him* in *his* affliction, and help *him* to cast *his* burden upon thee. Bless this cup of sorrow to *his* spiritual good. Bend *his* will to thine that *he* may hear thy voice speaking to *his* soul in consolation and sympathy. Follow *him* with thy goodness and mercy all the days of *his* life and at last admit *him* to the blessed companionship of thy saints in glory everlasting; through Jesus Christ our Lord. Amen.

For Children bereaved of a Parent or Parents.

Almighty Father, who art full of tenderness and compassion; We pray thee to take these bereaved children under thy gracious protection. Commit them to the guidance of thy good Spirit, that they may be saved from all things hurtful to body and soul. Be near to them to deliver them in temptation, and ever in them to give them peace. Be more to them than

any earthly parent or friend. Be thou
their everlasting Defender and God. Give
them abundantly of thy grace in this life,
and finally bring them to the perpetual
joys of thy heavenly kingdom; through
Jesus Christ our Lord. Amen.

The Lessons of our Mortality

Almighty God, who bringest good out
of evil, and light out of darkness, and
dost nourish strength in the souls of those
who patiently endure chastening at thy
righteous hand, dispose us to an humble
and thankful use of all thy dealings with
us, even of those which are darkest to our
mortal sight, and so shall we glorify thy
holy Name; through Christ our Lord.
Amen.

O Lord Jesus Christ, who art the
Resurrection and the Life; who didst
thyself weep over the dead, and art
touched with the feeling of all our griefs
and sorrows; Be with us, we beseech
thee, at this time, and sanctify to us the
removal of one from the midst of us.
Impress upon us the lesson of our
mortality and help us to turn to thee with
all our hearts in true repentance and lively
faith. Let no repining or murmuring
dishonor our Christian profession. Give
us sure confidence in thee for all that is to
come, and prepare our souls to meet thee
in that day when our spirits shall return to
him who gave them. Hear us for thy
great mercies' sake, our only Saviour and
Redeemer. Amen.

Almighty God, the Father of Spirits;
We pray thee to give us a right estimate
of our temporal surroundings. May we
not put our trust in them, or place them
before the claims of thy kingdom. So
separate us from the love and idolatry of
worldly things, that we may never be
surprised by the coming of death, but

with a glad heart may welcome the hour when thou dost call us away. These petitions we ask in the Name and for the sake of thy Son Jesus Christ our Lord. Amen.

Service in a Private House at the Funeral of a Child.

Scripture Selections.

A voice was heard in Ramah, lamentation, *and* bitter weeping; Rachel weeping for her children, refused to be comforted for her children, because they *were* not.

Thus saith the Lord; Refrain thy voice from weeping, and thine eyes from tears: for thy work shall be rewarded, saith the Lord; and they shall come again from the land of the enemy. And there is hope in thine end, saith the Lord, that thy children shall come again to their own border.

He shall feed his flock like a shepherd: he shall gather the lambs with his arm, and carry *them* in his bosom.

Like as a father pitieth *his* children, *so* the Lord pitieth them that fear him.

For he knoweth our frame; he remembereth that we *are* dust.

As for man, his days *are* as grass: as a flower of the field, so he flourisheth.

For the wind passeth over it, and it is gone; and the place thereof shall know it no more.

But the mercy of the Lord *is* from everlasting to everlasting upon them that fear him, and his righteousness unto children's children;

To such as keep his covenant, and to those that remember his commandments to do them.

David perceived that the child was dead: therefore David said unto his servants, Is the child dead? and they said, He is dead. Then David arose from the earth, and washed and annointed *himself*, and changed his apparel, and came into the house of the Lord and worshipped: then he came to his own house; and when he required, they set bread before him, and he did eat. Then said his servants unto him, What thing *is* this that thou hast done? Thou didst fast and weep for the child, *while it was* alive; but when the child was dead, thou didst rise and eat bread. And he said, While the child was yet alive, I fasted and wept: for I said, Who can tell *whether* God will be gracious to me, that the child may live? But now he is dead, wherefore should I fast? can I bring him back again? I shall go to him, but he shall not return to me.

And they brought young children to him, that he should touch them: and *his* disciples rebuked those that brought *them*.

But when Jesus saw *it*, he was much displeased, and said unto them, Suffer the little children to come unto me, and forbid them not; for of such is the kingdom of God.

Verily I say unto you, Whosoever shall not receive the kingdom of God as a little child, he shall not enter therein

And he took them up in his arms, put *his* hands upon them, and blessed them.

Take heed that ye despise not one of these little ones; for I say unto you, That in heaven their angels do always behold the face of my Father which is in heaven.

Verily I say unto you, Except ye be converted, and become as little children, ye shall not enter into the kingdom of heaven.

For the Sorrowing.

Father of Mercies and God of all consolation; We beseech thee to look in tenderness upon the bereaved [parent or parents] of the child, whom thou hast taken home. May there be no bitterness in *their* sorrow, and no questioning of thy love. Help *them* to feel that thou hast graciously delivered a lamb of thy fold from the sins and dangers of the present world, and granted *him* perpetual rest and safety. Sustain *them* by the encouragements of thy Word, and beyond the clouds of affliction may *they* see the wisdom of thy providence, and be at peace; through Jesus Christ our Lord. Amen.

Holy and compassionate Saviour, who didst take little children into thine arms and bless them, help us to be submissive to thy loving will when thou dost take our children to thyself, and grant us grace so to live that they may be ours again in thy heavenly kingdom, where with the Father and the Holy Spirit we shall praise thee, world without end. Amen.

Infinite and immortal God: We pray thee to teach us day by day that we are but strangers and pilgrims upon earth, and have here no abiding city. As the ties of family are broken one by one, and kindred and friends pass from sight, give us grace that we may place our affections more and more upon things spiritual and enduring; through Jesus Christ our Lord. Amen.

PRAYERS FOR THE FAITHFUL DEPARTED.

O God, who art the Lord of mercy, grant to the soul of thy servant [the anniversary of whose decease we celebrate] a place of refreshment, the blessedness of eternal peace and the brightness of heavenly light; through Jesus Christ our Lord. Amen

O Lord Jesus Christ, who didst put death under thy feet, didst destroy the power of the devil, and gavest thy life for the world, grant rest to the souls of thy departed servants (especially.........), in the place of light and refreshment, whence pain, sorrow and sighing are driven away; and in thy goodness and mercy pardon every sin committed by *them* in thought, word, and deed; thou who art the resurrection and the life, and who livest and reignest for ever and ever. Amen.

O God, whose property is ever to have mercy and to spare; We suppliants intreat thee for thy servant whom to-day thou hast called to depart from this world, that thou wouldest not deliver *him* into the hand of the enemy, but commend *him* to be received by holy angels, and led into the land of the living. Whereas *he* hath hoped and believed in thee, may *he* be found worthy to rejoice in the society of thy saints; through Jesus Christ thy Son our Lord. Amen.

O Lord Christ, who hast promised to come again in like manner as thou didst go into heaven; We pray thee to hasten the time of thine Advent, that sin and death may be overcome, and that we, with all thy faithful departed, may be perfected in blessedness in that day when thou makest up thy jewels; through thy mercy, O our God who art blessed, and livest and reignest for ever and ever. Amen.

O Lord Jesus Christ, God of our fathers; We bless thy holy Name, thy grace and mercy, for all those who have gone before us to rest in thee: pious fathers, devout mothers, zealous priests, chaste virgins, harmless infants, all in all vocations who have pleased thee. And we pray thee, give us also grace to walk before thee as they walked in righteousness and self-denial: that having laboured as they laboured, we may afterward rest as they rest. Grant this for thy mercies' sake O Saviour, who with the Father and the Holy Ghost art one God, world without end. Amen.

O God, the God of the spirits of all flesh, in whose embrace all creatures live, in whatsoever world or condition they be; We beseech thee for those whose names and dwelling-places and every need thou knowest. Lord, vouchsafe them light and rest, peace and refreshment, joy and consolation in Paradise, in the companionship of saints, in the presence of Christ, and in the ample folds of thy great love. Grant that their lives (so troubled here) may unfold in thy sight, and find sweet employment in the spacious fields of eternity. If they have ever been hurt or maimed by any unhappy word or deed of ours, we pray thee of thy great pity to heal and restore them, that they may serve thee without hindrance. Tell them, O gracious Lord, if it may be, how much we love them and miss them, and long to see them again; and, if there be ways in which they may come, vouchsafe them to us as guides and guards, and grant us a sense of their nearness in such degree as thy laws permit. If in aught we can minister to their peace, be pleased of thy love to let this be; and mercifully keep us from every act which may deprive us of the sight of them as soon as our trial-time is over, or mar the fullness of our joy when the end of the days hath come. Pardon, O gracious Lord and Father, whatsoever is amiss in this our prayer, and let thy will be done, for our will is blind and erring, but thine is able to do exceeding abundantly above all that we ask or think; through Jesus Christ our Lord. Amen

Occasional Offices.

✠

OFFICE FOR THE ADMISSION OF CHORISTERS.

¶ *After special psalms and lessons these questions follow:*

Dost thou desire to become a member of this Choir, appointed to direct the praises of Almighty God?
Answer. I do.
Dost thou promise to be attentive and reverent, and to conduct thyself in all things as becometh one who is in the house of God?
Answer. I do.
Dost thou promise to exercise the spirit of brotherly love toward all those who are associated with thee in this service of praise?
Answer. I do.
Dost thou promise to be punctual and regular in attendance, unless reasonably prevented?
Answer. I do.
Dost thou promise to obey in all things lawful, the rules of this choir?
Answer. I do.
Dost thou promise to be obedient to those, to whom the direction of this choir has been given?
Answer. I do.

¶ *Then shall the Priest say,*

I admit thee into this choir, In the Name of the Father, and of the Son, and of the Holy Ghost. Amen. The praises of God be in thy heart and in thy mouth. The grace of God sanctify and keep thee, that thou mayest hereafter be numbered among those, who having washed their robes and made them white in the Blood of the Lamb, stand before the throne of God and serve day and night in the heavenly temple.

¶ *The Priest then giving the Psalter to each says,*

Receive this book, and see that what thou singest with thy lips, thou believe in thy heart and practice in thy life.

Let us pray.

Almighty God, who hast ordained the faculties of man to be the eternal instruments of rendering to thee glory and praise: We thank thee that thou hast moved the hearts of these thy servants to desire to serve thee, in singing the praises of thy Name in thy holy Church. Bless them, we beseech thee, in their ministry of song. Endue them with the spirit of worship in thy holy fear, that through the presence and power of the Holy Ghost, they may edify themselves and all thy congregation in psalms and hymns and spiritual songs, singing and making melody in their hearts. Hear us, for the sake of Jesus Christ, to whom with thee and the Holy Ghost, be glory and praise, world without end. Amen.

Grant, O Lord Jesus Christ, that those who are set apart to lead thy worship upon earth may be admitted to join in the ceaseless songs of heavenly worship with thine elect; let their white robes be to them a constant memorial of the purity which thou requirest, and their association with thy priests on earth remind them of their nearness to thee, the great High Priest, by whom alone our praises are acceptably offered to the Father, that so their lives, as well as their psalms, may be found to thine honor and glory, who ever livest to make intercession for us, our Mediator and Advocate, our Lord and our God. Amen.

The blessing of God Almighty, the Father, the Son, and the Holy Ghost, be with thee, now and for evermore. Amen.

OFFICE FOR LAYING A CORNER STONE.

SUITABLE PSALMS.—84, 122, 87, 48, 118.
SUITABLE LESSONS.—Genesis xxviii. 10; 1 Chronicles xxix 10-18; 2 Chronicles ii 1-13; Ezra iii 10; 1 Corinthians iii. ; 1 Peter ii.

¶ *After the Psalms and Lessons the Priest shall say.*

Behold I lay in Zion a chief Corner Stone elect, precious:
R. And he that believeth in him shall not be confounded.
The Stone which the builders refused,
R. Is become the head stone of the corner.
This is the Lord's doing,
R. And it is marvelous in our eyes.
Glory be to the Father, etc.,
R. As it was in the beginning, etc.
I believe, etc.
Let us pray.
Our Father, etc.

Almighty and everlasting God, mercifully be pleased to bless this stone, which we are about to place for a foundation in the Name of him who is the tried and precious Stone; and grant that all they who, to the furtherance of this work, shall have faithfully offered to thee of their substance, may ever be preserved both in body and soul; through Jesus Christ our Lord. Amen.

¶ *Then shall the Priest, striking the stone three times, say,*

In the faith of Jesus Christ, we place this stone in the foundation, In the Name of the Father,✠ and of the Son,✠ and of the Holy Ghost.✠ Amen.

May the voice of prayer and praise continually be heard here. May many souls through faith in Jesus Christ, a devout hearing of the Word of God, and a right reception of the Holy Sacraments, find this place none other than the house of God, and the gate of heaven. Amen.

Let us pray.

Bless, O Lord, this stone, and grant through the invocation of thy holy Name that this work begun in thee may be fulfilled to thy glory; through Jesus Christ our Lord. Amen.

Let thy Holy Spirit, O Lord our God, descend and rest upon this place, that our gifts and all our services may be sanctified, and our hearts, and the hearts of all who labor upon this building may be cleansed and purified; through Jesus Christ our Lord. Amen.

O God, who art the shield and defence of thy people, be ever at hand, we beseech thee, to protect and succor the builders of this house; that the work which, through thy mercy, hath now been begun, may by their labor be brought to a happy end; through Jesus Christ our Lord. Amen.

O God, who hast built the living temple of thy Church upon the foundation of the Apostles and Prophets, Jesus Christ himself being the chief corner-stone; Grant unto the work of thine own hands continual increase of glory and spiritual strength, and daily make thy people more meet for the eternal tabernacle of thy rest in the heavens; through Jesus Christ our Lord. Amen.

O God, we humbly beseech thee to accept the services of all who contribute of their substance toward building here a house of prayer. Let thy blessing rest upon them and upon those who labor in erecting it, and grant that the progress of this work may be secured against every accident and carried forward without hindrance unto completion; through Jesus Christ thy Son our Lord. Amen.

O Lord, we beseech thee to pour thy heavenly blessing on all those who are engaged in doing and furthering good works in thy holy Church; prosper their undertakings, grant them perseverance therein, and stimulate others by their example to like zeal in thy service; through Jesus Christ our Lord. Amen.

O Lord Jesus Christ, who art the temple of the New Jerusalem; Guide, we pray thee, wandering souls into that earthly Jerusalem which is thy holy Catholic Church. Let thy compassions overflow all bounds, and gather into the sanctuary of thy love every soul which can be made capable of loving thee. And at last give us, O Lord, part in the worship of that blessed company to whom thou, in the Unity of the adorable Trinity, shalt be All in all. grant this, O our God, who art blessed and liveth and reigneth for ever and ever. Amen.

The grace, etc.

BENEDICTION OF A RECTORY OR CLERGY HOUSE.

O eternal God, without whom nothing is strong, nothing is holy: Bless ✠ to the use of this Parish for the years to come, this house which loving hearts and willing hands have erected for the honor and glory of thy great Name. May it ever be like a dwelling of Jacob, from which a hallowed influence shall go forth to bless and strengthen thy people in this place. May they, in the spirit of Christian love regard this home, and ever bring to those who dwell therein the support of true sympathy and devotion; all which we ask through Jesus Christ our Lord. Amen.

O Lord, our Heavenly Father; Let thy loving mercy and compassion ever descend upon the dwellers in this house. Give them health of body, soul and spirit, and a competent portion of temporal blessings. Drive away darkness and give them light. Defend them from evil, and support them in adversity. Vouchsafe them peace, cheerfulness and a living faith. Abide with them through all the changes of their mortal state, and grant them in the world to come, life everlasting; through Jesus Christ our Lord. Amen.

BENEDICTION OF AN ALTAR.

Almighty and everlasting God, who didst manifest thyself in the Temple with great glory: We invoke thy blessing ✠ upon this altar. Grant that the prayers and oblations offered here may be acceptable to thy divine Majesty. Kneeling here may thy people in times of trouble find relief; in sickness of body and soul, health; in unbelief, faith; in weakness, strength; in hours of darkness, light; and when depressed by sin and worldliness, spiritual refreshment and peace; through Jesus Christ our Lord, who with thee and the Holy Ghost liveth and reigneth one God, world without end. Amen.

Grant, Almighty God, that all who minister at the altars of thy Church may have the abundance of thy grace. May they be holy, loving and blameless in their lives, and may the blessed Sacrament of the Body and Blood of Christ administered by them, be to the great and endless comfort of thy people; through the same Jesus Christ our Lord. Amen.

BENEDICTION OF HOLY COMMUNION VESSELS.

Almighty God, we acknowledge that we are not worthy to offer unto thee anything belonging unto us; Yet we beseech thee to accept, bless, sanctify, and hallow, ✠ these vessels that are to be used in commemorating the love of thy Son in dying for us. We ask it through the same Jesus Christ our Lord. Amen.

O eternal God, by whose command the temple was adorned and beautified; We bless thy holy Name that it hath pleased thee to put it into the hearts of thy servants to contribute to the beauty, honor, and reverent worship of thine house through this memorial. Enlarge, we beseech thee this spirit of free will offerings in all thy people, that thy kingdom may be advanced and the salvation of men be accomplished; through Jesus Christ our Lord. Amen.

Grant, O Lord, that whosoever shall receive through these gifts the blessed Sacrament of the Body and Blood of Christ, may come to that holy ordinance with faith, charity, and true repentance; and being filled with thy grace and heavenly benediction may obtain remission of their sins, and all other benefits of the Eucharistic Feast. Grant this for the sake of Jesus Christ thy Son our Lord. Amen.

BENEDICTION OF A SANCTUARY LAMP.

Almighty and everlasting God, who didst command thine ancient people Israel to burn a lamp continually in the tabernacle of the congregation; We beseech thee to bless and hallow ✠ this lamp. By its light may it symbolize thy presence in thy holy temple, and teach us, that in thee there is no darkness at all; through Jesus Christ our Lord. Amen.

O Lord Jesus Christ, who art the Brightness of the Father's glory, and the Light of the world; Shine upon us, we beseech thee, and grant that those who have the Light may walk as children of Light; and that those who sit in darkness and the shadow of death may know thee, the one true Light and the Sun of righteousness; who, with the Father and the Holy Ghost, livest and reignest one God, world without end. Amen.

BENEDICTION OF A FONT.

Almighty God, we beseech thee to hallow ✠ by thy heavenly visitation and the radiancy of thy Holy Spirit this Font which we dedicate unto thee, that whoever shall be laved herein, being cleansed by the three-fold washing, may of thy bounty obtain the pardon of all his sins; through Jesus Christ our Lord. Amen.

We yield thee humble thanks, O heavenly Father, that thou hast vouchsafed to call us to the knowledge of thy grace and faith in thee. Increase this knowledge, and confirm this faith in us evermore. Give thy Holy Spirit to all who shall be baptized in this Font, that, being born again and made heirs of everlasting salvation through our Lord Jesus Christ, they may continue thy servants and attain thy promises; through the same thy Son Jesus Christ, who liveth and reigneth with thee in the unity of the same Holy Spirit everlastingly. Amen.

O God, by whom redemption and adoption are bestowed upon us, raise up unto thyself the hearts of thy believing people; that all who have been regenerated in holy Baptism may apprehend in their minds what they have received in mysteries; through Jesus Christ our Lord. Amen.

Almighty and everlasting God, bring us to the fellowship of heavenly joys; that thou mayest vouchsafe an entrance into thy kingdom to those that are born again of the Holy Ghost, and that the lowly flock may reach that place whither the mighty Shepherd hath gone before; through the same Jesus Christ our Lord. Amen.

BENEDICTION OF A PULPIT.

O Lord Jesus Christ, who didst command thy chosen ministers to go into all the world and preach the gospel to every creature; We pray thee to bless,✠ sanctify, and hallow this pulpit, and grant to all who shall speak therefrom, plainness of speech in rebuking vice, and persistency and boldness in declaring the whole truth. Grant this, blessed Saviour, for thy mercy's sake, who livest and reignest with the Father and the Holy Ghost one God, world without end. Amen.

Grant us, O Lord, attentive ears, and receptive hearts, that we may rejoice in thy preached Word, and loving more and more its holy precepts, may daily grow in grace until we come to thine everlasting kingdom; through Jesus Christ our Lord. Amen.

BENEDICTION OF A ROOD SCREEN.

Almighty God, who hast exalted the cross as the standard of our salvation; We beseech thee to bless ✠ and sanctify this Rood Screen. May its uplifting be acceptable to thee, and may it be to us a perpetual reminder of the passion of thy dear Son, Jesus Christ our Lord, to whom with thee and the Holy Ghost be glory and honor, world without end. Amen.

Blessed Saviour, who didst hang upon the cross, stretching forth thy loving arms; Grant that all mankind may look unto thee and be saved; through thy mercies and merits, who livest and reignest with the Father and the Holy Ghost, one God, world without end. Amen.

BENEDICTION OF A CROSS.

O God, who didst by the uplifting of thy beloved Son, draw all men unto him; We pray thee to bless and sanctify ✠ this cross, and grant that it may remind us of the humility and patience of him who suffered thereon, that we might obtain eternal life. This we ask in the Name of Jesus Christ our Lord. Amen.

Merciful and gracious God, who didst give thine only-begotten Son to die for us, the just for the unjust; Grant us grace that we may never be ashamed of the cross of Christ. May it be to us the emblem of our redemption, and fill us with love and gratitude toward him, who for our sakes endured the cross, despising the shame. We ask it through the same Jesus Christ our Lord. Amen.

BENEDICTION OF AN ORGAN.

Almighty God, who hast taught us in thy blessed Word to magnify thy holy Name; We offer thee this instrument of praise to assist in the services of thine house. We beseech thee to bless, ✠ hallow, and sanctify it, that it may be free from all secular and worldly purposes, and lead the minds of thy people up to thee; through Jesus Christ our Lord. Amen.

Grant, O Lord, that those who enter thy courts to worship thee, may engage in the prayers and praises with such solemnity, reverence and devotion, that their spiritual natures may be refreshed and strengthened; through Jesus Christ our Lord. Amen.

Grant, O Lord God, that our hearts may be so attuned to the songs of thine earthly house that we may at last be welcomed to the praises of that temple not made with hands, eternal in the heavens, where thou with the Son and the Holy Ghost livest and reignest one God, world without end. Amen.

BENEDICTION OF AN ALMS BASIN.

Almighty God, who delightest in the free will offerings of thy people; We pray thee to bless ✠ and hallow this alms basin; Grant that we may all offer thee of our substance according as thou hast blessed us. If we have much, may we give plenteously, and if little, may we give gladly of that little, thus laying up in store for ourselves a good foundation against the time to come, that we may attain eternal life; through Jesus Christ our Lord. Amen.

O God, who buildest for thy Majesty an eternal habitation out of living and elect stones; Assist thy suppliant people, that as thy Church gains in material extent, it may also be enlarged by spiritual increase; through Jesus Christ our Lord. Amen.

BENEDICTION OF A CHURCH BELL.

Almighty God, who dost sanctify material things to the honor and glory of thy Church; We entreat thee to bless ✠ and hallow this bell set apart for the services of thine house. May its voice be a joyful sound to all Christian people, bidding to prayer and praise, and a right keeping of holy days; through Jesus Christ our Lord. Amen.

We beseech thee, Almighty God, that this bell may speak in warning tones to the ungodly and the careless of the claims of thy house of prayer, and lead them to seek a new life in thee; through Jesus Christ our Lord. Amen.

We beseech thee, Almighty God, that the sound of this bell calling faithful souls to the Sacrament of the Body and Blood of Christ, may be heeded by us, that through the power of the Holy Eucharist, Christ may dwell in us, and we in him; through the same Jesus Christ our Lord. Amen.

Almighty God, we pray thee that those who are suffering from any sickness whereby they cannot appear in thy courts, may through this sounding bell have comforting and peaceful thoughts of thee; through Jesus Christ our Lord. Amen.

Almighty God, vouchsafe, we beseech thee, that the tolling of this bell at the passing away of any mortal life, may lead us to holy anticipations of that life which knows no ending; through Jesus Christ our Lord. Amen.

BENEDICTION OF PALMS.

O Lord Jesus Christ, who in the days of thy flesh, entered thy capital city, meek and lowly, sitting upon an ass, and upon a colt, the foal of an ass, and who afterward was seen by Saint John, going forth on a white horse, with a bow and a crown, conquering and to conquer; Bless ✠ these emblems of victory, and to those who carry them, grant that so far as the sufferings of Christ abound in them, their consolation may abound by Christ. Hear us, O blessed Saviour of mankind, who now livest and reignest with the Father, and the Holy Ghost, one God, world without end. Amen.

Almighty God, whose Son at the time of his entrance into Jerusalem was hailed as King, and his way strewn with palm branches; Grant that when the victorious Christ shall come again, we may be ready to meet him with Hosannas, and be made partakers with him of eternal victory, through the same Jesus Christ our Lord. Amen.

Various Benedictions.

Of a Marriage Ring.

Almighty God, we beseech thee to sanctify and hallow ✠ this ring, and grant that he who gives it, and she who receives it, may live each for the other, and both for thee; through Jesus Christ our Lord. Amen.

Of Choir or Guild Medals.

O God, Creator, Preserver, and Saviour of mankind, send down thy blessing ✠ on these medals, that whoever wears them may evermore stand fast in thy faith, love and fear, and may daily increase in thy Holy Spirit, more and more; through our Lord Jesus Christ. Amen.

Of Service Books.

O God, the source of all knowledge; We beseech thee to hallow ✠ these books now set apart for thy service. Grant that the blessed truths they contain may be gladly received and faithfully followed, to the glory of thy Name and our salvation; through Jesus Christ our Lord. Amen.

Of Candles.

Almighty God, who didst send thy Son to be the Light of the world; Bless ✠ we beseech thee, these candles, and grant, that we may walk as children of light, to the honor of thy holy Name; through Jesus Christ our Lord. Amen.

Of Vestments.

O God, whose power is Almighty who art the Creator and Hallower of all things; Graciously hear our prayers, and vouchsafe thyself to bless ✠ and hallow these garments for the use of thy ministers, and grant that all those who use them, attending in thy temple, and serving thee devoutly and reverently in them, may become well-pleasing unto thee; through Jesus Christ our Lord. Amen.

Of an Altar Cloth.

Almighty God, who hast appointed holy places for the administration of thy mysteries; Vouchsafe a blessing ✠ upon this cloth made to adorn the altar of thine house, and grant that it may deepen our reverence for all things sacred; through Jesus Christ our Lord. Amen.

Of Altar Linen.

Grant, Almighty God, that this linen may be hallowed ✠ by thy blessing, and that henceforth it may aid in making decorous the services that honor the Sacrament of the Body and Blood of Christ. We ask it through the same Jesus Christ our Lord. Amen.

Of a Church Banner.

Almighty God, who art honored in reverent worship and sacred appointments; We beseech thee to bless ✠ and sanctify this banner, that by its use, thy Church may be adorned and thy Name revered; through Jesus Christ our Lord. Amen.

Of a Funeral Pall.

Almighty God, in whose hand is the breath of man; We beseech thee to bless ✠ and hallow this funeral pall, and grant that its use may remind us of the shortness and uncertainty of our mortal life, and quicken us to seek that imperishable wisdom which thou hast revealed through thy Son Jesus Christ our Lord, to whom with thee and the Holy Ghost be all praise and glory, world without end. Amen.

Missionary Prayers.

✠

ORDER FOR A MISSIONARY SERVICE.

PROPER PSALMS.—Psalms 2, 45, 46, 72, 96, 110, 145.

SCRIPTURE LESSONS.—Isaiah xlix., lii. 7, liii. and lx.; St. Matthew ix. 35; St. John, xvii.; Romans, x.

COLLECTS.—For the Twenty-fifth Sunday after Trinity; St. Andrew's Day; Third Sunday in Advent; Second and Third Collects for Good Friday; Third Sunday after Easter; Fifth Sunday after Trinity; St. Simon and St. Jude's Day.

Almighty God, by whose heavenly inspiration we think those things that are right, even as by thy merciful guidance we perform the same; Quicken in the hearts of thy servants the Bishops and other Pastors of thy flock and the people committed to their charge, such a sense of their duty to all who are ignorant, erring and uncared-for in this land as shall move them to sacrifice and service in their behalf, without stint and without delay. Make us to see that souls are perishing for lack of the knowledge of Jesus Christ and him crucified, and since thou hast entrusted to us the knowledge of thy truth and the gifts of thy bounty, help us to use them as good stewards, that so thy Word may be proclaimed and thy kingdom enlarged, to the glory of thy Name and the salvation of men; through Jesus Christ our Lord. Amen.

Almighty God, who, by thy Son Jesus Christ, didst give commandment to the holy Apostles, that they should go into all the world, and preach the gospel to every creature; Grant to us whom thou hast called into thy Church a ready will to obey thy word, and fill us with a hearty desire to make thy way known upon earth, thy saving health among all nations. Look with compassion upon the heathen that have not known thee, and on the multitudes in our own land that are scattered abroad as sheep having no shepherd. O heavenly Father, Lord of the harvest, have respect, we beseech thee, to our prayers, and send forth laborers into thy harvest. Fit and prepare them by thy grace for the work of their ministry; give them the spirit of power, and of love, and of a sound mind strengthen them to endure hardship; and grant that both by their life and doctrine they may show forth thy glory, and set forward the salvation of all men; through Jesus Christ our Lord. Amen.

O Holy Father, who didst promise to thy well-beloved Son, "Desire of me and I shall give thee the heathen for thine inheritance and the utmost parts of the earth for thy possession;" Hear, we pray thee, his prevailing intercession for the souls which he has purchased with his precious blood; kindle our desires for the extension of his kingdom among men; pour upon us the spirit of supplication for the spread of the gospel; and so consecrate our lives to thy service, that we may gladly give ourselves and our substance to send the sound of the blessed gospel "into all lands and its words unto the ends of the world;" through Jesus Christ our Lord. Amen.

Gather together thine elect, O Saviour, from the four corners of heaven. Send forth thy ministers into all the world in the spirit and power of Elias, and bring in the fulness of the Gentiles. Quicken the dead in trespasses and sins; enlighten the ignorant; bring back the wandering; and as thou hast warned us that the day of the Lord so cometh as a thief in the night, grant us grace to be sober, and to watch always unto prayer, lest that day come upon us unawares; and evermore to live with our loins girded, as men who wait for their Lord; and thy Name shall be praised, world without end. Amen.

O most merciful Saviour and Redeemer, who wouldest not that any should perish, but that all men should be saved and come to the knowledge of the truth; Fulfil thy gracious promise to be present with those who are gone forth in thy Name to preach the gospel of salvation in distant lands. Be with them in all perils by land or by water, in sickness and distress, in weariness and painfulness, in disappointment and persecution. Bless them, we beseech thee, with thy continual favour; and send thy Holy Spirit to guide them into all truth O Lord, let thy ministers be clothed with righteousness, and grant that thy Word spoken by their mouths may never be spoken in vain. Endue them with power from on high; and so prosper thy work in their hands, that the fulness of the Gentiles may be gathered in, and all Israel be saved. Hear us, O Lord, for thy mercy's sake; and grant that all who are called by thy Name may be one in thee, and may abound more and more in prayers and in freewill offerings, for the extension of thy kingdom throughout the world, to thy honor and glory, who livest and reignest with the Father and the Holy Ghost, one God, world without end. Amen.

Almighty God, whose compassions fail not, and whose loving kindness reacheth unto the world's end; We give thee humble thanks for all the great things thou hast done and art doing for the children of men, for the opening of heathen lands to the light of thy truth, for making paths in the deep waters and highways in the desert, for knitting nation to nation in the bonds of fellowship, and for the planting of thy Church in all the earth. O merciful Father, in whom the whole family is named, fill full our hearts with grateful love for this thy goodness, granting us grace henceforth to serve thee better and more perfectly to know thee; through Jesus Christ our Lord. Amen.

Almighty God, who hast given to thy dear Son the heathen for an inheritance, and the utmost parts of the earth for a possession. Bless, we beseech thee, the missionary work of thy holy Church in all parts of the world. Have pity upon the peoples who are still calling upon gods that cannot save, and so touch their hearts and waken their consciences and rule their wills, that they may turn to thee the living God, who wouldest have all men to be saved and to come to the knowledge of the truth. Raise up among them, we pray thee, prophets and teachers of their own blood, men full of wisdom and of the Holy Ghost. Gather in the souls destitute of help. Set free the prisoners of darkness. Have pity upon the unthankful and the unholy. Forgive the evildoers who know not what they do; and out of many nations and peoples and kindreds and tongues assemble the congregation of thy saints. All which we ask for the sake of thy only Son our Saviour Jesus Christ. Amen.

O God, who hast made of one blood all nations of men to dwell on all the face of the earth, and didst send thy blessed Son to preach peace to them that are afar off, and to them that are nigh; Grant that the heathen peoples everywhere may seek after thee and find thee, and hasten, O Lord, the fulfilment of thy promise to pour out thy Spirit upon all flesh; through Jesus Christ our Lord. Amen.

Special Prayers for Missions.

For Indian Missions.

Almighty and most merciful God, the Father of the friendless and the helper of the helpless; Have pity, we beseech thee, upon the Indian tribes who dwell in this our land. Send to them the light and comfort of thy holy gospel. Bless all the means used to bring them to the knowledge of thy dear Son, who died for the salvation of all men. Guide with thy Spirit, guard with thy power, sustain with thy love, all those who minister to them in spiritual things, and bear to them the tidings of redemption. Stir up the hearts of all who profess and call themselves Christians to prayer and deeds of mercy in behalf of this perishing race. Give to our rulers a sense of honor, truth and justice in all their dealings with them, and fill this whole nation with compassion for this poor and scattered people; and so fetch them home, blessed Lord, to thy flock, that they may be saved among the remnant of true Israelites, and be made one fold under one Shepherd. All which we ask through Jesus Christ our Lord. Amen.

For Missions among Colored People.

Almighty and eternal God, whose love and care extendeth to all thy creatures; We pray thee to hear the prayers of thy Church in behalf of the missionary work now being carried on among the colored people of our land. Prosper every effort to advance their moral and spiritual condition. Save them from vice, superstition, and ignorance, and incite them to industry, self-reliance and faithfulness. Cause the light of thy gospel to shine into their hearts, and through the power of the Holy Spirit may they be lovers of purity, honesty and truthfulness. Grant that in all things they may live righteously, soberly, and godly in this present world, and finally by thy mercy enter upon the joys of the world to come; through Jesus Christ our Lord. Amen.

For the Jews.

O everlasting God, the God of Abraham, the God of Isaac, and the God of Jacob; We beseech thee to look upon thine ancient people, Israel, scattered abroad throughout the world, and to visit them with thy salvation. Take away the veil from their hearts, and bring them to a knowledge of Jesus Christ, their Messiah, their Prince, and their Saviour; and so fetch them home, blessed Lord, to thy flock, that they may be saved among the remnant of the true Israelites, and be made partakers of everlasting life; through the same Jesus Christ, thy Son, who liveth and reigneth with thee and the Holy Ghost, one God, world without end. Amen.

For our Fellow-country-men in distant Lands.

O Lord Jesus Christ, who hast commanded us by thy Apostles to walk worthy of the vocation wherewith we are called, and as we have received thy gift, so to minister the same one to another; Grant to all who are baptized into thy holy Name, and especially to our fellow-country-men who sojourn in distant lands, that they may show forth thy praises, who hast called them out of darkness into marvellous light. Preserve them, we beseech thee, from the sin of offending thy little ones who believe in thee, and from causing thy Word to be blasphemed among the heathen. Make them as the salt of the earth, and as a light in the world; that so, beholding their good works, and won by their holy lives, multitudes may be turned to thy truth, to glorify thee in the day of visitation, who with the Father and the Holy Ghost art one God, world without end. Amen.

For Persecuted Christians.

Almighty God, who hast knit together thine elect in one communion and fellowship in the mystical

Body of thy Son Christ our Lord; and hast taught us to bear one another's burdens and so fulfil the law of Christ; We beseech thee mercifully to remember thy servants, our brethren, who are suffering persecution for his Name. Strengthen those who stand, comfort and help the weak-hearted; if any fall, raise them up; and we pray thee to forgive their enemies and persecutors, and to turn their hearts; that the blood of these thy servants may be effectual to the conversion of souls and of the heathen land in which they dwell; through Jesus Christ our Lord. Amen.

For the Syrian Church.

Revive, O Lord, in the midst of the years, revive thy work, O Lord. Gather together thy dispersed sheep, scattered throughout the world, into one fold under one Shepherd; and grant that through the operation of the Holy Spirit the labors of the Syrian Church may be made effectual for the conversion of Asia. Send forth laborers into thy harvest, and defend them by thy mighty power, through Jesus Christ our Lord. Amen.

At the Sending forth of a Missionary.

Almighty God, who didst send thine only-begotten Son into the world for the redemption of mankind, and that the gospel of his kingdom might be made known unto men through the preaching of his Apostles; Send, we pray thee, thy Holy Spirit upon this thy servant whom thou hast called to labor in thy vineyard. Anoint him to preach the gospel to the poor, send him to heal the broken-hearted, to preach deliverance to the captives, and recovery of sight to the blind, to set at liberty them that are bruised, and to preach the acceptable year of the Lord. And grant that he may follow after righteousness, godliness, faith, love, patience, and meekness; through Jesus Christ our Lord. Amen.

For Seamen.

Almighty Father, with whom is no distance, and no darkness, and no power too strong for thy ruling; We beseech thee to bless on all seas the vessels of our fleet and merchandise, our sailors and our fishermen, with all that go to and fro and occupy their business in great waters; save them from dangers known and unforeseen; deliver them from strong temptation and from easily besetting sin; teach them to mark thy works and wonders on the deep, fill them with kindness, loyalty and faith, and make every man to do his duty; through Jesus Christ our Lord. Amen.

For Fallen Women.

O Almighty God, we thy unworthy servants beseech thee to bless the work of thy Church among those who have fallen through the temptations of fleshly sin. Stir up, O Lord, the hearts of devout men and women to minister to thy lost and helpless ones; support and comfort them in all their toil and anxiety, and vouchsafe them the increase of faith and love, and bring them to be of one mind and heart in the communion of thy saints, that they may work together for thee here, and finally be received into thy kingdom of peace; through the merits and mediation of thy dear Son, our only Saviour, Jesus Christ. Amen.

For the Increase of the Ministry.

O Almighty God, who hast in thy holy Church committed to the hands of men the ministry of reconciliation, to gather together a great flock in all parts of the world, to the eternal praise of thy holy Name; We humbly beseech thee that thou wilt put it in the hearts of many faithful men to seek this sacred ministry, appointed for the salvation of mankind; that so thy Church may rejoice in a due supply of true and faithful pastors, and the bounds of thy blessed kingdom may be enlarged; through Jesus Christ our Lord. Amen.

For City Missions.

O God, almighty and merciful, who healest those that are broken in heart, and turnest the sadness of the sorrowful to joy; Let thy fatherly goodness be upon all that thou hast made. Especially we beseech thee to remember in pity such as are, at this time, destitute, homeless, or forgotten of their fellow-men. Bless the congregation of thy poor. Uplift those who are cast down, mightily befriend innocent sufferers, and sanctify to them the endurance of their wrongs. Cheer with hope all discouraged and unhappy people, and by thy heavenly grace preserve from falling those whose penury tempteth them to sin. Though they be troubled on every side, suffer them not to be distressed; though they be perplexed, save them from despair. Grant this, O Lord, for the love of him, who for our sakes became poor, thy Son, our Saviour Jesus Christ. Amen.

For Workers in City Missions.

Gracious God and Father, who willest not that any should perish, but that all men should be saved and come to a knowledge of the truth; Bless and encourage all workers, clerical and lay, who are ministering to the poor, the destitute, the Christless and cast down in our great cities. Give them patience in dealing with the vicious and forsaken, and persistency in seeking the sheep that have wandered from thy fold. May they be as lights illuminating homes of darkness and vice. May they speak peace to troubled hearts and bring many souls, now burdened with sin into the liberty and joy of the gospel. Fill these workers and helpers

with love and courage, that they may never despair
of any of thy creatures, but be animated to greater
devotion and exertion by the sin and wretchedness
of the world. Grant this for the sake of him who
went about doing good, thy Son Jesus Christ our
Lord. Amen.

Prayers for Women Workers.

Almighty God, who didst call Phœbe and other
holy women to be helpers and workers in thy
service; We pray thee to bless these thy servants
whom thou hast called to a like ministration. Give
them hearts of thankfulness for the honor thou hast
put upon them. Fill them with all Christian graces,
that by their zeal and good example, they may faithfully serve thee, to the glory of thy Name, and the
good of thy Church; through Jesus Christ our Lord.
Amen.

Vouchsafe thy blessing, O Lord, upon all women
who are engaged in good works, and devoted to the
enlargement of thy kingdom. Give them wisdom
and patience, diligence and fortitude, and an unceasing regard for all who may be made thine.
Lift them above every discouragement and give
them an abundant harvest of souls, through him who
came to seek and save the lost, thy Son Jesus Christ
our Lord. Amen.

For the Woman's Auxiliary.

O Lord, without whom our labor is but lost, and
with whom thy little ones go forth as the mighty;
We humbly beseech thee to prosper all works in thy
Church undertaken according to thy holy will,
(especially the work of the Woman's Auxiliary,) and
grant to thy laborers a pure intention, patient faith,
sufficient success upon earth, and the blessedness of
serving thee in heaven; through Jesus Christ our
Lord. Amen.

For the Daughters of the King.

O eternal Father, who hast sent us thy Son to
teach us things pertaining to thy heavenly kingdom;
Give thy blessing, we beseech thee, to this order
wherever it may be throughout the world; vouchsafe that these, thy Daughters, ever may discern thy
sacred truth, and bear with sturdy mind, the cross,
thy royal emblem, through the battles of their
earthly life; give them strength to overcome, and
grace that they may strive to spread thy kingdom
and to gather thy dispersed sheep within thy fold;
pour out upon them the seven-fold gifts of thy Holy
Spirit, that they may never forget that it is thy
work which they are called upon to do, that they

may think nothing, do nothing, and say nothing which may injure themselves, their neighbors or thy holy work, and that amid all temptations they may be ready always to forget self by obeying thy most blessed will, and finally, upon them, faithful unto death, bestow thy crown of everlasting life. We ask it all for his sake, for whom we work, who died for us, who lives for us and intercedes, our Saviour Jesus Christ. Amen.

For Sisterhoods.

O God, who inhabitest and keepest pure hearts, grant to Christian virgins to know the excellence of virginity, to love that which they know, to preserve faithfully that which they love, that going forth to meet the Bridegroom with kindled lamps, they may be admitted to his heavenly marriage; through the same Jesus Christ our Lord. Amen

For Deaconesses.

Grant, O Lord, we beseech thee, to thine handmaidens called to the office of Deaconess, the grace of perseverance in their ministry; Bestow on them the gifts of wisdom and sound judgment, of simplicity and singleness of heart, of sympathy with those among whom they dwell and work, of ready obedience to all lawful rule and authority, and of courtesy and mildness toward all with whom they have to do. Be thou, O Lord, their guide in all doubt, their support in weariness, and their comfort in sorrow, that thou mayest be also unto them an exceeding great reward in the day of the revelation of thine only-begotten Son; to whom with thee and the Holy Ghost be glory and honor, world without end. Amen.

PRAYERS FOR GENEROUS GIVING TO MISSIONS.

I

Almighty God, and gracious Father, the source of all our blessings; We pray thee to make us sensible of our duty to thee in the use of the gifts intrusted to us. If our material resources increase, may there be a like increase of our generosity. If our resources diminish, we beseech thee to save us from the sin of beginning our economy at thy Church. Help us to reduce our personal comforts and gratifications, and to make ready sacrifices for the sake of giving toward the spread of thy kingdom and the salvation of men; through Jesus Christ our Lord. Amen

O Heavenly Father, who openest thine hand and fillest all things living with plenteousness; We glorify thy holy Name for thy loving care of us thine unworthy children. May a grateful sense of thy mercy and pity move us to love thee truly, and to offer to the service of thy kingdom, prayerfully, intelligently, and generously of the earthly treasures which thou hast committed to our hands; through Jesus Christ our Lord. Amen.

Almighty Saviour, who art ascended to the right hand of the Father, and hast poured forth the manifold gifts of the Spirit upon thy Church; Dispose thy people faithfully to use all that thou givest them in the furtherance of thy kingdom; for the glory of thy Name, who livest and reignest with the Father and the Holy Ghost, one God, forever and ever. Amen.

Almighty God, who alone art the Author and Giver of all good things; Grant unto thy people a willing mind, that of all thou givest them they may surely give a tenth to thee, and may offer to thee free-will offerings, with an holy worship; that so, proving thee according to thy holy Word, thou mayest open the windows of heaven and pour out the fulness of thy blessing upon thy Church, for his sake who gave himself a sacrifice for the sins of the world; Jesus Christ our Lord. Amen.

O Lord Jesus Christ, builder and maker of the city which hath foundations, preserve thy Church, we entreat thee, by thine almighty power. Let her walls be salvation and her gates praise; let her be all-glorious within, by the indwelling of the Holy Ghost; let her raiment be of wrought gold, even of the alms, precious self-denying gifts and free-will offerings of thy ransomed people; through thy mercy, O Lord, to whom, with the Father and the Holy Ghost, be endless praises. Amen.

Prayers for the Church and the Clergy.

✠

PRAYERS FOR THE CHURCH THROUGHOUT THE WORLD.

O eternal God and merciful Father, we humbly pray for thy holy Church throughout the world, that it being purged from false philosophy and vain deceit, we may live and act as befits the members of the mystical Body of thy Son, and in the end be found acceptable unto thee; through the same Jesus Christ our Lord. Amen.

O gracious Father, we humbly beseech thee, for thy Holy Catholic Church, that thou wouldest be pleased to fill it with all truth in all peace. Where it is corrupt, purify it; where it is in error, direct it; where in anything it is amiss, reform it; where it is right, strengthen it; where it is in want, provide for it; where it is divided, make up the breaches of it, for the sake of him who died and rose again, and ever maketh intercession for it, Jesus Christ our Lord. Amen.

Defend thy Church, O Lord, we beseech thee, with thy continual help, that we may be enabled hereafter to triumph over every outward enemy, having here prevailed over every error that makes war within; through Jesus Christ our Lord. Amen.

Almighty and everlasting God, who hast revealed thy glory, by Christ, among all nations, preserve the works of thy mercy; that thy Church, which is spread throughout the world, may persevere with stedfast faith in the confession of thy Name; through Jesus Christ our Lord. Amen.

PRAYERS FOR CHURCH COUNCILS.

At a Council or Conference of Bishops.

O Lord God Almighty, Father of Lights, and Fountain of all Wisdom; We humbly beseech thee that thy Holy Spirit may lead into all truth thy servants the bishops now [to be] gathered together in thy Name. Grant them grace to think and do such things as shall tend most to thy glory and the good of thy holy Church; direct and prosper, we pray thee, all their consultations, and further them with thy continual help, that the true Catholic and Apostolic Faith once delivered to the saints being maintained, thy Church may serve thee in all godly quietness; through Jesus Christ our Lord. Amen.

At a Diocesan or General Council.

Almighty and everlasting God, who by thy Holy Spirit didst preside in the Councils of the blessed Apostles, and hast promised, through thy Son Jesus Christ, to be with thy Church to the end of the world; We beseech thee to be with the Council of thy Church *here* assembled in thy Name and Presence. Save *us* from all error, ignorance, pride, and prejudice; and of thy great mercy vouchsafe, we beseech thee, so to direct, sanctify, and govern *us* in *our* work, by the mighty power of the Holy Ghost, that the comfortable gospel of Christ may be truly preached, truly received, and truly followed, in all places, to the breaking down the kingdom of sin, Satan, and death; till at length the whole of thy dispersed sheep, being gathered into one fold, shall become partakers of everlasting life; through the merits and death of Jesus Christ our Saviour. Amen.

O almighty and everlasting God, who hast given the Comforter to thy Church, that he should abide with it for ever; Pour forth the blessing of thy Spirit on our prelates and pastors now assembled in thy Name; defend their hearts from all hindrances of this world, and from all earthly feeling. Grant them abundantly stedfastness of faith, purity of love, sincere desire for peace, and firmness of authority, that they, by the help of thy Son Jesus Christ our Lord, may both rule thy flock committed to their care, according to thy will, and may also, together with their people, receive from the great Shepherd and Bishop of us all the rewards which are promised to thy saints, and be united to the number of thine elect; through the same Jesus Christ our Lord. Amen.

PRAYERS FOR THE DIOCESE.

O Lord, we beseech thee to bless thy Church and household in our Diocese. Grant to our Bishop a holy zeal in thy service. By diligent discharge of every duty, may he truly profit the clergy and the people over whom he is placed in thy Name. Bless all who minister in holy things. May they, declaring all thy counsel and living to thy glory, have many souls as their crown of rejoicing. O thou Lord of the harvest, send forth more laborers into thy harvest. Give to our congregations unity, liberality, zeal and holiness. May every parish look not on its own things alone but also on the things of others. Graciously behold the families, the communicants, and the children. Guide and further all who are in any special administration to order our affairs and enlarge our borders. May we all be so joined together in unity of spirit, and in the bond of peace, that we may be an holy temple acceptable unto thee; through Jesus Christ our Lord. Amen

O Lord Jesus Christ, Shepherd and Bishop of our souls, bless, we pray thee, thy servants the clergy of this Diocese; Give them holiness and wisdom in their hearts and words, that they may faithfully serve at thine altars, and truly preach thy Word, to us, their flocks, give the grace of humility, that we may gladly obey them for thy sake; give us, also, peace and love among ourselves, and purity in our lives; and so may we all, both priests and people, be found meet, at thy coming, to receive thine eternal rewards; who livest and reignest God, world without end. Amen

Prayers for the Bishop of the Diocese.

O Lord God, Father Almighty, who by the unspeakable bounty of thy grace alone, hast appointed thy servant to rule over this Diocese; Grant him, we beseech thee, by the grace of thy Holy Spirit, fitly to discharge the ministry of the priestly office before thee, duly to dispense the Sacraments of the Church, and worthily to govern the flock entrusted to him, to the glory of thy holy Name; through Jesus Christ our Lord. Amen.

O God, the Pastor and Ruler of thy faithful servants; Look down in mercy on thy servant, our Bishop, to whom thou hast given charge of this Diocese, and evermore guide, defend, comfort, sanctify, and save him; and grant him by thy grace so to advance in word and good example, that he may with the flock committed to him, attain to everlasting life; through Jesus Christ our Lord. Amen.

Prayers for a Clerical Retreat.

Almighty God, who hast given to thy Church pastors and teachers for the guidance of thy people; Grant us grace to be faithful stewards of the mysteries of thy kingdom. Make us diligent in the study of thy Word, and incline us to seek frequently places of retirement for holy meditation and prayer. Separate us from the contaminations of the world, and give us patience, lowliness of heart, watchfulness, zeal, and all other things that contribute to holiness of life. Inspire us with a love for the souls of men, and strengthen our efforts for their salvation. We ask all through him who came to seek and save the lost, thy Son, Jesus Christ our Lord. Amen.

O God, who hast given us thine only-begotten Son to be our High Priest, and hast joined unto him other priests to be his ministers to make a pure sacrifice unto thee; Grant that we who have been counted worthy of this holy calling, may devoutly serve at thine altar, and present ourselves as a pure and living offering; through the same Jesus Christ our Lord. Amen.

O Lord Jesus Christ, who didst say to thy disciples, Come ye apart into a desert place and rest awhile; Grant, we beseech thee, to thy servants now gathered together, so to seek thee whom our souls desire to love, that we may both find thee and be found of thee, and grant such love and such wisdom to accompany the words which shall be spoken in thy Name, that they may not fall to the ground, but may be helpful in leading us onward through the toils of our pilgrimage to that rest which remaineth, where, nevertheless, they rest not day nor night from thy perfect service, who livest and reignest God for ever and ever. Amen.

Prayers for Church Unity.

O God, the Father of our Lord Jesus Christ, our only Saviour, the Prince of Peace; Give us grace seriously to lay to heart the great dangers we are in by our unhappy divisions. Take away all hatred and prejudice, and whatsoever else may hinder us from godly union and concord; that, as there is but one Body, and one Spirit, and one hope of our calling, one Lord, one Faith, one Baptism, one God and Father of us all, so we may henceforth be all of one heart, and of one soul, united in one holy bond of truth and peace, of faith and charity, and may with one mind and one mouth glorify thee; through Jesus Christ our Lord. Amen.

O God, who art one God, yet Three Persons, blessed for evermore, who hast called us to glorify thee in one Body in thy only-begotten Son; We earnestly pray thee for the restoration of visible unity of worship and communion between the divided members of the Catholic Church, both east and west; and that all who confess thy holy Name, and are called Christians, may be re-united, as at the beginning, "in the Apostles' doctrine, and the fellowship, and in the breaking of the Bread, and in the Prayers." Remove, we beseech thee, from us, and from all others, whatsoever may hinder or delay this blessed re-union, all suspicions, prejudices, hard thoughts and judgments; endue us with such ardent love toward thee, and toward each other, that we may be one in heart, even as thou, Lord, art one with the Father, to whom in the unity of the Holy Ghost, be all praise, glory and thanksgiving for ever and ever. Amen.

Almighty God, who didst send thy only-begotten Son into the world, that he might draw all men unto him; Gather again, we beseech thee, thy scattered people into one communion and fellowship, that the world may believe that thou hast sent him and thy kingdom come; through the same thy Son Jesus Christ our Lord. Amen.

O almighty God, who hast built thy Church upon the foundation of the Apostles and Prophets, Jesus Christ himself being the chief corner-stone; Grant that, by the operation of the Holy Ghost, all Christians may be so joined together in unity of spirit, and in the bond of peace, that they may be an holy temple acceptable unto thee. And especially to this Congregation present, give the abundance of thy grace; that with one heart they may desire the prosperity of thy holy Apostolic Church, and with one mouth may profess the faith once delivered to the Saints. Defend them from the sins of heresy and schism; let not the foot of pride come nigh to hurt them, nor the hand of the ungodly to cast them down. And grant that the course of this world may be so peaceably ordered by thy governance, that thy Church may joyfully serve thee in all godly quietness; that so they may walk in the ways of truth and peace, and at last be numbered with thy saints in glory everlasting; through thy merits, O blessed Jesus, thou gracious Bishop and Shepherd of our souls, who art with the Father and the Holy Ghost one God, world without end. Amen.

O Lord Jesus Christ, who saidst unto thine Apostles, Peace I leave with you, my peace I give unto you; Regard not our sins, but the faith of thy Church, and grant to her that peace and unity which is agreeable to thy will; who livest and reignest God for ever and ever. Amen.

Prayers for the Parish and Parish Organizations.

✠

Prayers for the Parish.

Almighty and everlasting God, who dost govern all things in heaven and earth, mercifully hear our prayers, and grant to this parish all things needful to its spiritual and temporal welfare. Bless him who ministers to us in holy things, and grant that his work may be accompanied with the demonstration of the Spirit and of power. Bless our Sunday School, and may both teachers and scholars be taught of thee. Help thy people to give abundantly of their means according to their ability and opportunity. Strengthen and confirm the faithful, visit and relieve the sick, turn and soften the wicked, arouse the careless, recover the fallen, and restore the penitent. Remove every hindrance to the advancement of thy truth, and bring us all to be of one heart and mind within the fold of thy holy Church, to the honor and glory of thy Name; through Jesus Christ our Lord. Amen.

O Father of mercies and God of all grace, in whose hands are the hearts of men; Pour down, we beseech thee, on this parish the healthful dew of thy blessing. Give power and success to the ministration of thy Word and Sacraments, and prosper every design consistent with thy will for the spiritual or temporal welfare of thy people. Convert the sinful, reclaim the erring, instruct the ignorant, strengthen the weak-hearted, and make true piety and virtue to abound and flourish among us. Make the rich liberal, and the poor patient; relieve and succor the sick and afflicted, and give thankfulness to the prosperous and happy. Grant that we may be all knit together in the bond of Christian love, that we may dwell together in unity, and finally meet in thine eternal kingdom; through Jesus Christ our Lord. Amen.

O God, Holy Ghost, Sanctifier of the faithful; Visit, we pray thee, the members of this parish with thy love and favor; enlighten their minds more and more with the light of the everlasting gospel; graft in their hearts the love of thy Name; increase in them true religion; make them to delight to visit thy holy temple and to behold thy fair beauty; strengthen the weak in faith; reclaim all wandering and careless communicants; preserve our families in peace and concord; cherish our infants; instruct our youth; sustain the aged; comfort the feeble-minded; convert the ungodly; gather thy dispersed children and unite them to thy holy, Catholic and

Apostolic Church; nourish them with all goodness and of thy great mercy keep them in the same; through Jesus Christ our Lord. Amen.

For a Parish in Debt.

Almighty God, who has taught us that we are to owe no man anything, in mercy deliver us from the debt now resting upon this parish. Give us the grace of self-denial, to enable us to contribute generously of our means, and bless the Church work in which we engage to pay the debt; but above all, as the Israelites in Egyptian bondage cried to thee for deliverance, make us to rely on thee for deliverance from this and all other debts, through the merits of him who died to ransom us from the power of the grave, our Saviour, Jesus Christ. Amen.

For the Endowment of a Parish.

Almighty God, the source of all our blessings, and the author of every good, we commend to thy favor, our parish in this time of its need. Be pleased to encourage and strengthen every effort for its endowment. If we possess little may we give of that little for the upbuilding of thy Holy Church. If thou hast bestowed abundantly upon us the things of this life, may we give abundantly, so that having a keen sense of our accountability, and making a wise use of our stewardship, we shall at last obtain the enduring riches of thy heavenly kingdom. We ask it in the Name of Jesus Christ our Lord. Amen.

For an unfinished Church.

O Heavenly Father, who art the author of every good thought and deed, the only giver of health and wealth, and in whose hand are the hearts of all men, as thou hast put it into our mind to build to thee a holy and beautiful house, so give us courage and strength to finish the work which we have undertaken. Open our hearts and hands that we may gladly give thee of thine own. Hasten the time when this building completed, and freed from every debt, shall be consecrated to thy service forever. Make this Church an abiding place of thine honor, a bond of unity and peace to thy people, and a gate of heaven. As thy servants build and give to thee, so build thou in them thy spiritual temple and fill it with thy presence; through Jesus Christ our Lord. Amen.

At the Restoration of a Church.

O God, who didst put into the heart of thy prophet Ezra, to rebuild thy temple; We thank thee that thou hast blessed our endeavor in the restoration of this Church. Abide in it evermore, and make it a place of spiritual joy and peace to countless souls; through Jesus Christ our Lord. Amen.

At the Anniversary of a Parish.

O God, who year by year renewest the consecration day of this thy holy temple, and bringest us again in safety to thy holy mysteries; Hear the prayers of thy people, and grant that whosoever entereth this temple to offer his petitions, may rejoice in their fulfilment; through Jesus Christ our Lord, who liveth and reigneth with thee and the Holy Ghost, world without end. Amen

---

PRAYERS FOR THE RECTOR OF THE PARISH.

O most gracious God, let thy blessing rest upon thy servant, the Rector of this parish. Grant him by the special help of thy grace to be holy in his life, to be zealous in his work, and to minister to thy people according to thy will. We ask it for the sake of Jesus Christ our Lord. Amen.

O Lord, our heavenly Father, almighty, everlasting God; Vouchsafe to bless thy servant, the Rector of this parish. Make him as thy messenger, energetic and zealous; as thy watchman, vigilant for the great interest of thy flock; as thy steward, faithful in dispensing those treasures of thy Word and Sacraments committed to him. Give him fervency in prayer, and diligence in study. Give him knowledge to be sound and accurate in doctrine. Give him courage to maintain the truth boldly, and discretion to declare it seasonably, persuasively and effectively. Grant that he may do all that lieth in him to bring such as are committed to his charge unto the knowledge of God in Christ, that there be no place left among them either for error in religion, or for viciousness of life. This we beseech thee, through Jesus Christ our Lord. Amen.

For the Rector when Sick.

O Lord Jesus Christ, who hast given to thy Church pastors and teachers, for the perfecting of the saints, and for the edifying of the Body of Christ, who didst, when on earth, heal all manner of sickness and disease, and art the same yesterday, to-day, and for ever; We come unto thee in behalf of him who is appointed to minister in holy things among us, and who is now laid on a bed of sickness. Have mercy, we beseech thee, on him and on us also; and, if it be thy will, restore him to his former health and strength; and bless this affliction to his and to our good, and to thy glory, for thy mercy's sake, our only Saviour and Redeemer. Amen.

Prayers for a Parish Without a Rector.

O almighty and most gracious Father, in whose hands are the hearts of men, and from whom cometh every good and perfect gift; We pray thee to bestow on this parish the gift of a faithful minister of thy Word and Sacraments. Grant us one who shall labor diligently for thee, to the saving of those committed to his care, who shall be loving, but fearless in reproof, and an example of holiness to the flock. Vouchsafe, O Lord, that such good works as have been undertaken in this place for the promotion of thy glory may be not only carried on, but increased in number and efficiency, for the sake of thy dear Son Jesus Christ, our only Advocate and Redeemer. Amen.

Almighty and everlasting God, who dost govern all things in heaven and earth, mercifully hear the supplications of us thy servants, and of thy loving-kindness grant, we pray thee, a Priest to this parish, who by faithfulness in teaching and holiness of life may be well pleasing unto thee, and who by watchfulness and zeal may promote thy glory and the salvation of souls; through Jesus Christ our Lord. Amen.

Prayers for a Vestry Meeting.

Almighty and eternal God, the giver of grace and strength; We beseech thee to bestow thy blessing upon us, who have been placed in positions of trust in thy holy Church. Give us a clear sense of our duty, and lead us to a faithful discharge of the same. Grant us gentleness, forbearance, a right judgment and personal consecration, that by precept and example, as well as by our official actions, the temporal and spiritual good of thy Church may be enlarged. Especially direct us in our counsels by thy gracious Spirit, so that all things may be done to the glory of thy Name, and for the unity, peace, and prosperity of this parish. We ask it for the sake of Jesus Christ our Lord. Amen.

Vouchsafe, O Lord, to these thy servants to whom the affairs of this parish are committed, prudence, justice, and charity, that they may be of one mind and of one heart in the upbuilding of thy Church, and in the spread of thy kingdom; through Jesus Christ our Lord. Amen.

Prayers for Parochial Missions.

O God, our heavenly Father, we humbly pray thee, for thy dear Son's sake, to bless abundantly at this time whatever efforts may be made to turn the hearts of thy children to more sincere repentance, and more living faith. Give a double portion of thy Holy Spirit to all the Ministers of thy Church; and more especially to him who now comes to preach thy Word to us. Prepare all hearts to receive the seed of thy Word. Grant that it may take deep root, and bring forth fruit to thy glory. Alarm the careless among us, humble the self-righteous, kindle the lukewarm, soften the hardened, encourage the fearful, relieve the doubting, and bring many souls in loving faith to thyself; through Jesus Christ our Lord. Amen.

Have mercy, good Lord, on all in this parish during this special season of prayer and consecration. Let thy Spirit be poured out among us; the Spirit of Light and Truth, to shed abroad in the hearts of the people holiness, wisdom, peace and love; the Spirit of grace and supplication, to teach them earnestly to pray unto thee. Let thy blessing rest on every head, that all may be brought unto thee in faith and love; through Jesus Christ our Lord. Amen.

Almighty God, who hast promised to hear the petitions of those who ask in thy Son's Name, we earnestly beseech thee to send thy blessing upon the Mission held among us. Give thy Holy Spirit to all whom thou shalt call to proclaim the message of salvation, and dispose our hearts gladly to attend to and receive the same. Prosper this and every other endeavor to extend the knowledge of thy Name, so that thy glory may be advanced, and many souls may be won through the merits and for the sake of thy blessed Son Jesus Christ, our Lord, who liveth and reigneth with thee and the Holy Ghost, one God, world without end. Amen.

O Lord Jesus Christ, the Great Shepherd of the sheep, who seekest those that are gone astray, bindest up those that are broken, and healest those that are sick; Bless, we beseech thee, the effort now being made to convert souls unto thee. Open the deaf ears of the wanderers, that they may hear the words which belong unto their salvation; and grant that those whom thou dost raise to newness of life, may through thy grace persevere unto the end: of thy mercy, O our God, who art blessed, and livest with the Father and the Holy Ghost, one God, world without end. Amen.

Prayers with the Choir.

Before the Processional.

Almighty God, whose eyes are upon all our ways; We beseech thee to bless us as we enter upon the worship of thy Church. Help us to remember the sacredness of this place, and the solemnity of our duties. Keep us from wandering thoughts, worldly desires, and all irreverence. Kindle within us an increasing love of prayer and praise, and may the words we sing impress our hearts and influence our lives; through Jesus Christ our Lord. Amen.

O thou who art the true light of faithful souls, and perfect brightness of the blessed; Grant that our hearts may render unto thee thanksgiving and always glorify thee with the offering of praise; through Jesus Christ our Lord. Amen.

Almighty God, who art worshipped by the heavenly host with hymns that are never silent, and with thanksgivings that never cease; Fill our mouths with thy praise, that we may magnify thy holy Name; and grant us, with all those that fear thee and keep thy commandments, to be partakers of the inheritance of thy saints in light; through Jesus Christ our Lord, to whom, with thee and the Holy Ghost, be all glory, honor, and worship, now and forever. Amen.

Fill us, heavenly Father with the true spirit of praise, that the worship we render unto thee may be acceptable in thy sight, and bring lasting joy and peace to our hearts; through Jesus Christ our Lord. Amen.

O God, open thou our lips and purify our hearts, that we may fitly, reverently, and devoutly join in this service, and worthily magnify thy holy Name; through Jesus Christ our Lord. Amen.

After the Recessional.

Grant, O God, that what we have said and sung with our lips we may believe in our hearts, and what we believe in our hearts we may shew forth in our lives; through Jesus Christ our Lord. Amen.

Accept, O God and Father, the praises we have offered thee this day, and may they be sanctified to thy glory, and our eternal good; through Jesus Christ our Lord. Amen.

Gracious Father, make permanent the lessons we have heard in this house devoted to thy honor and glory. May we go away wiser and better than when we came, and serve thee in songs of gladness all our days. We ask it through our only Advocate and Redeemer, Jesus Christ our Lord. Amen.

Almighty God, grant that we who have been permitted to sing thy praises here, may through thy grace hereafter sing the songs of redemption before thy throne; through our Lord and Saviour Jesus Christ. Amen.

For the increase of the Ministry.

O heavenly Father, thou Lord of the harvest; We commend to thy love and protection, these thy youthful servants, engaged in the service of song. If thou hast need of any of them in the ministry of thy holy Church, graciously incline their hearts to this sacred office. May they count the pleasures and attractions of the world as nothing, compared with the joy and blessedness of turning many souls to righteousness. We pray thee to confirm them in all holy ways, and if it be thy blessed will make them faithful stewards of thy mysteries; through Jesus Christ our Lord. Amen.

Service for Choir Meetings, before and after practice.

In the Name of the Father, and of the Son, and of the Holy Ghost. Amen.
V. The Lord be with you.
R. And with thy spirit.
Let us pray: Our Father, etc.
V. O Lord, open thou our lips.
R. And our mouth shall show forth thy praise.
V. Let the people praise thee, O God.
R. Yea, let all the people praise thee.

Let us pray: O Heavenly Father, who hast given us a voice with which to make melody unto thee, teach us to sing of thy loving kindness unto us; and help us to serve thee, not only with our lips, but with our hearts, all the days of our life; through Jesus Christ our Lord. Amen.

Direct us, O Lord, in all our doings with thy most gracious favor, and further us with thy continual help; that in all our works begun, continued, and ended in thee, we may glorify thy holy Name; through Jesus Christ our Lord. Amen.

At the close, an evening hymn may be sung. Then:
V. The Lord be with you.
R. And with thy spirit.

Let us pray: O God, who didst call Samuel when a child to serve in thy holy temple; Be pleased to accept the service which we shall offer to thee in thy house; and may our words and our thoughts be such as thou approvest; for Jesus Christ's sake. Amen.

V. I will always give thanks unto the Lord.
R. His praise shall ever be in my mouth.

Let us pray: O Heavenly Father, who hast taught us to go into thy house and sing praise unto thee; Help us to tell of thy love with heart and voice, until we sing the new song in the company of those who serve and praise thee continually in thy heavenly courts; through Jesus Christ our Lord. Amen.

V. Let us depart in peace. Amen.

PRAYERS FOR THE SUNDAY SCHOOL.

For the Superintendent.

Almighty God, who didst teach the hearts of thy faithful people, by sending to them the light of thy

Holy Spirit; Grant to the Superintendent of this school by the same Spirit to have a right judgment in all things; may he know perfectly thy Son Jesus Christ to be the way, the truth, and the life; leave him not destitute of thy manifold gifts, nor yet of grace to use them always to thy honor and glory; and enable him to lead the lambs of thy flock committed to him for instruction, in the way that leadeth to everlasting life; through the same, thy Son Jesus Christ our Lord. Amen.

O God, without whose illumination and guidance we cannot please thee; Withhold not thy help from those who occupy places of trust in thy holy Church. Bless especially him who has been called to direct the interests of these children. Give him plenteously of thy Spirit, that he may be earnest, faithful, and zealous. May he rule with gentleness and firmness, and so shape the lives of those committed to his care that they may become the instruments of thy glory; through Jesus Christ our Lord. Amen.

For the Teachers.

Almighty God, we pray thee to bestow upon the teachers of this school that wisdom which cometh from above. Give them an abiding love for thy holy word, and may thy blessed Spirit help them in communicating thy truth to others. May they be kind, patient, and tender toward the lambs of thy flock, leading them by precept and example to love him who came to seek and save the lost. We ask it through the same, thy Son Jesus Christ our Lord. Amen.

Almighty God, the giver of every good and perfect gift; We beseech thee to regard with thy love and blessing those who are here engaged in the instruction of youth. Give them a deep sense of their responsibilities, and may they come to the special duties of this place with careful preparation of mind and heart. Give them the spirit of prayer and faith and of thorough consecration. Sustain them under any discouragements, and gladden them with the consciousness that they are directing the young in the paths of peace and righteousness. This we ask for the sake of Jesus Christ our Lord. Amen.

O Lord Jesus Christ, the child born unto us; Grant, we entreat thee, that in memory of thy holy infancy, and of the love thou bearest to thy little ones, all children may be sacred in our eyes. Make us heedful not to offend one of thy little ones; help parents with much patience to correct their children in love; make our infants holy Innocents, and teach us ourselves to become as little children; to the honor of thy Name, who livest and reignest with the Father and the Holy Ghost, one God, world without end. Amen.

We beseech thee, O blessed Saviour, to help us in the work we are doing for thee, in teaching thy little ones to know thy love and to live for thee, and help them to learn according to thy will. Give us thy

Holy Spirit, that we may really feel the depth of thy love and the happiness of a holy life, and so may teach others both by word and example. When thou shalt call us to account for our work, may we do it with joy; and may both teachers and scholars meet hereafter, to live with thee for ever and ever, who with the Father and the Holy Ghost art one God, world without end. Amen.

For the Children.

Gracious Saviour, we pray thee to look with favor upon the children of our Sunday School, and grant that the instruction they receive may be to thy glory and their welfare and happiness. Make them to be obedient to their parents and teachers, and diligent in all their duties. May they grow in grace and in the knowledge of thyself, that so they may be useful in their generation, and finally be received into thy heavenly kingdom, there to dwell with thee and the Father and the Holy Ghost for ever and ever. Amen

Merciful Father, we entreat thee to strengthen in these children all things that are good, and save them from all things that are evil. Drive from their hearts every corrupting thought, and keep their lips from idle, impure and unseemly words. Preserve them from evil companions, and deliver them from the temptations of youth. Bring them to true repentance, and help them to forsake their sins. May they love and reverence thy house, delighting in its prayers and praises and early heeding its messages of salvation. As they grow in years may they rejoice more and more in doing thy will, and in walking in the way of thy commandments. Hear us, we beseech thee, in the Name of thy Son Jesus Christ our Lord. Amen.

Blessed Jesus, who hast said, Suffer the little children to come unto me and forbid them not; Grant that these children may hear thy gentle voice and gladly and faithfully serve thee all the days of their life. Be thou their Ruler and Guide, their Friend, Mediator and Redeemer. And thy Name with that of the Father and the Holy Ghost shall have all the glory and honor for ever and ever. Amen.

O Lord Jesus Christ, who wast subject unto thy parents; Give, we pray thee, to all children grace after thine example reverently to love their parents, and lovingly to obey them. Teach us all that filial duty never ends or lessens: and bless all parents in their children, and all children in their parents; hear us, O Saviour, who with the Father and the Holy Ghost livest and reignest one God, world without end. Amen.

O God of Abraham, God of Isaac, God of Jacob; Bless these thy children, and sow the seed of eternal life in their hearts; that whatsoever in thy holy Word they shall profitably learn, they may in deed fulfil the same. Look, O Lord, mercifully upon them from heaven, and bless them, that they obeying thy will, and always being in safety under thy protection, may abide in thy love unto their lives' end ; through Jesus Christ our Lord. Amen.

Almighty and most merciful Father, bless, we humbly beseech thee, the children of this school with healthful bodies and good understandings, with the graces and gifts of thy Holy Spirit, and with sweet dispositions and holy habits. May thy mercy and thy providence lead them through all the dangers and temptations of this evil world, and sanctify them wholly in their bodies, souls and spirits, and keep them unblamable unto the coming of our Lord and Saviour Jesus Christ. Amen.

O Lord God, giver of heavenly increase, who by thy Spirit's might dost confirm the first efforts of feeble souls; Encourage in the hearts of these thy children every good intent, and carry them from strength to strength. Cleanse their consciences, and stir their wills gladly to serve thee, the living God. Leave no room in them for spiritual wickedness, no lurking place for secret sins; but so establish and sanctify them by the power of thy holy Word, that, evermore taking heed unto the thing that is right, and speaking and doing the truth, they may find godliness their gain both in the life which now is, and in that which is to come; through Jesus Christ our Lord. Amen.

For the Work of the School,

Almighty God, bless, we beseech thee, the work of this school, that it may be to thy glory, and that whatsoever we do, we may do it heartily as unto thee. Give thy blessing to those who teach, that they may be wise and patient, and ever concerned for the salvation of their scholars ; and to those who learn, give thy grace that they may increase in the knowledge of all good things, and in the love of our Lord and Saviour Jesus Christ, to whom, with thee and the Holy Spirit, be praise and glory now and forever. Amen.

For neglected Children.

Regard, O Lord God, with thy mercy all destitute and neglected children, who live in homes of vice, where thy Word is never read, and the voice of prayer is never heard. Raise up friends, we pray thee, who will seek them out, and bring them within the blessed influences and holy instruction of thy Church, that they may know thee, and walk in the way of eternal life; through Jesus Christ our Lord. Amen.

For the increase of the Ministry.

Almighty and everlasting God, who didst call Samuel to thy service in his youth; We beseech thee to incline parents early to consecrate their sons to the ministry of reconciliation, that thy holy Church may be supplied with true and faithful

Pastors to the glory of thy Name and the spread of thy kingdom; through Jesus Christ our Lord. Amen.

Prayers for the Young Men of a Parish.

Heavenly Father, we plead with thee especially in behalf of young men. Thou knowest how critical is the period of life through which they are passing, and how great are the dangers by which they are surrounded. Regard with pity and compassion those who need so much thy care. Those who are living godless lives, pluck as brands from the burning. May thy Holy Spirit show them the sinfulness of their hearts, and lead them to him whose blood cleanseth from all sin. Those who are trying to serve thee, build up more and more in faith. Protect them in time of danger. Strengthen them in time of temptation, and give them wisdom in times of uncertainty and doubt. May they put on the whole armor of God, that so they may overcome the wicked one, and finally receive the crown of life which thou hast promised to those who are faithful unto death. We ask it for Christ's sake. Amen.

Quicken, O Lord God, in the hearts of young men the spirit of devotion. May they gladly seek the services and duties of thy holy Church, and by their example and zeal lead others to the same privileges. Strengthen them in all good habits, and make their lives useful and happy; through Jesus Christ our Lord. Amen.

Almighty God, whose blessed Son didst take our nature upon him, leaving us an example that we should follow his steps; Look graciously with thy favor upon all young men, and make them to grow in wisdom and stature and in favor with thee their God. Give them grace to remember thee now in the days of their youth, and to consecrate their strength to thy service; preserve them from the sins which easily beset them, and deliver them out of all temptations; keep them pure in heart, upright in life, and diligent in the work to which they have been called. Looking unto Jesus, the author and finisher of their faith, may they go from strength to strength and at last, having finished their course and kept the faith, receive from thee the crown of life that fadeth not away; through Jesus Christ our Lord. Amen.

Prayers for the Brotherhood of Saint Andrew.

O almighty and eternal God, we humbly pray thee to vouchsafe thy blessing to this Brotherhood, that all its members being inspired with lively faith and love, may earnestly strive to promote the honor due to thy dear Son, the spread of his Church, and the gathering of wanderers into the fold. Give us grace to fulfil, in our lives, what we profess with our lips. Deliver us, O God, from false doctrine and slackness of living, and grant that, persevering unto the end, we may obtain everlasting life; through Jesus Christ our Lord. Amen.

Vouchsafe, we beseech thee, merciful Lord, to bless and prosper the work of our Brotherhood. Grant that we may labor together for the advancement of thy glory and the good of thy holy Church, doing always that which is well-pleasing in thy sight. Bless us in our own souls, and make us a blessing to the souls of others, and bring us at last to thy heavenly kingdom, and grant us the reward which thou hast promised to those who turn many to righteousness; through Jesus Christ our Lord. Amen.

God be gracious unto us, and give us all a heart to serve him, and to do his will with a good courage and a sound mind. Amen.

Heavenly Father, thou knowest the weakness and cowardliness of our hearts. Thou knowest how much we care for the opinion of men. Help us, we beseech thee, to care more for what will please thee. Make us strong and courageous, that we may never be afraid to do our duty. Give us grace and courage to speak when and as we should. Let us never shrink from our duty through the fear of man. Let the love of Jesus fill our hearts, that in his strength we may be strong. Give us the constant guidance and assistance of the Holy Spirit. We ask all in the Name and for the sake of thy dear Son Jesus Christ. Amen.

At the admission of a new Member.

Give ear, Lord, to our prayers, and vouchsafe to bless this thy servant, whom we have now received, in thy holy Name, to the companionship of the Brotherhood of St. Andrew; and grant that by thy grace he may lead a godly life in thy Church, and, laboring for the extension of thy kingdom, may finally inherit eternal life; through Jesus Christ our Lord. Amen.

Prayers for the Boys' Department of the Brotherhood of Saint Andrew.

Heavenly Father, have mercy, we beseech thee, upon our youth. Keep them continually under thy protection, and direct them, according to thy gracious favor, in the way of everlasting salvation. Assist them with thy heavenly help, that they may ever diligently serve thee, and by no temptations be separated from thee; through Jesus Christ our Lord, Amen.

Almighty and most merciful Father, whose paths always lead to peace and truth; Grant, we pray thee, that the members of this Brotherhood may be fostered by thy tenderness, sustained by thy grace, and quickened to every holy thought and deed in thy service; through Jesus Christ our Lord. Amen.

Prayers with a Confirmation Class.

O eternal God, who didst send thy Holy Spirit upon thy Church on the day of Pentecost, and hast promised that he shall abide with it for ever; Grant that the same gracious Spirit may be vouchsafed to these thy servants who are about to renew their baptismal vows. May he lead them into all truth, defend them from all sin, and enable them to do thy will; through Jesus Christ our Lord. Amen.

Grant, we beseech thee, O Lord, that thy servants may faithfully renew that vow which they pledged to thee in their baptism, renouncing the devil and all his works, and firmly resolving to fulfil the law of Christ; and vouchsafe that they may receive at thine altar the pledge of that life immortal which thou hast promised us, and derive therefrom continual increase in the life of holiness which they have vowed; through Jesus Christ our Lord. Amen.

Almighty and everlasting God, in whose Church the Bishops, after the example of the holy Apostles, in due season lay their hands on thy children and bless them; We make our humble supplications unto thee in behalf of all those who are about to receive the holy rite of Confirmation, that they may shew forth the fruits of their regeneration in a good profession; and, being strengthened with might by thy Spirit in the inner man, may be enabled to fulfil their vows, and to grow up unto the perfection of the Christian life; through Jesus Christ our Lord. Amen.

Prayers with a Parish Bible Class.

O gracious God and most merciful Father, who hast vouchsafed us the rich and precious jewel of thy holy Word, convert us with thy Spirit, that it may be written in our hearts to our everlasting comfort, to reform us, to renew us according to thine own image, to build us up and edify us into the perfect building of thy Christ, sanctifying and increasing in us all heavenly virtues. Grant this, O Heavenly Father, for Jesus Christ's sake. Amen.

O Lord God, with whom is the fulness of salvation and the perfection of blessing; Have mercy upon those who fail to meditate upon the inspired Word of thy truth; quicken us all with an increasing love of thy revelation; grant that, delighting by day and night to exercise ourselves therein, we may bring forth fruit in this world as trees of thy planting, nourished by the waters of thy grace, which may be found unto holiness and ripen unto everlasting life; through Jesus Christ our Lord. Amen.

O Lord Jesus Christ, who art the Truth incarnate and the Teacher of the faithful; let thy Spirit overshadow us in reading thy Word, and conform our thoughts to thy revelation; that learning of thee with honest hearts, we may be rooted and built up in thee; who livest and reignest with the Father and the Holy Ghost one God, world without end. Amen.

O God the Holy Ghost, open thou our eyes, that we may see the wondrous things of thy law. Let thy holy Word be a lantern unto our feet, and a light unto our paths; so that by thy help we may walk in the narrow way of eternal life; through Jesus Christ our Lord. Amen.

O God, whose blessed Word was given us for our edification, that we might attain to eternal life in the knowledge of thyself, pardon the sin of those who quote it heedlessly, and for unworthy ends, whether of falsehood or of amusement. Grant unto them grace so to reflect upon its hidden mysteries, that they may abstain from every expression which shall tend to destroy the sanctity of its language in the ears of others, and assist them in their meditations thereon, that they may be nourished by thy divine teaching; through Jesus Christ our Lord. Amen.

Give us, O Lord our God, a firm and living faith in thee, that we may believe all that thou teachest in the sacred Scriptures and in thy holy Church; for the sake of Jesus Christ our Lord. Amen.

Prayers for Parish Guilds.

O Almighty God, who art the source of all strength and goodness; We beseech thee to bless this Guild in all its doings. To us, thy servants who are united in its fellowship, wilt thou show the right way and incline our hearts steadily and faithfully to walk in it. Stand thou ever at our right hand, defending us against all evils that may beset us from within or without. In our counsels wilt thou counsel us. In our actions wilt thou go before and follow us. Engage and consecrate all our faculties of soul and body to the high calling wherewith we are called, keeping always alive in our memory the hallowed vows and promises of our holy Baptism. Freely we have received the inestimable gifts of thy gospel and thy Church; freely may we give them to others. May nothing ever seem too hard or too humble to do or to suffer, in following our crucified and glorified Master. We ask it for his sake who hath loved us and given himself for us, our only Mediator and Advocate, Jesus Christ our Lord. Amen.

Almighty, everlasting God, we beseech thee to pour thy continual blessing upon this Guild, and upon every member thereof, both present and absent. Knit our hearts in gentleness, forbearance, and brotherly love, after the example of thy saints. Grant that zeal, devotion and self denial may here flourish, to the glory of thy Name, the comfort of our hearts, and the salvation of our souls; through Jesus Christ our Lord. Amen.

O God, who art perfect love, grant unto thy servants to bear one another's burdens with sincere affection, that thy peace, which passeth all understanding, may keep our hearts and minds; through Jesus Christ our Lord. Amen.

For an Altar Guild before Vesting the Altar.

O Lord God Almighty, dwelling in light unapproachable, yet sanctifying by thy presence the house which is called by thy Name; Grant unto thy servants, the members of this Altar Guild, the spirit of consecration and joy, of reverence and faith, that ministering about holy things, and living of Christ our sacrifice, our souls may be temples of the Holy Ghost; through the same Jesus Christ our Lord. Amen.

CONFESSION AND ABSOLUTION OF PENITENTS IN PRIVATE.

* *Before confession the Priest may say:*

The Lord be in thy heart and on thy lips, that thou ✠ mayest rightly confess thy sins, in the Name of the Father, and of the Son, and of the Holy Ghost. Amen.

¶ *Any one of the following forms of confession may be used.*

I confess to God Almighty, the Father, the Son, and the Holy Ghost, in the sight of the whole company of heaven, and to thee, father, that I have sinned exceedingly in thought, word and deed, of my fault, of my own fault, of my own grievous fault; therefore I pray God to have mercy upon me, and thee, father, to pray for me.

I confess before you, and before Almighty God, that I have greatly sinned against his holy commandments, in thoughts, words and deeds, and that I am by nature sinful and unclean and deserve everlasting condemnation. On this account my heart is troubled. I sincerely lament that I have offended the Lord my God, and earnestly pray him for Christ's sake graciously to forgive me, and by his Holy Spirit to create in me a new heart, according as I believe and trust in his Word. And inasmuch as you have command from the Lord Jesus, as a Priest of the Church, to absolve all that are truly penitent, I entreat of you to instruct and comfort me out of God's Word, to declare unto me in the Name of Jesus Christ the forgiveness of my sins, and to admit me to the Sacrament of his Body and Blood for the strengthening of my faith, as I purpose, with the help of God, to amend and better my sinful life.

I confess to Almighty God that I have sinned in thought, word and deed. In humility and contrition I plead his forgiveness and ask for the benefit of your prayers.

¶ *Any one of the following forms of absolution may be used.*

Almighty God, have mercy upon you, forgive you your sins, and bring you to everlasting life. Amen

The Almighty and merciful Lord grant you absolution and forgiveness of your sins, time for repentance, amendment of life, and the grace and comfort of his Holy Spirit. Amen.

Almighty God, our heavenly Father, who of his great mercy hath promised forgiveness of sins to all those who, with hearty repentance and true faith, turn unto him; Have mercy upon you; pardon and deliver you from all your sins; confirm and strengthen you in all goodness; and bring you to everlasting life; through Jesus Christ our Lord. Amen.

Almighty God, our heavenly Father, is merciful and gracious, and ready to forgive thee all thy sins, for the sake of his Son Jesus Christ, who suffered and died for thee; therefore in his Name, in obedience to his command, and by virtue of his words: "Whosoever sins ye remit, they are remitted unto them," I declare thee, being penitent, absolved and free from all thy sins. They are forgiven, as abundantly and completely as Jesus Christ hath merited by his sufferings and death, and commanded to be preached by the gospel throughout the world. Take to thyself then, for thy comfort and peace, the assurance which I now give thee in the Name of the Lord Jesus, and believe without doubt, that thy sins are forgiven thee, in the Name of the Father, and of the Son, and of the Holy Ghost Amen.

As the servant of our Lord Jesus Christ, I declare thee freed from thy sins, in the Name of the Father, ✠ and of the Son, and of the Holy Ghost. Amen.

EUCHARISTIC PRAYERS.

O Lord Jesus Christ, God that hidest thyself, give us grace, we implore thee, to discern thee spiritually in the most blessed Sacrament of thy Body and Blood; to receive thee into souls prostrate in adoration, to entertain thee with our utmost love, and not to let thee go except thou bless us. Grant this, O Saviour, who with the Father and the Holy Ghost liveth and reigneth one God, world without end. Amen.

Defend, O Lord, with thy protection those whom thou satisfiest with heavenly gifts; that being set free from all things hurtful, we may press onward with our whole heart to the salvation which cometh from thee; through Jesus Christ our Lord. Amen.

Grant, O Lord, that what we have taken with our mouth we may receive with our soul, and let that which has been a temporary gift become to us an everlasting remedy; through Jesus Christ our Lord. Amen.

We give thee thanks, O Lord, Holy Father, almighty, eternal God, who hast refreshed us by the participation of the most holy Body and Blood of thy Son our Lord Jesus Christ. And we pray that this Sacrament of our salvation which we have received, may not turn to our condemnation, but that it may be to the perfecting of body and soul for eternal life; through Jesus Christ our Lord. Amen.

O God, who, of old, didst command the offering of the daily sacrifice in thy temple, and who dost accept the perpetual offering of thy Son once made upon the cross; Grant, we beseech thee, that in thy good time the daily Sacrifice may be offered on the altars of the Church's Seminaries, to the glory of thy great Name and the salvation of our souls; through the same thy Son Jesus Christ our Lord. Amen.

Almighty God, who didst give thine only Son to be a propitiation for the sins of the world by his sacrifice upon the cross; We beseech thee to hasten the time when there shall be restored to all the altars of thy Church, the reservation of the blessed Sacrament of the Body and Blood of Christ, that thereby faith in thee may be strengthened, holy mysteries exalted, true and reverent worship increased, and thy kingdom enlarged; through Jesus Christ our Lord. Amen.

Prayers for the Home.

✠

*FAMILY PRAYERS.

Mornings.

O Lord, who hast renewed unto us the light of the sun; We beseech thee in thy loving kindness, to pour the light of thy holy Word into our souls; that we may ever be devoted to thee, by whose wisdom we were created, and by whose providence we are governed; through Jesus Christ our Lord. Amen.

O God, who hast commanded that no man should be idle, but that we should all work with our hands the thing that is good; Look graciously upon thy servants now going forth to do their duty in that station of life unto which thou hast been pleased to call them. May thy blessing be upon our persons, upon our labors, upon our substance and upon all that belongs to us. Enable us to resist the temptations of the world, the flesh and the devil, to follow in all things the motions of thy good Spirit, to be serious and holy in our lives, true and just in our dealings, watchful over our thoughts, words and actions, diligent in our business, and temperate in all things. Give us grace, that we may honestly improve all the talents thou hast committed to our trust, and grant that no worldly business, nor worldly pleasure may ever divert us from the thought of the world to come; through Jesus Christ our Lord. Amen.

Almighty God, make us truly sensible of, and penitent for, all the sins that we have committed against thy divine Majesty, in thought, word or deed. Wash away their guilt with the precious blood of thy dear Son. Be reconciled to us for his sake and save us from the wrath to come. Draw our minds from a love of this world, and teach us to use it with temperance, sobriety and moderation, with an entire trust and dependence on thy fatherly care and good providence, and with a perfect submission to thy blessed will in all things. Root out of our hearts all pride and envy, all hatred, malice and ill will. Put away from us all censoriousness and uncharitableness, all lying and slandering, and whatever else is contrary to a truly Christian spirit. Endue us, we most humbly pray thee, with that meekness and that humility which in thy sight are of great value, and with all those holy and Christian dispositions which thou delightest in. Hear us for the sake of Jesus Christ our Lord. Amen.

---

*Subjects in great variety may be found in other parts of this book that can be used to supplement family worship.

O Lord Jesus Christ, thou Lord of glory, who didst empty thyself of glory for our sakes; Give us grace, we beseech thee, with willing hearts to offer ourselves to thee, all we are and all we have. Raise up according to thy will and for thy glory, saintly priests, heroic missionaries, self-denying rich and poor, men and women devoted to thy service, virgins espoused to thee, married persons loving thee above all and each other as thy precious and cherished gift. Guide us by that wisdom which is pure, peaceable, gentle, easily entreated, merciful, fruitful, without partiality or hypocrisy. And prosper, Lord, thy work in our hands; through thy mercy, O our God who art blessed, and livest and reignest for ever and ever. Amen.

Regard, O Lord, with thy favor all the members of this household. Bind us together in love, sympathy and forbearance. Brighten our daily existence with those endearing graces that come from thee. Help us to live each for the other, and to find our happiness in doing good and in denying ourselves; through Jesus Christ our Lord. Amen.

Be with us, O Lord, through the whole day, in our going out and in our coming in. Be with us in every place, and in every duty to which thy providence may call us. Bless all our lawful undertakings, and grant that in all our works begun, continued, and ended in thee, we may glorify thy holy Name, and finally, by thy mercy, obtain everlasting life; through Jesus Christ our Lord. Amen.

Grant us, O Lord, in all our duties, thy help, in all our perplexities, thy counsel, in all our dangers, thy protection, and in all our sorrows, thy peace; for the sake of Jesus Christ our Lord. Amen.

O Lord God, who art our Guide even unto death; Grant us, we pray thee, grace to follow thee whithersoever thou goest. In little daily duties to which thou callest us, bow down our wills to simple obedience, patience under pain or provocation, strict truthfulness of word and manner, humility and kindness. In great acts of duty or perfection if thou shouldest call us to them, uplift us to self-sacrifice, heroic courage, laying down of life for thy truth's sake or for a brother. Hear us in the Name of thy Son Jesus Christ our Lord. Amen.

O Lord God, gracious and merciful, give us this day, we entreat thee, a humble trust in thy mercy, and suffer not our hearts to fail us. Though our sins be seven, though our sins be seventy times seven, though our sins be more in number than the hairs of our head, yet give us grace in loving penitence to cast ourselves down into the depth of thy compassion; through Jesus Christ our Lord. Amen.

O heavenly Father, keep before us the daily inspiration of thy Son's life upon earth, till we ennoble our duties by the spirit in which we do them. Subdue all selfish ambitions in us, and hallow the uneventfulness of our surroundings by the companionship of Jesus Christ; teach us to fit our spirits to the circumstances in which thy ordering places us, and bring our hearts into reconciliation with what we have to do. From morning until evening keep us in the way which thou hast prepared for us to walk in, by the strength that cometh from the holy cross of Jesus Christ our Lord. Amen.

We praise thee, O Lord, for our family mercies; for bestowing on us a quiet habitation; for life, health, and strength, and the daily provisions of thy good providence. Grant that we may receive them all with grateful and sanctified hearts, enjoy them in the light of thy countenance, and freely give them back to thee when thou art pleased to require them Lord, take us as thine own, and show us the favor thou bearest to thy people, that we may rejoice with thy heritage, and ever adore the exceeding riches of thy grace in Christ Jesus our Lord. Amen.

Heavenly Father, we beseech thee to bless us in the personal influence, both conscious and unconscious, which we exert from day to day. May we be a hindrance to no one either by word or example, but by the purity, gentleness and unselfishness of our lives, may we lead many to serve and glorify thee; through Jesus Christ our Lord. Amen.

O God, at whose word man goeth forth unto his work and to his labor until the evening; Be merciful to all those whose duties are difficult or burdensome, and comfort them concerning their toil. Shield from bodily accident and harm the workmen at their work. Protect the efforts of sober and honest industry, and suffer not the hire of the laborers to be kept back by fraud. Incline the hearts of employers and of those whom they employ to mutual forbearance, fairness and good will. Give the spirit of governance, and of a sound mind to all in places of authority. Bless all those who labor in works of mercy and schools of good learning. Care for all aged persons, and all little children, the sick, and the afflicted, those who travel by land or by sea, all strangers, and emigrants and outcasts. Remember all who by reason of weakness are overtasked, or by reason of poverty are forgotten. Let the sorrowful sighing of the prisoners come before thee, and according to the greatness of thy power, preserve thou those that are appointed to die. Give ear unto our prayer, O merciful and gracious Father, for the love of thy dear Son our Saviour Jesus Christ. Amen.

Almighty God and heavenly Father, who art gracious and merciful, slow to anger and of great kindness; We would remember before thee all those who are in any trial, sorrow or adversity. Shelter the defenceless, feed the hungry, comfort the mourner, raise up the fallen, strengthen the weak, restore the backslider, humble the proud, give wisdom to the foolish, repentance and faith to the hardened and careless. Pity the widow and the fatherless. Defend all who may be in peril, whether temporal or spiritual. Be nigh to those who are

sick, and sanctify their afflictions to their eternal
good, and let thy sustaining grace be vouchsafed to
the dying, that when heart and flesh fail, thou
mayest be the strength of their heart, and their
portion forever. We ask all through Jesus Christ
our Lord. Amen.

O Lord, hear us from heaven, thy dwelling place.
Forgive the sins of our persons, and the sins of our
prayers, and do more for us than we are worthy to
expect at thy hands, for his sake who alone is
worthy, even Jesus Christ, our Mediator and
Redeemer. Amen.

Evenings.

We praise thee, O Lord, who givest the day for
labor, and the night for rest, that thou hast bestowed on us those things that are needful for us,
and hast not withheld thy Spirit from us during
these hours of light. Dispose us ever to make
mention of thy goodness. What things we miss may
we patiently, by thy grace, forego, and what things
we have, may we thankfully ascribe to thy mercy;
through Jesus Christ our Lord. Amen.

Thou hast made, O Lord, the outgoings of another morning and evening to rejoice. Thou hast
crowned the day with thy goodness. Let the night
witness thy care and kindness, and may we enter on
another portion of our time, not only under fresh
obligations, but with new desires and resolutions to
be forever thine; through Jesus Christ our Lord.
Amen.

O Lord God Almighty, in whose hand is our
breath, and whose are all our ways, we come to
thank thee, for thy merciful preservation of us
through another day. We know not, in our utter
ignorance of things unseen, the dangers that surround us by night and by day. We know not how
often there is but a step between us and death. But
all is known to thee, and thy gracious hand has often
turned away from us the danger which thine eye
alone could see. We praise thee, then, O Lord our
God, who redeemest our lives from destruction, and
crownest us with mercy and loving kindness.
O thou, who art slow to anger and plenteous in
mercy, pardon, we humbly pray thee, for Christ's
sake, all our sins, negligences and ignorances. Blot
them all out of the book of thy remembrance. Enter
not into judgment with us on account of them.
There is forgiveness with thee. May we hear thy
gracious voice saying to us, "Be of good cheer; thy
sins are forgiven thee." In every time of need and
trouble be thou, O God, a very present help.
Sanctify to us all thy fatherly chastisements. We
know that thou dost not afflict willingly, nor grieve
the children of men. Thou chastenest us for our
profit, to make us partakers of thy holiness. Teach
us then, O Lord our God, to profit by all thy dealings with us. Subdue every proud and stubborn
thought within us. May our wills be conformed to
thine. When we are called to suffer, may we trust

and be still. When the night of weariness is upon
us, may we be enabled patiently to wait for the
morning of joy. O most merciful Father, who
despisest not the sighing of a contrite heart, receive
and comfort us who are wearied with the burden of
our sins. Blessed Saviour, who callest the weary
and heavy-laden unto thee, give us the rest which
thou alone canst give. Lord, we believe, help thou
our unbelief. Of thy great mercy scatter all our
doubts and fears, and shed abroad in our hearts the
comforts of thy good Spirit, that we may have joy
and peace in believing. Take this household under
thy care this night. Be pleased to give us all refreshing sleep. May our minds be peaceful, and
may our waking thoughts be thoughts of praise.
These things we humbly ask in the Name of Jesus
Christ our Saviour. Amen.

O most gracious God, we confess that we have
most justly provoked thy wrath and indignation
against us. O Lord, we have displeased thee by the
sins of our youth, and the sins of our riper years, by
the sins of our souls and the sins of our bodies, by
our negligences and ignorances, by the evil things
we have done to please ourselves, and the evil things
we have done to please others, by the sins we know
and remember, and the sins we have forgotten, by
the sins we have kept secret from others, and the
sins by which we have made others to offend. But,
O Lord, be not angry with us forever. Spare us,
good Lord, who with true and hearty sorrow confess
our sinfulness, and forgive us, we beseech thee, all
that we have done amiss, for his sake, who died for
our sins, and rose again for our justification, and
now standeth at thy right hand, to make intercession
for us, Jesus Christ our Lord. Amen.

Enlighten, O Lord, our minds that we may know
thee, and let us not be barren nor unfruitful in that
knowledge. May we be thankful for thy mercies,
humble under thy corrections, and devoted to thy
service. Put into our hearts a true faith, a purify-
ing hope and an unfeigned charity; and let no
Christian grace be wanting in us. Give us meekness, humility and contentedness of mind. Make us
diligent in our duty, watchful against all temptations, and temperate in our most lawful enjoyments. Grant us grace to perform all parts of
justice, yielding unto every man, whatsoever, by any
kind of right, becomes his due; and put also into our
hearts such mercy and compassion that we may be
ever ready to do acts of charity, both to our friends
and enemies, according to the commandment and
example of our blessed Saviour. Sanctify us
throughout, that our whole spirits and souls and
bodies may be preserved blameless unto the coming
of our Lord Jesus Christ, to whom with thee and the
Holy Ghost be all honor and glory, world without
end. Amen.

Extend, O Lord, thy pity and compassion to the
whole race of mankind. Enlighten the Gentile
world with a knowledge of thy truth, and bring into
the flock thine ancient people, the Jews, and let all

who name the Name of Christ, depart from all iniquity. Be gracious to thy holy Catholic Church. Grant that she may always preserve that doctrine and discipline, which thou hast delivered to her, and let not the gates of hell ever prevail against her. Grant that all our governors in Church and State may be useful and serviceable to thy glory, and the public good, remembering the great account they must one day give. Be merciful to all that are in affliction or distress, that labor under poverty or persecution, under bodily pains or diseases, or under temptation or trouble of mind. Be pleased to support and comfort them, and in thy good time to deliver them according to thy great mercy. Bless all our friends, relations and acquaintances. Those that are in sin, convert, and those that are in grace, confirm and strengthen. Unite us all, O God, to one another by mutual love, and to thyself by the constant practice of piety and holiness; through the merits of thy blessed Son Jesus Christ our Lord. Amen.

Almighty God, who hast knit together thine elect in one communion and fellowship, in the mystical body of thy Son our Saviour Jesus Christ; Give us grace evermore to draw our supplies of life and peace from him, who is the head over all things to his Church; and so fill us with love to him and all his members, that we may abound in sympathy and kindness. Make us willing to deny ourselves, that others may be enriched. Help us to bear the burdens of the weak, and to minister to the wants of all. Grant that this mind may be in us which was also in Christ Jesus, who came not to be ministered unto, but to minister. Save us from pride, envy and selfishness, and fill us with kindness, consideration, and humility; for the sake of thy dear Son Jesus Christ our Lord. Amen.

Almighty God, who art of purer eyes than to behold iniquity; We beseech thee to fill us with sorrow for our sins of omission this day. If we have not thought of others rather than of ourselves, if we have not been patient under the pressure of trials and cares, if we have not been stedfast when tempted, if we have not been spiritually minded while surrounded with the worldly and thoughtless, we implore thy forbearance and forgiveness. Be pleased to grant us the aid of the Holy Spirit, that we may daily grow in grace, and render thee a higher and better service the longer we live. These things we ask in the Name of our blessed Lord and Saviour Jesus Christ. Amen.

Now, Lord, we commend ourselves to thy gracious care. Preserve us safely from all the dangers and perils of this night. Let not the sons of violence approach to hurt us, nor the devouring flame consume our dwelling. Except the Lord keep the city, the watchman watcheth in vain, but he that keepeth Israel neither slumbereth nor sleepeth. Be then, O God, our helper during the hours of darkness. Preserve us in body and soul from all evil, and grant us at last an abundant entrance into the everlasting kingdom of our Lord and Saviour Jesus Christ. Amen.

In the covenant of our Baptism and in the Name of the holy and undivided Trinity, we close our eyes to sleep. The Father bless us and keep us; the Son make his face to shine upon us, and be gracious unto us; the Spirit lift up his countenance upon us, and give us peace, now and evermore. Amen.

FAMILY PRAYERS FOR EACH DAY OF THE WEEK.

BY THE RT. REV. F. D. HUNTINGTON, D.D., LL.D., L.H.D.

Sunday.

MORNING.

This is the day which the Lord hath made; we will rejoice and be glad in it. Ye shall keep my Sabbaths, and reverence my Sanctuary. Hallow my Sabbaths, and they shall be a sign between me and you, that ye may know that I am the Lord your God. Come before his presence with thanksgiving, and enter into his courts with praise. Worship the Lord in the beauty of holiness. God is a Spirit, and they that worship him must worship him in spirit and in truth.

O Lord, most gracious Saviour, who as on this holy day didst rise from the dead, raise up our souls, we beseech thee, to newness of life, transforming us in the likeness of thy resurrection. Bestow upon each member of this family, upon all who are related to us and dear to us, and upon our fellow-worshippers, such a blessing through thy worship that the days which follow may be spent in thy service and thy favor. Feed us with the Bread of Life which cometh down from heaven. Give wisdom from above and courage and meekness, O blessed Lord, to thy ministers, and give power to their message. May thy truth be received into believing and faithful hearts, and bear fruit in holy and charitable lives. And the praise shall be given to the Father, the Son, and the Holy Ghost, world without end. Amen.

EVENING.

Whoso dwelleth under the defence of the most High shall abide under the shadow of the Almighty. At evening time it shall be light. Thou shalt not be afraid for any terror by night, nor for the arrow that flieth by day, for the pestilence that walketh in darkness, nor for the sickness that destroyeth in the noon-day. The beloved of the Lord shall dwell in safety by him, and the Lord shall cover him all the day long, and he shall dwell between his shoulders. This is the confidence that we have in him, that if we ask anything according to his will, he heareth us.

Abide with us, O blessed Spirit of the living God, we entreat thee, and so cleanse our consciences that our Lord Jesus Christ when he cometh may find us waiting and prepared for his appearing, who by his dying overcame death and by his rising again has opened for us the gate of everlasting life. Accept our thanks for this hallowed day, for the covenants of thy grace and for the ordinances of thy Church. Pardon the sins of our holy things. Remember this night all who are dear to us, and may they be dear to thee. Shine with thy light upon the dark places of the earth. Let healing and sight be given to the nations that they may walk no more in the shadow of death. And to those who labor and witness for thee in heathen or Christian lands give thy strength and heavenly benediction, that they may live according to thy will, set forth thy holy faith, and hasten the coming of thy glorious kingdom ; through Jesus Christ our Lord. Amen.

Monday.

MORNING.

Blessed be the Lord God who turneth the shadows into the morning. Cause me to hear thy lovingkindness in the morning, for in thee do I trust. They that trust in the Lord shall be as Mount Zion which cannot be removed, but abideth for ever. Hast thou not known, hast thou not heard, that the everlasting God, the Lord, fainteth not, neither is weary ? Even the youths shall faint and be weary, and the young man shall utterly fall. But they that wait upon the Lord shall renew their strength. They shall mount up with wings as eagles. They shall run and not be weary ; they shall walk and not faint.

O Almighty God who art the life and light of men ; We give thee humble thanks that thou hast refreshed us with rest and sleep, and hast now touched us and wakened us with thine unseen Hand. Drive away all dullness, we beseech thee, from our minds, and help us to look up in faith and prayer to the true light of the world, which is Jesus Christ. Keep us this week from all injury and accident, mischief and wrong-doing. Make us watchful against the enemy of our souls, stedfast in every good work, content with our lot, and conquerors of our appetites and passions, through the power of thy Holy Spirit always present in our hearts. In all our anxieties and perplexities as to the necessities of this mortal life, be thou our guide and our comforter. Help us to go on in our Christian way, without stumbling and without stain, always both ashamed and afraid to offend our heavenly Master who so loved us as to die for us, and who will judge us in the last day. These things we ask through him, our blessed Mediator and Redeemer. Amen.

EVENING.

O Lord, thou hast searched me out, and known me; thou knowest my down-sitting and mine uprising; thou understandest my thoughts long before. Thou art about my path, and about my bed, and spiest out all my ways. For there is not a word in my tongue, but thou, O Lord, knowest it altogether. Yea, the darkness is no darkness to thee, but the night is as clear as the day. The darkness and light to thee are both alike. How dear are thy counsels unto me, O God; O how great is the sum of them. If I tell them, they are more in number than the sand. When I wake up I am present with thee.

O God, who by making the evening to follow the day hast bestowed the gift of repose on human weakness; Grant, we beseech thee, that while we enjoy these timely blessings we may acknowledge him from whom they come. Thine is the day, O Lord, and thine is the night; grant that, as the natural sun goes down, the Sun of righteousness may abide in our hearts, to drive away the darkness of wicked thoughts. Visit, we beseech thee, this habitation with thy mercy, and us thy children with thy grace and salvation, that no illusion of the night may abuse us, the spirits of darkness may not come near to hurt us, no evil or sad accident oppress us; and may thy blessing, most blessed God, be upon us forever, through Jesus Christ our Lord. Amen.

Tuesday.

MORNING.

Put them in mind to obey magistrates, to be ready to every good work, to speak evil of no man, to be no brawlers, but gentle, showing all meekness unto all men. And we beseech you, brethren, to know them which labor among you and are over you in the Lord, and admonish you, and to esteem them very highly in love for their work's sake. And be at peace among yourselves. See that none render evil for evil unto any man. Provide things honest in the sight of all men. Study to be quiet and to do your own business, and to work with your own hands. And the very God of peace sanctify you wholly.

We entreat thee, O God of all wisdom, and Fountain of all goodness, that thou wilt show us the right way, and incline us steadily and faithfully to walk in it. Engage all our powers and faculties in observing thy commandments. Make our bodies fit temples for thy Holy Spirit to dwell in, so that, with temperance and purity, all our desires and appetites may be subdued to thine incorruptible will, and no excess or sloth darken our minds or deaden our consciences. Teach us to prize honor more than comfort, and usefulness to our fellow-men more than their favor. Lift us above a weak or wicked fear of human opinions. Set us free from foolish fashions and wrong customs. Restrain us from following any multitude to do evil. Grant us patience whenever we are provoked, courage when we are ready to despair, and perseverance unto the end. May nothing ever seem too hard for us to do, or to suffer, in following him, our crucified and glorified Master, who bore the cross and laid down his life for us. And this we beg in the Name of him, our Redeemer, who, with thee and the Holy Ghost, liveth and reigneth, one God, world without end. Amen,

EVENING.

The fruit of the Spirit is love, joy, peace, long-suffering, gentleness, goodness, faith, meekness, temperance: against such there is no law. And they that are Christ's have crucified the flesh with the affections and lusts. As many of you as have been baptized into Christ have put on Christ. If any man be in Christ he is a new creature. Every man's work shall be made manifest; for the Day shall declare it, and the fire shall try every man's work of what sort it is. If any man defile the temple of God him shall God destroy; for the temple of God is holy, which temple ye are.

O thou, Lord, who never slumberest nor sleepest, we humbly and heartily thank thee, for all thy goodness and loving-kindness this day. This night let thy holy angels be ministering spirits around us; and keep thou far from us all dangers and mischiefs and the fear of them, that we may enjoy such refreshing sleep as may fit us for the duties of the following day. Pardon, for thy dear Son's sake, all which we have done amiss this day, and help us to be truly sorry for every known sin. Remember for good all forsaken and troubled souls, all homeless children and all who have gone out from their homes into a world full of temptation. Remember the sick and friendless; the Bishop and all the Clergy of this Diocese; and all thy whole Church. May thy kingdom come on earth, and prepare us all by thy Holy Spirit, and through the merits and death of thy dear Son, for thy eternal kingdom in glory. All which we ask for Jesus Christ's sake. Amen.

Wednesday.

MORNING.

Let us, who are of the day, be sober, putting on the breast-plate of faith and love, and for an helmet the hope of salvation. If we live in the Spirit let us also walk in the Spirit. Let us not be desirous of vain glory, provoking one another, envying one another. Bear ye one another's burdens, and so fulfil the law of Christ. Be kindly affectioned, one to another, with brotherly love, in honor preferring one another. For as we have many members in one body, and all members have not the same office, so we being many are one body in Christ, and every one members one of another.

Bless, O Lord, we beseech thee, this household with thy love and favor. Be very gracious to all our dear relatives wherever they may be. Give joy and health in their dwellings. Gather into the one

Catholic and Apostolic Church our companions and friends, bringing into the way of truth all such as have erred and are deceived. Multiply ministers and missionaries who by a holy life and sound doctrine shall diligently and earnestly preach thy Word and rightly and duly administer thy holy sacraments. Preserve our nation and defend our land. Purge it of profanity, drunkenness, violence and crime. May all the laws and institutions of our country be conformed to the principles of that everlasting kingdom which is righteousness, liberty and peace. And wilt thou fill the whole world with thy love and thy glory, for Jesus Christ's sake. Amen

EVENING.

There is one Body and one Spirit, even as ye are called in one hope of your calling; one Lord, one Faith, one Baptism, one God and Father of all, who is above all and through all, and in you all. It was needful for me to write unto you and exhort you that ye should earnestly contend for the faith. Woe unto that man by whom the Son of man is betrayed. Examine yourselves whether ye be in the faith: prove your own selves. For we can do nothing against the truth but for the truth. And I pray God your whole body, soul and spirit may be preserved blameless unto the coming of our Lord Jesus Christ.

Lighten our darkness, we beseech thee, O Lord, and take us into thy holy care and keeping for this night. We thank thee for wonderfully and patiently preserving us, all this day, from seen and unseen dangers both of the body and the soul. We thank thee for all that we have learned and enjoyed. May thy continual goodness move us more and more to love and serve thee. Cleanse our evil hearts by the precious blood of our Saviour Jesus Christ, the Lamb of God who taketh away the sins of the world. Pity our weakness, and strengthen us with the might of thy Holy Spirit in the inner man. Permit us to go to our rest with trust in thee, our Heavenly Father, and in peace with each other and all mankind, forgiving any who may have offended or injured us, as we hope to be forgiven. And inasmuch as our blessed Lord, as on this day of the week, was betrayed into the hands of wicked men, save us, we pray thee, from all heartlessness towards him and from acting treacherously towards one another. May we be ready always with holy courage to confess and defend the faith handed down to us as our heritage in thy Church. And being found stedfast unto the end may we have mercy in thy judgment, through Jesus Christ our Lord. Amen.

Thursday.

MORNING.

Jesus said, I am the Bread of Life. He that cometh to me shall never hunger, and he that believeth on me shall never thirst. Verily I say unto you, he that heareth my word, and believeth on him that sent me, hath everlasting life, and shall not come into condemnation, but is passed from death unto life.

Blessed Lord, who hast given us a new commandment, that we should love one another, write that law of love, we beseech thee, on our hearts. Help us by thy Holy Spirit that all our affections may be pure and without dissimulation. Keep us from uncharitable judgments, words and actions. Dispose us to give gladly of such good things as thou hast given us for the needy and distressed, for the enlargement of thy kingdom, and for the glory of thy great Name; through him who gave himself for us, Jesus Christ, thy Son, our Lord. Amen.

EVENING.

Charity suffereth long and is kind; Charity envieth not; Charity vaunteth not itself, is not puffed up, doth not behave itself unseemly, seeketh not her own, is not easily provoked, thinketh no evil, rejoiceth not in iniquity but rejoiceth in the truth; beareth all things, believeth all things, hopeth all things, endureth all things. Charity never faileth. And now abideth faith, hope, charity, these three; but the greatest of these is charity.

O Lord God, Judge of all men, whose eyes are everywhere, beholding the evil and the good, we confess to thee our sins of this day, and our unworthiness of thy constant care. Thy mercy, O Father, is greater than our offences. Lead us to true sorrow for them, and hearty repentance. Grant us, for Christ's dear sake, pardon for them all, and especially for our too frequent loss of that love which is the fulfilling of thy Law; for thou art love. Make us strong henceforth to do thy holy will. Help us to live every day as if it were to be our last, and make us to be thy true and loving children, for Jesus Christ's sake. Amen.

Friday.

MORNING.

Behold the Lamb of God, which taketh away the sin of the world. This Man, after he had offered one sacrifice for sins forever, sat down on the right hand of God. Let this mind be in you which was also in Christ Jesus, who being in the form of God thought it not robbery to be equal with God, but made himself of no reputation, and took upon him the form of a servant, and was made in the likeness of men; and, being found in fashion as a man, he humbled himself and became obedient unto death, even the death of the cross. Wherefore God hath highly exalted him

O Father of mercies, whose beloved Son was, as on this day of the week, crucified for us, the just for the unjust, to bring us to thee, give grace, we beseech thee, to every member of this family to look in faith upon that cross, and to crucify ourselves upon it to every impure desire and unchristian temper. May we each learn, in humble devotion to our Master's service, to deny ourselves daily, for his sake, and for one another's sake, that we may follow him. Remove from us every corrupt and unfaithful affection. May we never be afraid to do right, and never dare to do wrong. And so, out of the good treasure of the heart, may we be ever bringing forth good things, to the praise and glory of thy Name, through Jesus Christ our Lord. Amen

EVENING

Having therefore boldness to enter into the holiest by the blood of Jesus, by a new and living way which he hath consecrated for us, through the vail, that is to say his flesh, and having an high priest over the house of God, let us draw near with a true heart in full assurance of faith, having our hearts sprinkled from an evil conscience, and our bodies washed with pure water. Let us hold fast the profession of our faith without wavering, for he is faithful that promised. And let us consider one another, to provoke unto love and to good works: not forgetting the assembling of ourselves together, as the manner of some is, but exhorting one another, and so much the more as ye see the day approaching.

O thou good and faithful Shepherd, who didst not leave thy sheep but didst die for them, and who, in order to save us thy people from eternal death, didst suffer every bitter pain of body and soul, look mercifully upon us; leave us not to the punishments which our self-indulgence and wrong-doing deserve; continue thy loving kindness to us; hide us under the shadow of thy wings; put away from us anger, envying, and the lusts of the flesh and the pride of life; give us more and more of thine own patience, gentleness, long-suffering and humility; graciously accept our poor endeavors to draw near to thee, and bring us to that everlasting day, where thou, O Christ, with the Father and the Holy Ghost livest and reignest, world without end. Amen.

Saturday.

MORNING.

Draw nigh to God and he will draw nigh to you. Ask and ye shall receive; seek and ye shall find. Let us search and try our ways, and turn again unto the Lord. The eyes of the Lord are over the righteous and his ears are open unto their prayers. God shall bring every work into judgment, with every secret thing, whether it be good or whether it be evil. They said unto Peter and to the rest of the Apostles, Men and brethren, what shall we do? Then Peter said unto them, Repent and be baptized, every one of you, in the Name of Jesus Christ. For the promise is unto you and to your children, and to all that are afar off, even as many as the Lord our God shall call.

O Lord God Almighty, who art without beginning of days and end of years, grant unto us thy children such a measure of thy grace that running in the way of thy commandments we may attain at length to the fulfillment of thy heavenly promises. Thou who hast declared to us in thy holy Word that except a man be born of water and of the Holy Ghost he cannot enter thy kingdom, may we be saved at last by that true baptism which is the answer of a good conscience towards God. Cleanse our hearts that our outward lives may be clean. Guide us by thy counsel here and afterwards receive us to thy glory, through Jesus Christ our Lord. Amen.

EVENING.

Lord, thou hast been our dwelling place in all generations. A thousand years in thy sight are but as yesterday when it is past, and as a watch in the night. So teach us to number our days that we may apply our hearts unto wisdom. Let thy work appear unto thy servants, and thy glory unto their children. Let the beauty of the Lord our God be upon us, and establish thou the work of our hands upon us. The Lord is at hand. Be careful for nothing, but in everything, by prayer and supplication, with thanksgiving, let your requests be made known unto God. And the peace of God, which passeth all understanding, shall keep your hearts and minds through Jesus Christ.

O holy and most merciful Father, whose most dear Son Jesus Christ, did as on this day of the week lie in the grave, all the travail of his soul and the agonies of his body being past, grant that by his blessed ministry and mediation we may become dead unto sin and freed from all its power. Give us grace while yet we have our dwelling and our daily and our weekly tasks in this world to be ever looking forward to that rest which remaineth for thy people. Receive our humble and hearty thanks for all thy forbearing goodness to us through this week now drawing to a close. Prepare us for the sacred employments and the reverent worship of another of the days of the Son of man. Seeing how short our time is, may we be found diligent in thy work, fervent in spirit, serving the Lord. Suffer no stain of unforgiven sin to linger in our hearts, but pardon and accept us for the sake of Jesus Christ thy Son our Lord. Amen.

SPECIAL PRAYERS FOR THE FAMILY.

For Mutual Love.

O God, who art the God of all the families of the earth, and who hast so constituted our households that they may be aids to holiness and to heaven, breathe thy Holy Spirit into each of our hearts, and help us to feel the power of personal godliness. Knit us together in Christian love and mutual kindness. Help each one to fill the position which thou hast assigned him with a single eye to thy glory, and a sincere desire for the benefit of all those who are associated with us. Give us grace to cultivate personal communion with thee, that so we may walk together in unity and godly love, and help each other on in the way to heaven. Bless us and make us a blessing, that our home on earth may be a preparation for our home in heaven. Grant this, O Lord, for thy dear Son's sake. Amen.

On Removing to a new Home.

O Lord our God, who hast determined the times before appointed and the bounds of our habitation; We pray unto thee to prosper this change in our dwelling-place, not only to our spiritual and temporal good, but also to that of others. We heartily thank thee for all thy past mercies, and beseech thee to grant that, with a new abode, we may begin a new life, and still more abundantly partake of thy grace and goodness. May this house be to us a peaceable habitation, and a sure dwelling, and a quiet resting-place. Above all, be thou, O Lord, our dwelling-place in all generations, and our strong habitation whereunto we may always resort, for the sake of Jesus Christ, our Saviour and Redeemer. Amen.

For an Husband and Wife.

O merciful God, we humbly beseech thee to send thy blessing continually upon us, and to make us thankful for all that thou hast already vouchsafed unto us; and as thou hast made us one in the mystical grace of matrimony, grant that we may be also inwardly of one heart and of one mind, paying due honor one to another, united in love to thee and to each other in thee; living together in peace and holiness as faithful members of thy Church, denying ourselves, and being a mutual help, comfort and support to each other all the days of our life. [Give us grace to train our children in thy faith and fear] Bless us with health and strength, if it be thy will; and with whatever else thy good providence shall see to be best for our souls and bodies. Fit and prepare us day by day for our departure hence, that we may together inherit eternal life in thy heavenly kingdom, through the merits of Jesus Christ our Lord and Saviour. Amen.

At the Birth of a Child.

Lord Jesus Christ, thou tender Shepherd of the sheep, who dost carry the lambs in thine arms, and gently lead them that are with young, be gracious to the lamb thou hast added to thine earthly flock. Take the infant into thine arms as thou didst take the children in the days of thy humiliation, and didst bless them. Temper the wind to the shorn lamb, and give it covert beneath the shadow of thy wings. Grant that it may be written in heaven, as it was recorded of thyself, that the child grew in wisdom and in stature, and in favor with God and man. And to thee, O Saviour, with the Father and the Holy Spirit, be all the praise now and forever. Amen.

Before the Baptism of a Child.

O Almighty God and heavenly Father, we humbly commend to thy fatherly blessing and care, the child of this family, who is this day to be brought to thy holy Baptism. Bless *him*, and sanctify *him*, we beseech thee, and grant that, being baptized with the Holy Ghost and received into thy Church, *he* may continue thy servant unto *his* life's end, and finally be united to all the saved in thy kingdom; through Christ our Lord. Amen.

For Children of the Family.

O Lord Jesus Christ, who hast redeemed us with thy most precious blood; Visit and quicken, we humbly beseech thee, the children of this household, whom thou by holy Baptism hast made members of thee, their Head and Saviour, and united into thy family. As thou hast thus brought them into thy fold, so do thou help them by thy right hand: count them with thy lambs, govern them by thy love, direct them in thy way. Make them reverent and holy; teachable and observant of all heavenly precepts; temperate and chaste in their lives; dutiful and loving toward their parents; gentle, patient, and courteous to all. So, Lord, do thou adorn them with the graces of thy Spirit, assist them with thy tender compassion, and sanctify them by thy truth, that they may grow up in thy holy ways, and render acceptable praise and adoration to thee, with the Father, and the Holy Ghost, world without end. Amen.

For Children at School.

Almighty God, from whom cometh every good and perfect gift; We pray thee to direct, assist, and bless the children of this family who are under instruction. Father of lights, enlighten their minds; preserve them from error, and lead them into the right knowledge of all truth. Grant that they may earnestly devote themselves to whatsoever studies or pursuits thy providence shall call them; and adorn them with that modesty and humbleness of spirit which thou delightest to reward. Give them healthy minds, upright and faithful hearts, singly devoted to please thee; that they may be comforts to their parents, and sincere members of Christ's Body, the Church. Imbue their spirits with the heavenly treasures of wisdom laid up in thy holy Scriptures, which are able to make them wise unto salvation: and let thy Word be their ruler and guide in so discharging the duties of this life, that they may not fail to attain the heavenly life; through the merits of our Lord and Saviour Jesus Christ. Amen.

Sponsors for Children.

O heavenly Father, look graciously, we beseech thee, upon thy children to whom by thy calling we stand in the holy relationship of sponsors, that the life of thine incarnate Son into whom they are new-born by the operation of the Holy Ghost, may ever perfect them according to thy will. Grant that they, with pure hearts, attaining the years of discretion, may speedily receive the strengthening of Confirmation, the nourishment and support continually of the Holy Communion, and that, renouncing all sin, believing all thy truth, seeking all thy commandments, they may in the grace of the Holy Sacraments attain everlasting life; through Jesus Christ our Lord. Amen.

For Absent Members of the Family.

O God, who art everywhere present, look down with thy mercy upon those who are absent from us. Give thy holy angels charge over them, and grant that by the light of thy divine inspiration, and the gifts of thy bountiful providence, they may be protected in body, soul and spirit, and presented faultless before the presence of thy glory with exceeding joy; through Jesus Christ our Lord. Amen.

After the Marriage of any Member of the Family.

O Lord God, who hast this day joined together thy servants in holy matrimony, be merciful unto them, and bless them; that being more and more united to one another in thy dear Son, they may serve thee in all holy fear and love, and living together as heirs of the same grace, may become meet for the inheritance of the saints in glory. Grant this, O heavenly Father, for Jesus Christ's sake. Amen.

At a Marriage Anniversary.

Almighty God, who didst institute the holy estate of matrimony for the mutual help and comfort of thy children; We thank thee that thou hast preserved these thy servants to this hour. We praise thee for thy goodness to them in making their union one of love, peace and happiness, and that through thy grace they have been enabled to keep the vow and covenant betwixt them made. Protect them, we beseech thee, through the years to come, and multiply thy blessings upon them. May they abound in love, and bear together willingly the burdens of life. Encourage and sustain them in all godly living, and may their home continue to be a place of prayer, consecration and joy. Let thy benediction rest upon them to their life's end, and finally give them a joyful entrance into thy blessed kingdom; through Jesus Christ our Lord. Amen.

After a Death in the Family.

O God, who orderest all things in heaven and in earth, who hast been pleased in thy wise providence to take out of this world the soul of our deceased *brother*, enable us to submit in faith and patience to this thy dispensation, and both to see and feel thy love and mercy in it. Teach us, O Lord, the shortness and uncertainty of human life, and so to remember our days that we may apply our hearts unto wisdom. Protect, sanctify, and guide us to the end, that, living in thy faith and fear, we may at last be gathered to thy saints in peace; through him who died for us, Christ Jesus our Redeemer. Amen.

For Resignation when Calamity Befalls a Family.

O Lord God, good and gracious, whose mercy endureth for ever; Give us now a surer trust in thee, and an entire submission to thy divine will. Support us under our present trial, and suffer us not to be dispirited and cast down by fears and anxieties about the future. If this trial is permitted to punish us for our past sins, to render us more humble, or to exercise our patience and trust in thee, make us submissive and content to bear it; and grant that, setting our affections on things above and not on things on the earth, we may be enabled by thy grace to live a life of faith, of fortitude, and duty, and die in thy favor; through Jesus Christ our Lord. Amen

Prayers for the State and Nation.

✠

PRAYERS FOR THE STATE.

Save, O God, the State from evil and designing men, from corruption in social and political life, from crime, intemperance, dishonesty and every false way. Prosper every good purpose and overturn every evil one, that thy Name may be honored; through Jesus Christ our Lord. Amen.

Vouchsafe thy blessing, Almighty God, on this Commonwealth. Build it up, and sustain it in righteousness. Give the spirit of obedience to law to all our people. Protect our homes, secure us our liberties, strengthen us in religion and education, surround us with uplifting influences and make our State the abode of peace and prosperity. Commit the guidance of our affairs to the hands of the upright and conscientious, so that every virtue may flourish and the kingdom of thy Son be exalted; through the same Jesus Christ our Lord. Amen.

For the Governor of the State.

Almighty God, by whom kings reign and princes decree justice, look with thy favor upon thy servant, the Governor of this Commonwealth. Endue him with thy Holy Spirit, and enrich him with thy heavenly grace. Dispose and turn his heart as it seemeth best to thy Godly wisdom, that he, knowing whose minister he is, may, above all things, seek thy honor and glory: Prosper him with all happiness, and bring him to thine everlasting kingdom; through Jesus Christ our Lord. Amen.

For the State Legislature.

Almighty and everlasting God, Creator and Ruler of men; We beseech thee to bless the members of the Legislature of this State, in all their consultations. Protect them from selfish interests and prejudices, and give them the spirit of true and wise statesmen. Guide them by thy heavenly counsel that their legislation may result in the maintenance of peace and prosperity, religion and justice. We ask it in the Name of Jesus Christ our Lord. Amen.

For Rulers and People.

O God, the Sovereign Lord and King, who hast given unto men the administration of government upon earth, we make our supplications unto thee, for all those who have that trust committed to their hands. Enable them, we pray thee, to fulfil the same to thy honor and the welfare of the nations among whom they rule. Especially we implore thy favor on thy servants, the President of the United States, the Governor of the State, and all who have the making or the executing of law in the land. Endue them with uprightness and wisdom, with firmness and clemency, remembering whose ministers they are, and the account which they must render at thy throne. To the people of all ranks and conditions among us, give the spirit of obedience to government, and of contentment under its protection, in leading peaceable and honest lives. Let the righteousness prevail which exalteth a nation, and, throughout our land, let the Name of thy Son be acknowledged as King of kings, and Lord of lords, to thy honor and glory, who art God over all, blessed for evermore. Amen.

O Almighty Lord, who fashionest the hearts of men and considerest all their works; Grant, we beseech thee, to us and to all the people of this land, the spirit of obedience to thy commandments; that, walking humbly in thy fear, we may, under thy mighty protection, continue to dwell in righteousness and peace. Defend our liberties; preserve our unity; save us from lawlessness, dishonesty and violence; from discord and confusion; from pride and arrogance, and from every evil way. Continue thy goodness to us, that the heritage received from our fathers may be preserved in our time and transmitted, unimpaired, to the generations to come; that all nations of the earth may know that thou, O Lord, art our Saviour and mighty Deliverer and our King forever. Grant this, we beseech thee, through Jesus Christ our Lord. Amen.

At the Raising of a Flag.

O Almighty and everlasting God, King of kings and Lord of lords, who hast constituted the services of angels and men in a wonderful order, and having divided the human race into nations, appointed the archangel Michael prince over Judah, as guardian and protector, continue, we beseech thee, the favor thou hast ever shown to the United States of America, since thou hast made us a nation; and may the guardianship of thy most powerful angels secure to us the respect of the peoples of the earth. Bless the flag, now to be raised heavenward, that it may ever wave as the symbol of a nation exalted by righteousness. And forasmuch as righteousness can only come through the gift of the Holy Ghost sent down upon thy holy Catholic Church, on the day of Pentecost, which Church thou hast made the way of salvation, bless with abundant blessings the Church of America. May it, by the power of the Holy Ghost, walk answerably to its high calling and leaven the nation. Bless all who love our Lord Jesus Christ in sincerity and truth, and prosper the works undertaken by them for the welfare of the people. As we look up to the flag, may the blue of its union direct our thoughts to the higher blue of the sky, reminding us that heaven is our home, in which the righteous shall shine as the stars in the firmament. Hear us for the sake of Jesus Christ, our Lord, who livest and reignest with thee and the Holy Ghost, ever one God, world without end. Amen.

In time of Civil Discord.

O God, our refuge and strength, who orderest all things in heaven and earth, we flee to thee for succor in this our time of trouble. Look down with thy mercy on us. Remember not our iniquities, nor the iniquities of our forefathers, neither take thou vengeance of our sins. Deliver us, O Lord, from blood-guiltiness; preserve us from open violence and secret conspiracy. Pour out upon us, and on all the people of this land, the spirit of grace and supplication, and join us together in piety, loyalty, and brotherly love. Direct the counsels, and strengthen the hands of all in authority, for the repression of crime and outrage, the maintenance of order and law, and of public peace and safety; so that leading quiet lives in all godliness and honesty, we may be thy people, and thou mayest vouchsafe to be our God; and that we may bless and glorify thee, our Defender and mighty Deliverer, through Jesus Christ our Lord. Amen.

For the Army and Navy.

Bless, O Lord, our soldiers and sailors, of whatever rank or quality; Grant that in the midst of every temptation which besets them they may fight manfully against the world, the flesh, and the devil; and resisting all evil by the spirit of thy ghostly strength, may acquire true courage in the victory of faith. Prosper them in the maintenance of our country's honor, and keep them safe from enemies spiritual and temporal, that they may glorify thee upon the earth until they are called to rest in the triumph of thy glory; through Jesus Christ our Lord. Amen.

For the Reign of Peace.

O Prince of Peace, govern in our hearts, dispelling all angry passions and ill-will, and all that is discordant with the harmony of thy rule. Sway the nations of the earth. Put an end to their enmities and strifes. Hasten the time when they shall prepare for war no more, and rest secure in thine empire of peace, to the glory of thee, and of the Father, and of the Holy Ghost, world without end. Amen.

Prayers for Colleges, Schools and Charitable Institutions.

✠

PRAYERS FOR COLLEGES AND SCHOOLS.

Almighty God, the fountain of all wisdom, the true light which lighteth every man that cometh into the world; We beseech thee, regard with thy favor and visit with thy blessing the colleges and schools in our land. Assist all who are guardians of their interests. Secure to them the means of their usefulness. Endue all those who are teachers with a serious sense of their charge, and wisdom and strength for its fulfilment. Bless the students with health; make them to be diligent and faithful in study. Guard their inexperience, and carry them safely through all temptations. Teach them how to cleanse their path so as to keep it according to thy Word. Inspire them with high hopes and worthy purposes, and so prepare them to fulfil their course with honor, fidelity and success in this life, that they may attain the glorious destiny to which thou dost call them in the life to come; through the redemption that is in Jesus Christ our Lord. Amen.

Bless, O Lord, this college, and grant that every one therein may perceive and know what things he ought to do, and also may have strength and power faithfully to perform the same. Give wisdom unto those who administer its government and discipline, and to all those who impart instruction, as also to all the students, according to their duties and the necessities of their youth. And grant that by thy special favor, on which we humbly depend, this college may be enriched with all temporal and spiritual good, to the great increase and welfare of thy holy Apostolic Church, and to the glory of thy holy Name; through Jesus Christ our blessed Saviour and Redeemer. Amen.

For Founders and Benefactors.

Blessed be thy Name, O Lord, for the happy memory of the founders and benefactors of this College, and for all who befriend it by their labors and their prayers. Raise up many helpers to enlarge and adorn it, granting unto them that wisdom through which an house is builded and the understanding by which it is established; that so by knowledge its chambers may be filled with all precious and pleasant riches. For the silver and the gold are thine, O Lord our God, and all things come of thee; therefore unto thee we look for all that we desire; as for all thou hast done for us, we praise and bless thy glorious Name; through Jesus Christ, our Strength and our Redeemer. Amen.

Daily Prayer for a School.

O God, who knowest that we are not able to believe or do what is right without thy special grace; Bless, we pray thee, our work in this school to-day; keep far from us all pride and covetousness, lust and anger, envy, impatience, discontent and idleness. Grant that those who teach may do it with earnestness and patience, as in thy sight, and for thy sake; and give to all thy children an humble and teachable spirit, that each in his appointed state, may learn more and more to love and serve thee, and finally, through that knowledge, may come to everlasting life; through our Lord Jesus Christ. Amen.

For past Members of a School.

Bless, O Lord, all who have ever belonged to this school, and who yet survive; and make precious unto us the good examples of such as have departed this life in thy faith and fear, that with them we may be partakers of thy heavenly kingdom. All which we beg through Jesus Christ our Lord. Amen.

For Students in Divinity.

O Lord Jesus Christ, bless, we beseech thee, all those who are preparing for the work of the ministry in thy holy Church. Give them that wisdom which cometh from above, and that gentleness which becometh the gospel of peace. Make them to be diligent in the study of thy Word, and teach them by thy Spirit that they may be enabled to teach others. Take from them the spirit of worldliness, and give them grace, that they may cultivate that holiness of life, which is required of those who bear the vessels of the Lord. May they be instant in season and out of season, willing to spend and be spent, in the great work to which they are called, and may they do all things to thy glory, who, with the Father and the Holy Ghost, art one God, world without end. Amen.

For Medical Students.

Almighty Lord, who hast made our bodies to be the temples of the Holy Ghost; Give, we pray thee, to all those who are engaged in the study of man's physical nature, that reverence for thee and for thy works which will lead them to love and adore thy Name. When called to minister to the suffering may they by their godly example influence the souls as well as the bodies of the sick. While they seek to heal others, may they also be healed of every spiritual ill; through the great Physician of souls, Jesus Christ our Lord. Amen.

For Reformatory Schools.

Deliver, O most merciful God, those little ones of thy flock who, whether through the neglect of their parents or the stubbornness of their own evil nature, have fallen into manifest sin. Remember not the offences of their youth, but set them free from the snare of the enemy. Prosper with the help of thy Holy Spirit the endeavors of all who are seeking to train them for good. Grant that, following after humility, and being made partakers of thy heavenly wisdom, they may be strengthened to the performance of thy will, and sheltered evermore by thy fatherly protection, so that in the joy of thy presence they may be restored as true penitents to the perfect fellowship of thy saints; through Jesus Christ our Lord. Amen.

For an Hospital.

O Lord Jesus Christ, the great and only Physician of the soul and the body; Send thy blessing upon the inmates of this institution who are suffering from sickness. Give them sorrow for sin and an humble dependence upon thy mercy, and grant that their afflictions may quicken their faith and love. If it be thy will, restore them to health and usefulness, that they may praise thee for thy goodness during the residue of their days. If in thy wisdom, thou hast appointed otherwise, give them a resigned will and a peaceful heart, that they may commit themselves to thy keeping, thou merciful Judge of the quick and dead; to whom, with the Father and the Holy Ghost, be all the glory, world without end. Amen.

For an Home for Orphan and Destitute Children.

O Almighty God, the Father of the fatherless, and the Friend of the friendless; We commend to thy protection the inmates of this Home, and all who pray, or give, or labor to help its loving work. Bless the children, and give them an heart ever thankful, a mind ever teachable, and a will always obedient to thee and to those whom thou hast in thy love placed over them. Keep them in health and strength; be with them in their studies, tasks and plays. Protect them under thy wing from every assault and temptation of the devil. Let thy Holy Spirit be with them and teach them more and more to renounce all the sinful desires of their hearts, to believe all the articles of the Christian faith, and obediently to keep thy holy will and commandments. May they be so truly children of God, and members of Christ, that they fail not finally to inherit thine everlasting kingdom. All which we ask for Jesus Christ's sake. Amen.

For the Insane.

O Lord, whose ways are past finding out; We pray thee of thy great goodness to look upon these thy servants whom thou hast afflicted with weakness and darkness of mind; grant unto them to be strengthened and enlightened with thy spirit in the inner man, that they to whom thou hast denied earthly wisdom may be filled with that knowledge of thee which passeth all understanding; through Jesus Christ our Lord. Amen.

For the Deaf and Dumb.

O God, our heavenly Father, whose dearly beloved Son Jesus Christ, when he dwelt on earth, went about doing good, unstopping the ears of the deaf, and loosening the tongues of the dumb; Look down with loving eyes upon all thy deaf and mute children, and give them the special blessing of thy mercy and grace. Let thy Fatherly hand ever be over them, let thy Holy Spirit ever be with them; so that they may learn the truth as it is in Jesus, and believe in and rest upon him as the Saviour of their souls, and find in him that joy and peace which the Holy Ghost alone can bestow. Be with them, we beseech thee, in all the trials and duties and dangers of this life, and may they so live in thy fear and love here, that in the world to come they may ever, with open ears and loving tongues, show forth thy praise in thy heavenly kingdom. Hear us, O Lord God, through thy Son Jesus Christ, to whom, with thee, O Father, and thee, O Holy Ghost, be all honor and glory, now and forever. Amen.

For the Blind.

O God, who hast sent thy Son to be the true Light of the world; Grant that they who cannot see the things of the world may be the more fully enlightened and comforted by his inward guidance. Cheer them in their blindness with thy heavenly manifestations. Show thyself to such as know thee not, and grant that they may thankfully accept the loss of earthly sight, as the means ordained of thee for bringing their hearts to the contemplation of their own misery and of thy holiness. Quicken those who know thee by faith to a deeper intuition of thy purity, that, beholding thee with increasing love, they may become the more conformed to thine image, until they behold thee as thou art, and awake to the full revelation of thy glory; through the same Jesus Christ our Lord. Amen.

For an Home for the Aged.

O Lord Jesus Christ, the strength of all that put their trust in thee; Vouchsafe unto these thy servants increase of spiritual might as their bodily vigor faileth, and grant that as their eyes become dim, and their ears dull to earthly things, their affections may be the more set on things above; through thy mercy, who liveth and reigneth with the Father and the Holy Ghost one God, world without end. Amen.

Prayers Relating to Social Subjects.

✠

PRAYERS FOR THE EMPLOYER AND THE EMPLOYED.

O God, merciful and just; We humbly beseech thee to sanctify the hearts of those who are in positions of authority and influence, that they may act justly toward all who are in their employ. Keep them from the spirit of oppression and wrong, and from forgetfulness of others. Help them to be tender-hearted to the suffering, liberal to the needy, and in all their dealings considerate and humane. Incline them rightly to use the influence thou hast given them, that at last they may give an account of their stewardship with joy and thankfulness; through Jesus Christ our Lord. Amen.

Almighty God, who hast made toil honorable among all men; We pray thee to bestow thy blessing upon those classes in the community who are engaged in the industries of life. Rectify whatever may be oppressive and unjust in their lot, and give them patience and contentment. Deliver them from rebellion and violence, and dispose them and their employers to peaceful measures that shall result in mutual concessions for their common interests. Hear us for the sake of Jesus Christ our Lord. Amen.

Prayers for the Harmony of Revelation and Science.

✠

PRAYERS FOR EXPLORATIONS IN ANCIENT LANDS.

Almighty God, who of old didst create the heavens and the earth, and breathed into man the breath of life; Inspire us, we beseech thee, in all our studies of nature and of man, to behold the harmony between Revelation and Science, and to hold fast to faith in thee, and to accept the blessed hope of immortality taught us in thy holy Word, through the resurrection of Jesus Christ, thy Son, our Advocate and Redeemer. Amen.

Almighty Source of all knowledge; Bless in larger measure every effort made to obtain a knowledge of truth through explorations in ancient lands, and in particular may Egypt, Assyria and Palestine yield more and more their hidden treasures, to the confirmation of the sacred Scriptures and the advancement of thy kingdom of righteousness on the earth; through Jesus Christ thy Son our Lord. Amen.

Grant, we beseech thee, Almighty God, unto thy servants in distant lands, who engage in research and exploration for the truth's sake, and unto all who labor in the cause, the spirit to think and to do those things which are pleasing in thy sight; through Jesus Christ, to whom with thee and the Holy Ghost be ascribed all honor and glory for ever and ever. Amen.

Almighty God, who openest thine hand and fillest all things living with plenteousness, so fill our hearts with gratitude for the discoveries of our age, which shed precious light on the Bible and the history of man, that we may open our hands liberally to support the societies engaged in the work. Grant this, O bountiful Giver of every good and perfect gift, through thy blessed Son, our Saviour Jesus Christ. Amen.

Prayers for Graces and Virtues.

✠

Prayers for Purity.

O God, whose blessed Son took upon him our flesh, and yet lived in this world without sin, leaving us an example that we should follow in his steps; Grant that we may be conformed more and more to his image. May thy Holy Spirit sanctify our hearts and minds, that we may be cleansed from the defilements of the world, and the lusts of the flesh. For Jesus Christ's sake give us grace that we purify ourselves even as he is pure, and thus attain to that holiness without which no man shall see the Lord. Answer thou our prayer, O merciful and gracious Father, for the love of thy dear Son Jesus Christ our Advocate and Redeemer. Amen.

O Almighty God, who hast taught us that our bodies are the temples of the Holy Ghost who dwells in our hearts; Give us grace to flee from all impurity of mind and body. Let the hope of heaven and the joys of eternity withdraw our hearts from all unholy thoughts; that we may enjoy that peace which is the fruit of holiness here, and hereafter receive the full reward of the pure in heart, and see thee, O blessed Lord, for ever and ever; for the sake of Jesus Christ our Lord. Amen.

O Lord Jesus Christ, who hast declared that when we have done all that is commanded us we are still unprofitable servants; Give us grace so to fix our eyes on thy most pure and holy life, that we may know our own impurity and sin, and seek in all humility to be conformed unto thy will; who livest and reignest with the Father and the Holy Ghost one God, world without end. Amen.

Kindle our hearts, O Lord, with the fire of thy Holy Spirit, that we may serve thee with chaste bodies, and please thee with pure souls; through Jesus Christ our Lord. Amen.

O God, who art of purer eyes than to behold iniquity, mercifully grant unto us such a sense of sin that we may receive cleansing, and such cleansing that we may be made pure in heart, and may see thee for evermore; through our Saviour Jesus Christ. Amen.

O Lord, our God, who hast commanded us to speak righteousness, and to judge uprightly; Grant that iniquity may not be found in our mouths, nor wickedness in our minds, but that, from pure hearts, we may speak those things that are right; through Jesus Christ our Lord. Amen.

Prayers for Reverence of God's Name.

Almighty God and heavenly Father, who hast given thy people commandment that they should not take thy Name in vain; Have mercy upon us and incline our hearts to keep this law. Save us from all carelessness and irreverence in thy holy temple, from all angry condemnation of our fellow-men, and from all thoughtless and trifling expressions. Help us so to use the precious gift of speech that our words may be always acceptable in thy sight; through Jesus Christ our Lord. Amen.

O Almighty and all-loving Father; Fill us with so deep a sense of thy goodness in creating, redeeming and preserving us, that we may never use thy holy Name except in devout supplication, joyful adoration and pious instruction. Grant us the spirit of the blessed angels who continually cry "Holy, Holy, Holy," before thee. Help us in our trials and vexations to keep before us the example of thy blessed Son, who glorified thy Name in dire anguish, and not to soil our Christian profession with evil words. Give us the loving spirit of dutiful children, and grant that our lips may be opened by thy Holy Spirit to show forth thy praise on earth, so that they may be trained here to glorify and praise thee in eternity. This we ask for Christ's sake. Amen.

O God, our heavenly Father, who hast magnified thy Name and thy Word above all things; Imprint upon our hearts such a sense of thy majesty, and such a reverence for thy holy Name that we may never take it lightly or carelessly upon our lips. Set a watch before our mouth and keep the door of our lips, that we may always speak soberly and thoughtfully. Let our yea be yea, and our nay, nay, remembering that whatsoever is more than these cometh of evil. Pardon us for all our sins of the tongue in time past, and do thou so open our lips through all the time to come that our mouth shall show forth thy praise; through Jesus Christ our Lord. Amen.

Prayers for Reverence of the Lord's Day.

O God, who in thine infinite wisdom didst appoint one day in seven as a day of rest, and who by the glorious resurrection of thy Son didst consecrate to thyself for all time the first day of the week; Give us grace that we may sacredly regard it as thine own day. During its holy hours separate our minds from worldly things, and help us to fix them upon themes belonging to eternal life, that we may be given such strength as shall fit us for the faithful discharge of the duties of the week. Grant, O Father, that each returning Lord's Day may be to us an earnest of that eternal rest which remaineth for thy people in heaven; through Jesus Christ our Lord. Amen.

Almighty God, the source of all wisdom and goodness; We thank thee that thou hast consecrated this day to thy service and commanded us to keep it holy. For thy glory and our good, help us faithfully to observe this command. Have mercy upon the careless and indifferent, the neglectful and hardened, whose feet are not turned toward thy holy House. Deliver our land, we pray thee, from worldly and wicked men, who mock at sacred things, and profane thy holy day, to the dishonor of thy Name and the great peril of souls. Increase the number of those who delight in keeping thy commandments, who seek thy courts, who rejoice in the sound of the gospel, who reverence thy Sacraments and who look forward to the eternal rest of thy kingdom. Hear us for the sake of thy Son Jesus Christ our Lord. Amen.

Prayers for Temperance.

Almighty God, who didst make man in thine own image, and afterwards didst sanctify our human nature by the incarnation of thy Son; Give us grace to resist all those sinful lusts whereby that which thou hast made and sanctified may be defiled. Send thy blessing in particular, we pray thee, upon the Church Temperance Society, that by its means many may be brought back from the ways of sin, and that all its members, living in mutual help and sympathy, may grow in holiness both of soul and body, until they come to thy perfect likeness; through the mediation of thy Son Jesus Christ our Lord. Amen.

Deliver our land, we beseech thee, O Lord, from the crying sin of drunkenness, whereby it is so grievously defiled, and grant that they who indulge in excess of drink may have grace to check themselves ere they have lost the power of self-control, and finding the unsatisfying nature of all earthly excitement, may come to hunger and thirst after righteousness, and attain to salvation; through Jesus Christ our Mediator and Advocate. Amen.

We beseech thee, O Lord, to renew thy people inwardly and outwardly, that as thou wouldest not have them to be hindered by bodily pleasures, thou mayest make them vigorous with spiritual purpose. Protect them, O Lord, in the time of temptation, support their weakness, and wash away their earthly stains; and while they walk amid the darkness of this mortal life, do thou ever quicken them by thy light; deliver them in thy mercy from all evils, and grant them to attain the height of good; through Jesus Christ our Lord. Amen.

Look down from heaven, O Christ, upon the lambs of thy flock, and bless their bodies and souls Grant that we who have received thy sign in our foreheads, may keep our bodies in temperance, soberness and chastity, and be found thine own in the day of judgment, who, with the Father and the Holy Ghost, art one God, for ever and ever. Amen.

Special Thanksgivings.

✠

HARVEST THANKSGIVING.

Most gracious God, by whose knowledge the depths are broken up, and the clouds drop down the dew; We yield thee unfeigned thanks and praise, as for all thy mercies, so especially for the returns of seed-time and harvest, and for crowning the year with thy goodness, in the increase of the ground, and the gathering in of the fruits thereof And, we beseech thee, give us a just sense of this great mercy; such as may appear in our lives, by an humble, holy and obedient walking before thee all our days; through Jesus Christ our Lord, to whom, with thee and the Holy Ghost, be all glory and honor, world without end. Amen.

O most merciful Father, who hast blessed the labors of the husbandman in the returns of the fruits of the earth; We give thee humble and hearty thanks for this thy bounty; beseeching thee to continue thy loving-kindness to us; that our land may still yield her increase, to thy glory and our comfort; through Jesus Christ our Lord. Amen.

Grant us, O Lord, so to bless thee with grateful hearts for the bounty of thine earthly harvest, that filled with thy love we may bring forth fruit to thee a hundredfold in this life, and in that harvest where the angels are the reapers we may be gathered as wheat into thy garner; through Jesus Christ our Lord. Amen.

For a Recovery from Sickness.

O God, who art the giver of life, of health, and of safety; We bless thy Name, that thou hast been pleased to deliver from *his* bodily sickness *this thy servant*, who now *desireth* to return thanks unto thee, in the presence of all thy people. Gracious art thou, O Lord, and full of compassion to the children of men. May *his heart* be duly impressed with a sense of thy merciful goodness, and may *he* devote the residue of *his* days to an humble, holy and obedient walking before thee; through Jesus Christ our Lord. Amen.

For a Child's Recovery from Sickness.

Almighty God and heavenly Father, we give thee humble thanks for that thou hast been graciously pleased to deliver from *his* bodily sickness the *child* in whose behalf we bless and praise thy Name, in the presence of all thy people. Grant, we beseech thee, O gracious Father, that *he*, through thy help, may both faithfully live in this world according to thy will, and also may be *partaker* of everlasting glory in the life to come; through Jesus Christ our Lord. Amen.

For a Safe Return from Sea.

Most gracious Lord, whose mercy is over all thy works; We praise thy holy Name that thou hast been pleased to conduct in safety, through the perils of the great deep, *this* thy *servant*, who now *desireth* to return *his* thanks unto thee in thy holy Church. May *he* be duly sensible of thy merciful providence towards *him*, and ever express *his* thankfulness by a holy trust in thee, and obedience to thy laws; through Jesus Christ our Lord. Amen.

For Peace and Deliverance from our Enemies.

O Almighty God, who art a strong tower of defence unto thy servants against the face of their enemies; We yield thee praise and thanksgiving for our deliverance from those great and apparent dangers wherewith we were compassed. We acknowledge it thy goodness that we were not delivered over as a prey unto them; beseeching thee still to continue such thy mercies towards us, that all the world may know that thou art our Saviour and mighty Deliverer; through Jesus Christ our Lord. Amen.

For Restoring Public Peace at Home.

O eternal God, our heavenly Father, who alone makest men to be of one mind in a house, and stillest the outrage of a violent and unruly people; We bless thy holy Name, that it hath pleased thee to appease the seditious tumults which have been lately raised up amongst us; most humbly beseeching thee to grant to all of us grace, that we may henceforth obediently walk in thy holy commandments; and, leading a quiet and peaceable life in all godliness and honesty, may continually offer unto thee our sacrifice of praise and thanksgiving for these thy mercies toward us; through Jesus Christ our Lord. Amen.

For Deliverance from great Sickness and Mortality.

O Lord God, who hast wounded us for our sins, and consumed us for our transgressions, by thy late heavy and dreadful visitation; and now, in the midst of judgment remembering mercy, hast redeemed our souls from the jaws of death; We offer unto thy fatherly goodness ourselves, our souls and bodies which thou hast delivered, to be a living sacrifice unto thee, always praising and magnifying thy mercies in the midst of thy Church; through Jesus Christ our Lord. Amen.

After Child-birth.

O Almighty God, we give thee humble thanks for that thou hast been graciously pleased to preserve, through the great pain and peril of child-birth, *this woman*, thy *servant*, who *desireth* now to offer *her* praises and thanksgivings unto thee. Grant, we beseech thee, most merciful Father, that *she*, through thy help, may both faithfully live and walk according to thy will in this life present, and also may be *partaker* of everlasting glory in the life to come; through Jesus Christ our Lord. Amen.

For an Escape from Special Peril.

O Lord God, in whose hand is the life of every thing, and the breath of all mankind; We magnify thy goodness in that thou hast been pleased to save from deadly hurt thy *servant*, who now *desireth* [*or*, for whom we desire] to offer thee the sacrifice of praise and thanksgiving. Give *him* grace, we humbly beseech thee, worthily to spend in thy service the days which thou hast so mercifully prolonged, that henceforth dwelling always under thy protection *he* may abide in thy love unto *his life's* end; through Jesus Christ our Saviour. Amen.

For a Minister's Recovery from Sickness.

O Lord our God, who alone bringest down to the grave and bringest up again; We give thee thanks and praise for restoring to health thy servant who is set over us in the Lord. Give unto him, we beseech thee, fresh and enlarged measures of thy Holy Spirit, that he may labor among us in the fulness of the blessing of the gospel of Christ. Unto us give more grace to value and to improve our spiritual privileges. While the day of salvation lasts, let none of us receive thy grace in vain, but learn to-day, while it is called to-day, more and more to obey thy gospel, and to walk in all thy commandments and ordinances blameless; through Jesus Christ our Redeemer. Amen.

A General Thanksgiving.

O God, of whose mercy there is no end, and the treasure of whose bounty is infinite; We give thanks to thy divine Majesty for the gifts of thy lovingkindness, humbly beseeching thee that the praise and thanksgiving which we begin here on earth we may, with all thy ransomed saints, continue in heaven; through Jesus Christ our Lord. Amen.

Prayers for the Beginning and the Ending of the Year.

✠

PRAYERS FOR NEW YEAR'S DAY.

Almighty God, give us grace, we beseech thee, to run the race which thou hast set before us. Deliver us from the sin and folly of an aimless life. Enable us to set Christ Jesus before us as our object and our hope, our example and our guide. Quicken us by the Holy Spirit to greater energy and earnestness in our Christian course. Grant that, day by day, and year by year, the world may loose its hold upon our hearts, and that we may be found pressing forward to our home above. May the year upon which we have now entered find us making progress in divine things; and, whether we see the end of it or not, enable us to use it as a help to heaven and to thee; through Jesus Christ our Lord. Amen.

Most merciful God, who hast graciously preserved us during the year which is past; Help us, we entreat thee, to serve thee henceforth with all our heart and mind and soul and strength; watch over us with thy divine providence; and, whether we live or whether we die, may we evermore be thine; through our Lord and Saviour Jesus Christ. Amen

O God, whose days are without beginning and without end; Grant us, we humbly pray thee, throughout this year whose beginning we dedicate to thee, such prosperity as thou seest to be good for us, and make us to abound in such works as may be pleasing unto thee. Renew in us, we humbly pray thee, the gifts of thy mercy, increase our faith, strengthen our hope, enlighten our understanding, enlarge our charity, and make us ever ready to serve thee, both in body and soul; through Jesus Christ thy Son, our Lord. Amen.

PRAYERS FOR THE LAST DAY OF THE YEAR.

Most gracious God, we thank thee that in thy great mercy thou hast kept us to the close of another year. We are brought thereby so much nearer to the end. Grant that it may bring us nearer to thee. We dare not venture into another year of our pilgrimage without thy presence and thy blessing. Give us grace to run in the way of thy commandments. Help us to live to thee; help us to labor for thee. Be thou our portion and our inheritance. Grant that we may stand complete in thee now through thy beloved Son, and finally be admitted to the kingdom of thy glory. All this we ask for Jesus Christ's sake. Amen.

Heavenly Father, draw near to us now, we beseech thee, and enable us to close this year with thee. Mercifully forgive all our sins and shortcomings in the past and graciously strengthen us with thy Holy Spirit for the time to come. Abide with us as our teacher, our guide, our friend. Show thyself unto us in all thy grace. Cause our hearts to burn within us as we hear thy loving voice. Be with us when the shadows of life's evening are closing around us, and finally bring us to abide with thee for ever, for the sake of thy dear Son Jesus Christ our Lord. Amen.

Collects of the Christian Year.

✠

COLLECTS FROM THE BOOK OF COMMON PRAYER, WITH OTHERS SELECTED, ADAPTED OR CONTRIBUTED.

The First Sunday in Advent.

Almighty God, give us grace that we may cast away the works of darkness, and put upon us the armor of light, now in the time of this mortal life, in which thy Son Jesus Christ came to visit us in great humility; that in the last day, when he shall come again in his glorious majesty to judge both the quick and the dead, we may rise to the life immortal, through him who liveth and reigneth with thee and the Holy Ghost, now and ever. Amen.

Mercifully hear, O Lord, the prayers of thy people; that as they rejoice in the Advent of thine only begotten Son according to the flesh, so when he cometh a second time in his majesty, they may receive the reward of eternal life; through the same Jesus Christ our Lord, who liveth and reigneth with thee and the Holy Ghost, ever one God, world without end. Amen.

O Lord Jesus Christ, who at the first coming of thy glory didst humble thyself because of our sins; Grant that at thy second coming, our sins done away by thy mercy, we may be numbered with thy saints in glory everlasting; through thy merits, O blessed Saviour, who, with the Father and the Holy Ghost, livest and reignest, ever one God, world without end. Amen.

The Second Sunday in Advent.

Blessed Lord, who hast caused all holy Scriptures to be written for our learning; Grant that we may in such wise hear them, read, mark, learn and inwardly digest them, that by patience and comfort of thy holy Word, we may embrace, and ever hold fast, the blessed hope of everlasting life, which thou hast given us in our Saviour Jesus Christ. Amen.

Enlighten our minds, we beseech thee, O God, by the Spirit which proceedeth from thee; that as thy Son hath promised, we may be led into all truth. We ask it through the same Jesus Christ our Lord. Amen.

Almighty God, our heavenly Father, whose property it is always to have mercy; We most earnestly beseech thee to visit with thy fatherly correction all such as have erred and gone astray from the truth of thy holy Word, and to bring them to a due sense of their error, that they may again with hearty faith receive and hold fast thine unchangeable truth; through Jesus Christ our Lord. Amen.

The Third Sunday in Advent.

O Lord Jesus Christ, who at thy first coming didst send thy messenger to prepare thy way before thee; Grant that the ministers and stewards of thy mysteries may likewise so prepare and make ready thy way, by turning the hearts of the disobedient to the wisdom of the just, that at thy second coming to judge the world we may be found an acceptable people in thy sight, who livest and reignest with the Father and the Holy Spirit ever, one God, world without end. Amen.

Almighty God, we beseech thee to clothe thy ministers with righteousness and salvation, that thy Word which is in their hands may not return unto thee void, but have free course and be glorified in the world; prospering in the thing whereunto thou hast sent it, and turning men from darkness to light and from the power of Satan unto thee, that they may receive forgiveness of sins, and inheritance among those who are sanctified by faith that is in Christ Jesus; to whom with thee and the Holy Ghost be honor and glory, world without end. Amen

Blessed Saviour, who didst send thine Apostles to preach the gospel of reconciliation throughout the world; Open our hearts to the gracious message, that through its power we may lead a life of holiness and true charity; through thy mercy, Jesus Christ our Lord, who livest and reignest, Father, Son and Holy Spirit, one God, world without end. Amen.

The Fourth Sunday in Advent.

O Lord, raise up, we pray thee, thy power, and come among us, and with great might succor us; that whereas, through our sins and wickedness, we are sore let and hindered in running the race that is set before us, thy bountiful grace and mercy may speedily help and deliver us; through the satisfaction of thy Son our Lord, to whom, with thee and the Holy Ghost, be honor and glory, world without end. Amen.

Almighty God, we beseech thee to incline thine ear to our prayers, and visit the darkness of our minds with the Dayspring from on high; that at the second coming of thy Son to judge the world, we may hasten with joy to meet him; who liveth and reigneth with thee and the Holy Ghost, ever one God, world without end. Amen.

Stir up our hearts, O God and Father, to make ready the way of thine only-begotten Son, so that by his coming we may be enabled to serve thee with pure minds; through the same our Lord Jesus Christ, who liveth and reigneth with thee and the Holy Ghost, ever one God, world without end. Amen.

Eve of the Nativity.

O God, who hast made this most holy night to shine with the brightness of the true Light; Grant, we beseech thee, that as we have known on earth the mysteries of that Light, we may also come to the fulness of its joys in heaven; through the same Jesus Christ our Lord. Amen.

We beseech thee, Almighty God, let our souls be enlightened by thy Spirit, that being filled as lamps, by the divine gift, we may shine as blazing lights in the day of the Saviour's coming and enter with him into his everlasting kingdom; through the same Jesus Christ our Lord. Amen.

The Nativity of our Lord, or the Birthday of Christ, commonly called Christmas-day.

Almighty God, who hast given us thine only-begotten Son to take our nature upon him, and as at this time to be born of a pure virgin; Grant that we being regenerate, and made thy children by adoption and grace, may daily be renewed by thy Holy Spirit; through the same our Lord Jesus Christ, who liveth and reigneth with thee and the same Spirit ever, one God, world without end. Amen.

O God, who makest us glad with the yearly remembrance of the birth of thine only Son Jesus Christ; Grant that as we joyfully receive him for our Redeemer, so we may with sure confidence behold him when he shall come to be our Judge, who liveth and reigneth with thee and the Holy Ghost, one God, world without end. Amen.

Grant, we beseech thee, Almighty God, that we who are filled with the new light of thy incarnate Word, may show forth in our works that faith which shineth in our minds; through Jesus Christ our Lord. Amen.

O God, who by angelic choirs wast pleased to announce the coming of thy Son, our Lord Jesus Christ, and didst, by the heralding of angels, proclaim, Glory to God on high, and on earth peace, good-will toward men; Grant that we may so pass our time here in thy love and fear, that at thy Son's second coming we may rejoice before him with exceeding joy; through thy mercy, O our God, who art blessed, and dost live, and govern all things, world without end. Amen.

Saint Stephen's Day.

Grant, O Lord, that, in all our sufferings here upon earth for the testimony of thy truth, we may stedfastly look up to heaven, and by faith behold the glory that shall be revealed; and, being filled with the Holy Ghost, may learn to love and bless our persecutors by the example of thy first Martyr Saint Stephen, who prayed for his murderers to thee, O blessed Jesus, who standest at the right hand of God to succor all those who suffer for thee, our only Mediator and Advocate. Amen.

O Lord Jesus Christ, who didst give unto thy first Martyr, Saint Stephen, grace to follow thine example both in suffering and in patience; Grant that, like him, in all our sufferings here for thee, we may not be terrified by our adversaries, but may pray for those who would do us harm to thee, O blessed Saviour, who, with the Father and the Holy Ghost, livest and reignest, ever one God, world without end. Amen.

Saint John the Evangelist's Day.

Merciful Lord, we beseech thee to cast thy bright beams of light upon thy Church, that it, being instructed by the doctrine of thy blessed Apostle and Evangelist Saint John, may so walk in the light of thy truth, that it may at length attain to everlasting life; through Jesus Christ our Lord. Amen.

O Lord Jesus Christ, who didst have for thine Apostle Saint John a special love; Grant us grace to love thee as truly as he loved, and make us to share in the love that thou hadst for him; through thy mercy, O our God, who art blessed, and dost live, and govern all things, world without end. Amen.

The Innocents' Day.

O Almighty God, who out of the mouths of babes and sucklings hast ordained strength, and madest infants to glorify thee by their deaths; Mortify and kill all vices in us, and so strengthen us by thy grace, that by the innocency of our lives, and constancy of our faith even unto death, we may glorify thy holy Name; through Jesus Christ our Lord. Amen.

Grant us, heavenly Father, the spirit of little children, that our faith may not be obscured by doubts, nor our love weakened and corrupted by the temptations of the world. Hear us, we beseech thee, through Jesus Christ our Lord. Amen.

The Sunday after Christmas Day.

Almighty God, who hast given us thine only-begotten Son to take our nature upon him, and as at this time to be born of a pure virgin; Grant that we, being regenerate and made thy children by adoption and grace, may daily be renewed by thy Holy Spirit; through the same our Lord Jesus Christ, who liveth and reigneth with thee and the same Spirit ever, one God, world without end. Amen.

O Lord Jesus Christ, the Lord our God; Give us grace, we pray thee, with adoring love to receive and hold fast the mystery of thy holy incarnation. Reveal this blessed truth to those who know it not; and let not Satan with all deceivableness of unrighteousness pervert our faith. Help us here, by the enlightening of thy most Holy Spirit, to discern thee hidden in thy blessed Sacrament; hereafter, in thy kingdom of glory, to behold thy glory and greatness face to face; and thy Name, with that of the Father and the Holy Spirit shall have all the praise and glory, world without end. Amen.

Grant, we beseech thee, Almighty God, that the new birth of thine only-begotten Son in the flesh, may set us free who are held in the old bondage under the yoke of sin; through the same, thy Son our Lord, who liveth and reigneth with thee and the Holy Ghost, ever one God, world without end. Amen.

The Circumcision of Christ.

Almighty God, who madest thy blessed Son to be circumcised, and obedient to the law for man; Grant us the true circumcision of the Spirit; that, our hearts, and all our members, being mortified from all worldly and carnal lusts, we may in all things obey thy blessed will; through the same thy Son Jesus Christ our Lord. Amen.

O Jesus, our Saviour and our Lord, who, by thy proclamation of thy grace, didst take from our necks the yoke of the law, and remove the burden from our shoulders to thine own; Grant to the prayers of thy Church, that it may joyfully serve thee here, and behold thy blissful presence with fulness of joy hereafter; through thy mercy, O our God, who art blessed, and dost live, and govern all things, world without end. Amen.

O eternal Jesus, who didst wear the crown of thorns and the purple robe, with which thy persecutors would mock thy heavenly majesty, may we ever adore, love and obey thee as the Lord of heaven and earth, and bow our knees at thy Name, as the only Name given among men whereby we may be saved. Grant this, through thy mercy, O our God, who art blessed, and livest and reignest, world without end. Amen.

The Epiphany, or the Manifestation of Christ to the Gentiles.

O God, who by the leading of a star didst manifest thine only-begotten Son to the Gentiles; Mercifully grant that we, who know thee now by faith, may after this life have the fruition of thy glorious Godhead; through Jesus Christ our Lord. Amen.

O God, our Protector, behold and look upon the face of thine anointed, who hath given himself for the redemption of all, and grant that from the rising of the sun to the going down thereof, thy Name may be great among the Gentiles, and that in every place sacrifice and a pure offering may be made unto thy Name; through Jesus Christ our Lord. Amen.

O God, who by the leading of a star didst manifest thyself in thy humanity to the Gentiles; Graciously illumine our hearts by the holy radiance of thy incarnation, that so we may escape the darkness of this world, and by thy guidance attain to the country of eternal brightness; through Jesus Christ our Lord. Amen.

The First Sunday after the Epiphany.

O Lord, we beseech thee mercifully to receive the prayers of thy people who call upon thee; and grant that they may both perceive and know what things they ought to do, and also may have grace and power faithfully to fulfil the same; through Jesus Christ our Lord. Amen.

Bestow, O Lord God, upon thy suppliant people the aids of thy heavenly grace; that they may see plainly before them the path of duty and meekly walk in the same all the days of their life; through Jesus Christ our Lord, who liveth and reigneth with thee and the Holy Ghost, ever one God, world without end. Amen.

Almighty God, our heavenly Father, who hast given us thy Son, that believing on him we might have everlasting life; Grant us, we beseech thee, thy Holy Spirit, that we may continue stedfastly in this faith to the end, and may come to the life immortal; through Jesus Christ our Lord. Amen.

The Second Sunday after the Epiphany.

Almighty and everlasting God, who dost govern all things in heaven and earth; Mercifully hear the supplications of thy people, and grant us thy peace all the days of our life; through Jesus Christ our Lord. Amen.

O God, the Fountain of all truth and grace, who hast called us out of darkness into marvelous light, by the glorious gospel of thy Son; Grant unto us power, we beseech thee, to walk worthy of this vocation, with all lowliness and meekness, endeavoring to keep the unity of the Spirit in the bond of peace, that we may have our fruit unto holiness, and the end everlasting life, through Jesus Christ our Lord. Amen.

Hear, we beseech thee, O Lord, our God, the prayer of thy suppliants, and spare those who confess their sins unto thee, that thou mayest bestow upon us both pardon and peace; through Jesus Christ our Lord. Amen.

The Third Sunday after the Epiphany.

Almighty and everlasting God, mercifully look upon our infirmities, and in all our dangers and necessities stretch forth thy right hand to help and defend us; through Jesus Christ our Lord. Amen.

O God, comforter of mourners, and salvation of them that hope in thee; Grant us, truly to lament our sins, and to obtain thy gracious pardon; through Jesus Christ our Lord. Amen.

We beseech thee, O God, in thy clemency, to show us thy unspeakable mercy; that thou mayest both set us free from our sins, and rescue us from the punishments which for our sins we deserve; through Jesus Christ our Lord. Amen.

The Fourth Sunday after the Epiphany.

O God, who knowest us to be set in the midst of so many and great dangers, that by reason of the frailty of our nature we cannot always stand upright; Grant to us such strength and protection, as may support us in all dangers, and carry us through all temptations; through Jesus Christ our Lord. Amen.

O God, who justifieth the ungodly, and who desireth not the death of the sinner; We humbly implore thy Majesty, that thou wouldest graciously assist, by thy heavenly aid, and evermore shield with thy protection, thy servants who trust in thy mercy, that they may be separated by no temptations from thee, and without ceasing, may serve thee; through Jesus Christ, thy Son our Lord. Amen.

Grant unto us, heavenly Father, to have a true love of thy holy Name, so that, trusting in thy grace, we may fear no earthly evil, and set our hearts upon no earthly good, but may rejoice at last in thy full salvation; through Jesus Christ our Lord. Amen.

The Fifth Sunday after the Epiphany.

O Lord, we beseech thee to keep thy Church and household continually in thy true religion; that they who do lean only upon the hope of thy heavenly grace may evermore be defended by thy mighty power; through Jesus Christ our Lord. Amen.

Grant, we beseech thee Almighty God, unto thy Church, thy Holy Spirit, and the wisdom which cometh down from above, that thy Word, as becometh it, may not be bound, but have free course and be preached to the joy and edifying of Christ's holy people, that in stedfast faith we may serve thee, and in the confession of thy Name abide unto the end; through Jesus Christ our Lord. Amen.

O God, who art the Restorer and the Ruler of mankind; Grant, we beseech thee, that thy Church may ever be increased by a new offering, and grow up by the devotion of all the faithful, and the indwelling of the Spirit; through Jesus Christ our Lord. Amen.

The Sixth Sunday after the Epiphany.

O God, whose blessed Son was manifested that he might destroy the works of the devil, and make us the sons of God, and heirs of eternal life; Grant us, we beseech thee, that, having this hope, we may purify ourselves, even as he is pure; that, when he shall appear again with power and great glory, we may be made like unto him in his eternal and glorious kingdom; where with thee, O Father, and thee, O Holy Ghost, he liveth and reigneth ever, one God, world without end. Amen.

O eternal Father, convert our hearts unto thyself, so that by thy help, we being heartily devoted to thy service, no manner of good things may be lacking to us, through thy grace and truth. We ask all in the Name of Jesus Christ our Lord. Amen.

Visit us, we beseech thee, O God, and cleanse our consciences, that thy Son our Lord Jesus Christ, when he cometh with all his saints, may find in us a mansion prepared for himself; through the same thy Son, Jesus Christ our Lord. Amen.

The Sunday called Septuagesima, or the third Sunday before Lent.

O Lord, we beseech thee favorably to hear the prayers of thy people; that we, who are justly punished for our offences, may be mercifully delivered by thy goodness, for the glory of thy Name; through Jesus Christ our Saviour, who liveth and reigneth with thee and the Holy Ghost ever, one God, world without end. Amen.

O God, the life of the faithful, the joy of the righteous, mercifully receive the prayers of thy suppliants, that the souls which thirst for thy promises may evermore be filled from thine abundance, to the glory of thy holy Name; through Jesus Christ our Lord. Amen.

O God, whose mercy is over all thy works, and whose truth is light to those that mourn, and a deliverance to captives, and sight to the blind; Grant to us all a free remission of our sins, and a portion among those who serve thee by faith, that they may behold thee in glory; through Jesus Christ our Lord. Amen.

The Sunday called Sexagesima, or the second Sunday before Lent.

O Lord God, who seest that we put not our trust in any thing that we do; Mercifully grant that by thy power we may be defended against all adversity; through Jesus Christ our Lord. Amen.

Grant, we beseech thee, Almighty God, that always pressing onward in thy way with devout minds, we may escape the snares of the sins that beset us; through Jesus Christ our Lord. Amen.

Look mercifully, O God, we beseech thee, on the afflicted of thy people, and let not our sins destroy us, but let thine almighty mercy save us; through Jesus Christ our Lord. Amen.

The Sunday called Quinquagesima, or the the next Sunday before Lent.

O Lord, who hast taught us that all our doings without charity are nothing worth; Send thy Holy Ghost, and pour into our hearts that most excellent gift of charity, the very bond of peace and of all virtues, without which whosoever liveth is counted dead before thee. Grant this for thine only Son Jesus Christ's sake. Amen.

O God, who hast taught thy Church to keep all thy commandments by loving first the eternal God, and next our neighbor as ourself; Grant us the spirit of peace and grace, that thine universal family may be both devoted to thee with their whole heart, and united to each other with a pure will; through thy Son Jesus Christ our Lord. Amen.

O God, the Author of peace; Grant, we beseech thee, that thy faithful people may be so held in the bonds of charity, that the peaceful may remain in peace, and that those who differ may be reconciled by thy mercy; through Jesus Christ, thy Son, our Lord. Amen.

The first day of Lent, commonly called Ash-Wednesday.

Almighty and everlasting God, who hatest nothing that thou hast made, and dost forgive the sins of all those who are penitent; Create and make in us new and contrite hearts, that we, worthily lamenting our sins and acknowledging our wretchedness, may obtain of thee, the God of all mercy, perfect remission and forgiveness; through Jesus Christ our Lord. Amen.

Almighty and everlasting God, we beseech thee to cleanse away the folly of our hearts, and to purify us from our sins, both open and secret, that we may be able to serve thee with a pure mind, to the honor of thy holy Name; through Jesus Christ our Lord. Amen.

O God, who desirest not the death of a sinner, but rather that he should turn and live; Look with pity upon the weakness of our mortal nature, and grant that we, who confess that we are but ashes, and that for our wickedness we must justly return to the dust, may obtain of thee the forgiveness of all our sins, and the blessings promised to the penitent; through Jesus Christ our Lord. Amen.

The First Sunday in Lent.

O Lord, who for our sake didst fast forty days and forty nights; Give us grace to use such abstinence, that, our flesh being subdued to the Spirit, we may ever obey thy godly motions in righteousness, and true holiness, to thy honor and glory, who livest and reignest with the Father and the Holy Ghost, one God, world without end. Amen.

We beseech thee, O Lord, by the mystery of our Saviour's fasting and temptation, to arm us with the same mind that was in him toward all evil and sin, and give us grace to keep our bodies in such holy discipline, that our minds may be always ready to resist Satan, and obey the motions of thy Holy Spirit; through Jesus Christ our Lord. Amen.

O God, whose blessed Son became obedient to the law for man, and underwent hunger and thirst in doing thy will, and fulfilling all righteousness; Give us grace in all patience and temperance so to bear and to forbear, that our flesh being subdued to the Spirit, we may ever obey thy holy guidance and control, in all righteousness, purity and soberness. Grant this for the sake of thy Son Jesus Christ our Lord, to whom, with thee and the Holy Ghost, be all the praise, world without end. Amen

The Second Sunday in Lent.

Almighty God, who seest that we have no power of ourselves to help ourselves; Keep us both outwardly in our bodies, and inwardly in our souls; that we may be defended from all adversities which may happen to the body, and from all evil thoughts which may assault and hurt the soul; through Jesus Christ our Lord. Amen.

O God, who hast vouchsafed to mankind the remedies that bring salvation, and the gifts of eternal life; Preserve to us, thy servants, the gifts of thy power, and grant that not only in our bodies, but also in our souls, we may experience thy healing, through Jesus Christ our Lord. Amen.

Grant, Almighty God, that our bodies may be healthful, and our souls pure, and give us remission of our sins through the sacrifice of thy Son, Jesus Christ our Lord, who liveth and reigneth with thee and the Holy Ghost, one God, world without end. Amen.

The Third Sunday in Lent.

We beseech thee, Almighty God, look upon the hearty desires of thy humble servants, and stretch forth the right hand of thy Majesty, to be our defence against all our enemies; through Jesus Christ our Lord. Amen.

Almighty God, who hast been the hope and confidence of thy people in all ages; Mercifully regard, we beseech thee, our supplications, and in all the issues of life, be unto us salvation and protection; through Jesus Christ our Lord. Amen.

We beseech thee, Almighty God, in thy loving kindness to set in order our life and conversation, that no adversaries may prevail against us, and no kind of spiritual good be wanting to us; through Jesus Christ our Lord. Amen.

The Fourth Sunday in Lent.

Grant, we beseech thee, Almighty God, that we, who for our evil deeds do worthily deserve to be punished, by the comfort of thy grace may mercifully be relieved; through our Lord and Saviour Jesus Christ. Amen.

O Lord God, merciful and gracious, long suffering and abundant in goodness and truth; Enter not into judgment with thy servants, we beseech thee, but be pleased of thy great goodness to grant, that we who are now righteously afflicted and bowed down by the sense of our sins, may be refreshed and lifted up with the joy of thy salvation; through Jesus Christ our Lord. Amen.

Hear us, O Lord our God, and separate the hearts of thy faithful people from the wickedness of the world, that they who call thee Lord with their own voice may not fall back into the service of any enemy of the soul. We ask all through him who loved us and gave himself for us, Jesus Christ thy Son our Lord. Amen.

The Fifth Sunday in Lent.

We beseech thee, Almighty God, mercifully to look upon thy people; that by thy great goodness they may be governed and preserved evermore, both in body and soul; through Jesus Christ our Lord. Amen.

Merciful God and Father, make us, we beseech thee, obedient to thy holy commandments, so that we may present thee a complete consecration of body, soul and spirit; through Jesus Christ our Lord. Amen

Renew us, O our God, day by day, that both inwardly and outwardly we may be made more and more like unto him who was the Son of man and the Son of God; through the same Jesus Christ our Lord. Amen.

The Sunday next before Easter.

Almighty and everlasting God, who, of thy tender love toward mankind, hast sent thy Son, our Saviour Jesus Christ, to take upon him our flesh, and to suffer death upon the cross, that all mankind should follow the example of his great humility: Mercifully grant, that we may both follow the example of his patience, and also be made partakers of his resurrection; through the same Jesus Christ our Lord. Amen.

O God, whose blessed Son entered Jerusalem amid the plaudits and hosannas of the people, and a little later was reviled and rejected by men; Give us grace, we beseech thee, not to place our trust in the applause of the world, but may our affections be fixed upon the things that shall endure forevermore at thy right hand; through Jesus Christ our Lord. Amen.

Grant, Almighty God, that amid the insincerity and fickleness of the world we may always exercise the spirit of humility and patience, following the example of our Lord and Saviour Jesus Christ, to whom, with thee and the Holy Ghost, be all dominion and power, world without end. Amen.

Monday before Easter.

Grant, we beseech thee, Almighty God, that we, who amid so many adversities do fail through our own infirmities, may be restored through the passion and intercession of thine only-begotten Son, who liveth and reigneth with thee and the Holy Ghost, ever one God, world without end. Amen.

O holy and most merciful Saviour, thou most worthy Judge eternal, who, as on this day didst curse the fig tree bearing leaves and no fruit; Take away from us all hollow, vain and false appearances, and make us plenteously to bring forth the fruit of good works, and of thee to be plenteously rewarded, through thy merits, who with the Father and the Holy Ghost livest and reignest, ever one God, world without end. Amen.

Tuesday before Easter.

Almighty and everlasting God, grant us grace so to pass through this holy time of our Lord's passion, that we may obtain the pardon of our sins; through the same, thy Son, who liveth and reigneth with thee and the Holy Ghost, ever one God, world without end. Amen.

Blessed Jesus, who as on this day, didst endure such contradiction of sinners; Grant to us, thy servants, not to wish to be above our Master, but to be as our Master, even like thee our only Lord and Saviour, to whom, with the Father and the Holy Ghost, be glory and dominion, world without end. Amen.

Wednesday before Easter.

Grant, we beseech thee, Almighty God, that we, who for our evil deeds are continually afflicted, may mercifully be relieved by the passion of thine only-begotten Son, who liveth and reigneth with thee and the Holy Ghost, ever one God, world without end. Amen.

Blessed Jesus, who as on this day wast sold into the hands of wicked men to redeem us from sin and death, root out of us the love of money, and make us content with such things as we have, through thy merits, who, with the Father and the Holy Ghost, livest and reignest, ever one God, world without end. Amen.

Thursday before Easter.

O God, who in this wonderful Sacrament hast left unto us a memorial of thy passion ; Grant to us, we beseech thee, so to venerate the sacred mysteries of thy Body and Blood, that we may always perceive in ourselves the fruit of thy redemption ; who livest and reignest with the Father in the unity of the Holy Ghost, one God, world without end. Amen.

Blessed Lord, who as on this day didst wash the feet of thy disciples, grant us, also, to be ready to wash one another's feet, and gladly to minister to our brethren with great humility and love. Hear us, O Saviour, who livest and reignest with the Father and the Holy Ghost, one God, world without end. Amen.

Good Friday.

Almighty God, we beseech thee graciously to behold this thy family, for which our Lord Jesus Christ was contented to be betrayed, and given up into the hands of wicked men, and to suffer death upon the cross ; who now liveth and reigneth with thee and the Holy Ghost, ever one God, world without end. Amen.

Almighty and everlasting God, by whose Spirit the whole body of the Church is governed and sanctified : Receive our supplications and prayers, which we offer before thee for all estates of men in thy holy Church, that every member of the same, in his vocation and ministry, may truly and godly serve thee ; through our Lord and Saviour Jesus Christ. Amen.

O merciful God, who hast made all men, and hatest nothing that thou hast made, nor desirest the death of a sinner, but rather that he should be converted and live ; Have mercy upon all Jews, Turks, infidels and heretics ; and take from them all ignorance, hardness of heart, and contempt of thy Word ; and so fetch them home, blessed Lord, to thy flock, that they may be saved among the remnant of the true Israelites, and be made one fold under one shepherd, Jesus Christ our Lord, who liveth and reigneth with thee and the Holy Spirit, one God, world without end. Amen

Almighty and everlasting God, who hast willed that thy Son should bear for us the pains of the cross, that thou mightest remove from us the power of the adversary ; Help us so to remember and give thanks for our Lord's passion that we may obtain remission of sin and redemption from everlasting death ; through the same, our Lord Jesus Christ. Amen.

O righteous and holy God, who hast manifested toward us thine unfathomable love, in not sparing thine own Son, but delivering him up for us all ; By the memory of his bitter death, by the awful mystery of his sorrows in the garden and upon the cross, we humbly beseech thee to have mercy upon us and upon all men, and to make known thy saving health among the nations, that he may see of the travail of his soul and be satisfied ; to whom, with thee and the Holy Ghost, be honor and glory, world without end. Amen.

Easter-Even.

Grant, O Lord, that as we are baptized into the death of thy blessed Son, our Saviour Jesus Christ, so by continual mortifying our corrupt affections we may be buried with him ; and that through the grave and gate of death, we may pass to our joyful resurrection ; for his merits, who died, and was buried, and rose again for us, thy Son Jesus Christ our Lord. Amen.

O God, who didst enlighten this most holy night with the glory of the Lord's resurrection ; Preserve in all thy people the spirit of adoption which thou hast given, so that renewed in body and soul they may perform unto thee a pure service ; through the same, our Lord Jesus Christ, who liveth and reigneth with thee and the Holy Ghost, ever one God, world without end. Amen.

O Lord Jesus Christ, who didst, for our sins, endure the cross and the grave, and then didst, on the third day, rise again from the tomb ; Grant that we, who have been buried and raised again with thee in Baptism, and washed from all our iniquities, may by thy blood be continually cleansed from all spot of sin ; through thy mercy, O our God, who art blessed, and dost live, and govern all things, world without end. Amen.

Easter-day.

Almighty God, who through thine only-begotten Son Jesus Christ hast overcome death, and opened unto us the gate of everlasting life ; We humbly beseech thee that, as by thy special grace preventing us thou dost put into our minds good desires, so by thy continual help we may bring the same to good effect ; through Jesus Christ our Lord, who liveth and reigneth with thee and the Holy Ghost ever, one God, world without end. Amen.

O God, who for our redemption didst give thine only-begotten Son to the death of the cross, and by his glorious resurrection hast delivered us from the power of our enemy ; Grant us so to die daily from sin, that we may evermore live with him in the joy of his resurrection ; through the same Jesus Christ our Lord. Amen.

Grant, we beseech thee, Almighty God, that we who celebrate the Paschal Feast, kindled with heavenly desires, may ever thirst for the Fountain of Life, Jesus Christ thy Son, our Lord. Amen.

Grant, we beseech thee, Almighty God, that we who celebrate the solemnities of the Lord's resurrection, may by the renewal of thy Holy Spirit rise again from the death of the soul; through the same Jesus Christ our Lord. Amen.

Monday in Easter-week.

Almighty God, who through thine only-begotten Son Jesus Christ hast overcome death, and opened unto us the gate of everlasting life; We humbly beseech thee that, as by thy special grace preventing us thou dost put into our minds good desires, so by thy continual help we may bring the same to good effect; through Jesus Christ our Lord, who liveth and reigneth with thee and the Holy Ghost ever, one God, world without end. Amen.

Grant, we beseech thee, Almighty God, that we who commemorate the Lord's resurrection, may by the help of thy grace, bring forth the fruits thereof in our life and conversation; through the same Jesus Christ, thy Son, our Lord, who liveth and reigneth with thee and the Holy Ghost, ever one God, world without end. Amen.

O Lord Jesus Christ, who wilt come again to judge the quick and the dead, and call forth all who sleep in their graves, either to the resurrection of life, or the resurrection of condemnation; We beseech thee to be gracious to us, and to raise us up to life everlasting, that we may abide with thee forever; who livest and reignest with the Father and the Holy Ghost, world without end. Amen.

Tuesday in Easter-week.

Almighty God, who through thine only-begotten Son Jesus Christ hast overcome death, and opened unto us the gate of everlasting life; We humbly beseech thee that, as by thy special grace preventing us thou dost put into our minds good desires, so by thy continual help we may bring the same to good effect; through Jesus Christ our Lord, who liveth and reigneth with thee and the Holy Ghost, ever one God, world without end. Amen.

Almighty and most merciful God, who hast appointed us to endure suffering and death with our Lord Jesus Christ, before we enter with him into glory; Grant us grace at all times to submit ourselves to thy holy will, to continue stedfast in the true faith unto the end, and to find peace and joy in the blessed hope of the resurrection of the dead, and the glory of the world to come; through Jesus Christ our Lord. Amen.

Almighty God, who by the humiliation of thy Son, didst raise up the fallen world; Grant unto thy faithful ones perpetual gladness, and those whom thou hast delivered from the danger of everlasting death, do thou make partakers of eternal joys; through the same Jesus Christ our Lord, who liveth and reigneth with thee and the Holy Ghost, ever one God, world without end. Amen.

The First Sunday after Easter.

Almighty Father, who hast given thine only Son to die for our sins, and to rise again for our justification; Grant us so to put away the leaven of malice and wickedness, that we may always serve thee in pureness of living and truth; through the merits of the same thy Son Jesus Christ our Lord. Amen.

Grant, Almighty God, that the power of the resurrection of thy Son may be manifested in the purity of our thoughts and the holiness of our daily lives; through Jesus Christ our Lord. Amen.

O Lion of the tribe of Judah, O Root of David; Enlighten our hearts and minds with thy true wisdom, that we, who now rejoice in thy resurrection, may, in thy kingdom, join with thy blessed ones, and with all the heavenly host, in praising thy glorious Name, who, with the Father, and the Holy Ghost, livest and reignest, ever one God, world without end. Amen.

The Second Sunday after Easter.

Almighty God, who hast given thine only Son to be unto us both a sacrifice for sin, and also an ensample of godly life; Give us grace that we may always most thankfully receive that, his inestimable benefit, and also daily endeavor ourselves to follow the blessed steps of his most holy life; through the same Jesus Christ our Lord. Amen.

O God, who, of thine abundant mercy, hast begotten us again unto a lively hope, by the resurrection of Jesus Christ from the dead; Let thy great love constrain us, we beseech thee, to rise up, forsake all, and follow him; that as we have been redeemed by his Blood, so we may walk also in the light of his holy example, and be joined to him evermore as the Shepherd and Bishop of our souls; to whom, with thee and the Holy Ghost, be honor and glory, world without end. Amen.

O Lord Jesus Christ, the Shepherd of souls, who leadeth thy flock into green pastures, and to refreshing streams; Help us to hear thy voice, and to follow thee, that we may evermore be the sheep of thy fold, and praise thee with the Father and Holy Spirit, world without end. Amen.

The Third Sunday after Easter.

Almighty God, who showest to them that are in error the light of thy truth, to the intent that they may return into the way of righteousness; Grant unto all those who are admitted into the fellowship of Christ's religion, that they may avoid those things that are contrary to their profession, and follow all such things as are agreeable to the same; through our Lord Jesus Christ. Amen.

God of all truth and grace, who hast caused the Sun of righteousness to arise upon a dark and benighted world, in bringing up thy Holy One from the grave; Be pleased graciously so to illuminate the souls of thy people with the beams of heavenly wisdom, that they may continually walk in thy light, and know both to avoid evil and to follow after that which is good; through Jesus Christ our Lord, who liveth and reigneth with thee and the Holy Ghost, ever one God, world without end. Amen.

O God, who delightest in the devotion of the faithful; Make thy people, we pray thee, to be devoted to holy things. Help them not only to depart from sin, but to refrain from the appearance of evil; through Jesus Christ our Lord. Amen.

The Fourth Sunday after Easter.

O Almighty God, who alone canst order the unruly wills and affections of sinful men; Grant unto thy people, that they may love the thing which thou commandest, and desire that which thou dost promise; that so, among the sundry and manifold changes of the world, our hearts may surely there be fixed, where true joys are to be found; through Jesus Christ our Lord. Amen.

O God, whose promises are the comfort, and thy graces the support of thy people; Grant that what is now their hope in time, may hereafter be their joy throughout eternity; through Jesus Christ our Lord. Amen.

O God, who hast founded the earth upon the seas, and established it upon the floods and whose Word is forever settled in heaven; Grant unto us grace, we beseech thee, to look beyond the things which are seen and temporal to the things which are not seen and eternal; that walking by faith more than by sight, we may not be unduly moved by any occasions in this world, but be able to endure unto the end in the way of life; through him who is the same yesterday and to-day, and forever, thy Son Jesus Christ our Lord. Amen.

The Fifth Sunday after Easter.

O Lord, from whom all good things do come; Grant to us thy humble servants, that by thy holy inspiration we may think those things that are good, and by thy merciful guiding may perform the same; through our Lord Jesus Christ. Amen.

Vouchsafe unto us, O Lord, the inspirations of thy salutary grace, and quicken us according to thy Word; that knowing what is right, and approving that which is good, we may, by patient continuance in well doing, seek for glory and honor and immortality; and so finally having escaped the corruption that is in the world through lust, find an entrance ministered unto us abundantly into the everlasting kingdom of our Lord and Saviour Jesus Christ, to whom, with thee and the Holy Ghost, be honor and glory, world without end. Amen.

Grant, O Almighty God, that as we are saved from all evil by partaking of thy thought, and becoming obedient to thy will, so we may ever be preserved by thy power, and enjoy the peace of thy kingdom; through Jesus Christ our Lord. Amen.

The Ascension-day.

Grant, we beseech thee, Almighty God, that like as we do believe thine only-begotten Son our Lord Jesus Christ to have ascended into the heavens; so we may also in heart and mind thither ascend, and with him continually dwell, who liveth and reigneth with thee and the Holy Ghost, one God, world without end. Amen.

O Lord, the king of glory, who, when thou hadst fulfilled all that the prophets had spoken of thee, didst, through the eternal doors, ascend to thy Father's throne, and open the kingdom of heaven to all believers; Grant that whilst thou dost reign in heaven, we may not be bowed down to the things of earth, but that our hearts may there be lifted up whither our redemption is gone before; through thy mercy, O our God, who, with the Father and the Holy Ghost, livest and reignest, ever one God, world without end. Amen.

Raise, Almighty God, our affections to things above, and though we walk upon the earth, may our conversation be in heaven, from whence also we look for the Saviour; to whom, with thee and the Holy Ghost be all honor and glory, world without end. Amen.

Sunday after Ascension-day.

O God, the King of glory, who hast exalted thine only Son Jesus Christ with great triumph unto thy kingdom in heaven; We beseech thee, leave us not comfortless; but send to us thine Holy Ghost to comfort us, and exalt us unto the same place whither our Saviour Christ is gone before, who liveth and reigneth with thee and the Holy Ghost, one God, world without end. Amen.

Almighty God, in whose sight to sin is to die, but in whom knowledge is life; Grant that as by necessity of nature we have borne the likeness of things earthly, so by the inward transformation of the Holy Spirit we may attain to things heavenly, and dwell in thy likeness forever; through Jesus Christ our Lord. Amen.

O Lord, strong and mighty, the Lord of hosts, the King of glory; Cleanse our hearts from sin, keep our hands pure, and turn away our minds from vanity, so that, at the last, we may stand in thy Holy Place, and receive blessing from thee, whom, with the Father and the Holy Ghost, we worship and glorify, as one God, world without end. Amen.

Whitsunday.

O God, who as at this time didst teach the hearts of thy faithful people, by sending to them the light of thy Holy Spirit; Grant us by the same Spirit to have a right judgment in all things, and evermore to rejoice in his holy comfort; through the merits of Christ Jesus our Saviour, who liveth and reigneth with thee, in the unity of the same Spirit, one God, world without end. Amen.

O Holy Ghost, who as at this time, didst descend upon the Apostles in the likeness of fiery tongues; Take away all vices from our hearts, and fill us with all wisdom and spiritual understanding; Grant this, O blessed Spirit, who, with the Father and the Son, livest and reignest, ever one God, world without end. Amen.

Almighty God, who hast given us commandment to pray for the gift of the Holy Ghost; Most heartily we beseech thee, through Jesus Christ our Advocate, to grant us thy Holy Spirit, that he may quicken our hearts by thy saving Word, and lead us into all truth, that he may guide, instruct, enlighten, govern, comfort and sanctify us unto everlasting life; through the same Jesus Christ our Lord. Amen.

Monday in Whitsun-week.

O God, who as at this time didst teach the hearts of thy faithful people, by sending to them the light of thy Holy Spirit; Grant us by the same Spirit to have a right judgment in all things, and evermore to rejoice in his holy comfort; through the merits of Christ Jesus our Saviour, who liveth and reigneth with thee, in the unity of the same Spirit, one God, world without end. Amen.

Grant, we beseech thee, Almighty God, that the brightness of thy glory may shine forth upon us, and that the light of thy light by the illumination of the Holy Spirit may stablish the hearts of all that have been born anew by thy grace; through Jesus Christ our Lord. Amen.

O Lord God, heavenly Father, who by the blessed light of thy divine Word, hast led us to the knowledge of thy Son; We most heartily beseech thee, so to replenish us with the grace of thy Holy Spirit, that we may ever walk in the light of thy truth, and rejoicing with sure confidence in Christ our Saviour, may in the end be brought unto everlasting salvation; through the same thy Son Jesus Christ our Lord. Amen.

Tuesday in Whitsun-week.

O God, who as at this time didst teach the hearts of thy faithful people, by sending to them the light of thy Holy Spirit; Grant us by the same Spirit to have a right judgment in all things, and evermore to rejoice in his holy comfort; through the merits of Christ Jesus our Saviour, who liveth and reigneth with thee, in the unity of the same Spirit, one God, world without end. Amen.

O God, the Protector and Guide of all who trust in thee; Turn away from us the false gleams of selfish and worldly wisdom, that under the teaching of the Holy Spirit we may find pleasure in the simplicity of thy truth, and have the wisdom which comes of thy holy fear; through Jesus Christ our Lord. Amen.

Almighty and everlasting God, who of thy great mercy in Jesus Christ thy Son, dost grant us forgiveness of sin, and all things pertaining to life and godliness; Grant us, we beseech thee, thy Holy Spirit, that he may so rule our hearts, that we, being ever mindful of thy fatherly mercy, may strive to mortify the flesh, and to overcome the world, and serving thee in holiness and pureness of living, may give thee continual thanks for all thy goodness; through Jesus Christ thy Son, our Lord. Amen.

Trinity-Sunday.

Almighty and everlasting God, who hast given unto us thy servants grace, by the confession of a true faith, to acknowledge the glory of the eternal Trinity, and in the power of the divine Majesty to worship the Unity; We beseech thee that thou wouldest keep us stedfast in this faith, and evermore defend us from all adversities, who livest and reignest, one God, world without end. Amen.

O God, the Creator and Saviour of the world, who hast made thyself known in the work of man's redemption, as the mystery of the ever adorable Trinity, Father, Son and Holy Ghost, Three in One and One in Three; Reveal in us, we beseech thee, the full power of this faith, into which we have been planted by Baptism, that being born of water and the Spirit, we may, by a life of holiness, be formed into thine image here, and rise to thy blissful presence hereafter; there to join with the song of the seraphim, in praising thee, world without end. Amen.

O Father, Son and Holy Ghost, Three Persons, and One God; Enlighten, we pray thee, our hearts and minds, that we, stedfast in the true faith, and ever shining in good works, may attain at last to the life everlasting; through thy mercy, O our God, who art blessed, and dost live, and govern all things, world without end. Amen.

The First Sunday after Trinity.

O God, the strength of all those who put their trust in thee; Mercifully accept our prayers; and because, through the weakness of our mortal nature, we can do no good thing without thee, grant us the help of thy grace, that in keeping thy commandments we may please thee, both in will and deed; through Jesus Christ our Lord. Amen.

Confirm and strengthen in us, O God, sincere and upright purposes, foster in us warm and true affections, and help us to bring to good effect the holy desires which by thy grace arise in our hearts. When we are tempted, strengthen us, when we are weak, encourage us, when we are cast down, raise us up. Leave us not without thy grace, but perfect thy work in us, and grant that we may do thee true and faithful service in this world, and may enter at the last into thy eternal peace; through Jesus Christ our Lord. Amen.

Guide, Almighty God, our steps into the paths of righteousness, that we may behave ourselves according to thy will, and observe thy commandments all the days of our life, and come to a blessed end; through Jesus Christ our Lord. Amen.

The Second Sunday after Trinity.

O Lord, who never failest to help and govern those whom thou dost bring up in thy stedfast fear and love; Keep us, we beseech thee, under the protection of thy good providence, and make us to have a perpetual fear and love of thy holy Name; through Jesus Christ our Lord. Amen.

O God, the author of all freedom and salvation, hear the voices of thy people, and grant that those whom thou deliverest from evil may both live by thee, and in thee enjoy perpetual peace; through Jesus Christ our Lord. Amen.

Almighty and everlasting God, the source of all life and joy, who by the glad sound of the gospel, hast called us to have part in thy kingdom and glory; Shine powerfully into our hearts, we beseech thee, by thy Word and Spirit, and draw us with the cords of thy constraining grace, that we may heartily choose that good part which shall not be taken away from us, and give all diligence to make our calling and election sure; through Jesus Christ our Lord. Amen

The Third Sunday after Trinity.

O Lord, we beseech thee mercifully to hear us; and grant that we, to whom thou hast given an hearty desire to pray, may, by thy mighty aid, be defended and comforted in all dangers and adversities; through Jesus Christ our Lord. Amen.

O Lord our God, who alone foreseest and bestowest things needful for our salvation; Do thou both bestow on our souls the hearty desire of imploring thy mercy, and graciously vouchsafe us what will be for our good; through Jesus Christ our Lord. Amen.

O God, the Lord, strong to deliver and mighty to save, who hast been the refuge and dwelling place of thy people in all generations; Perfect and fulfill in us, we beseech thee, the work of thy converting grace, and be pleased to confirm in us every good purpose and deed; that having been called into the way of righteousness, we may have power to continue stedfastly in the same until the day of Jesus Christ; to whom with thee and the Holy Ghost, be all honor and praise, world without end. Amen.

The Fourth Sunday after Trinity.

O God, the protector of all that trust in thee, without whom nothing is strong, nothing is holy; Increase and multiply upon us thy mercy; that, thou being our ruler and guide, we may so pass through things temporal, that we finally lose not the things eternal. Grant this, O heavenly Father, for Jesus Christ's sake, our Lord. Amen.

O God, who only art holy, and who dost by thy grace purify the unholy; Cleanse us, we humbly beseech thee, from every spot of sin, so that, justified by thee, our names may be written in heaven; Grant this, for the sake of Jesus Christ, our most blessed Lord and Saviour. Amen.

O God, whose favor is life and in whose presence there is fulness of peace and joy; Vouchsafe unto us, we beseech thee, such an abiding sense of the reality and glory of those things which thou hast prepared for those that love thee, as may serve to raise us above the vanity of this present world, both in its pleasures and in its necessary trials and pains, so that under thy guidance and help all things here shall work together for our everlasting salvation; through Jesus Christ our Lord. Amen.

The Fifth Sunday after Trinity.

Grant, O Lord, we beseech thee, that the course of this world may be so peaceably ordered by thy governance, that thy Church may joyfully serve thee in all godly quietness; through Jesus Christ our Lord. Amen.

O God, favorably receive the prayers of thy Church, that being delivered from all adversity and error, it may serve thee in safety and freedom; and grant us thy peace in our time; through Jesus Christ our Lord, who liveth and reigneth with thee and the Holy Ghost ever, one God, world without end. Amen.

O God, who art both the Restorer and Ruler of mankind; Grant, we beseech thee, that thy Church may ever be increased by a new offspring, and grow up by the devotion of all the faithful, through the indwelling of the Holy Spirit; to whom, with thee and thy Son Jesus Christ, be all the glory and honor, world without end. Amen.

The Sixth Sunday after Trinity.

O God, who hast prepared for those who love thee such good things as pass man's understanding; Pour into our hearts such love toward thee, that we, loving thee above all things, may obtain thy promises, which exceed all that we can desire; through Jesus Christ our Lord. Amen.

O God, who makest all things work together for good to those that love thee; Grant to our hearts an invincible power of love, that the desires which have been conceived by thine inspiration may not be changed by any temptations; through Jesus Christ our Lord. Amen.

Give us, Almighty God, a heart to love and serve thee, and enable us to show our thankfulness for all the goodness and mercy thou hast granted us, by giving up ourselves to thy service, and cheerfully submitting in all things to thy blessed will; through Jesus Christ our Lord. Amen.

The Seventh Sunday after Trinity.

Lord of all power and might, who art the author and giver of all good things; Graft in our hearts the love of thy Name, increase in us true religion, nourish us with all goodness, and of thy great mercy keep us in the same; through Jesus Christ our Lord. Amen.

Almighty God, the Former of our bodies and Father of our spirits, in whom we live, move and have our being; Shed abroad thy love in our hearts, we beseech thee, and cause the comfort of thy heavenly grace to abound in us, as the earnest and pledge of joys to come, that casting away all anxious thought for the transitory things of this life, we may seek first thy kingdom and righteousness, and labor only for that meat which endureth unto everlasting life; through Jesus Christ our Lord. Amen.

Increase in our hearts, O God, the power of faith and love, that no temptations may overcome us and no evils deter us in thy service; through Jesus Christ our Lord. Amen.

The Eighth Sunday after Trinity.

O God, whose never-failing providence ordereth all things both in heaven and earth; We humbly beseech thee to put away from us all hurtful things, and to give us those things which are profitable for us; through Jesus Christ our Lord. Amen.

O God, who dividest the day from the night, separate our deeds from the gloom of darkness that, ever meditating on holy things, we may continually live in thy light; through Jesus Christ our Lord. Amen.

Keep alive within us, O God, that fire which thy blessed Son came to kindle upon earth, that we also may be anointed with his Spirit of peace, holiness and obedience; through the same Jesus Christ our Lord. Amen.

The Ninth Sunday after Trinity.

Grant to us, Lord, we beseech thee, the spirit to think and do always such things as are right; that we, who cannot do any thing that is good without thee, may by thee be enabled to live according to thy will; through Jesus Christ our Lord. Amen.

We beseech thee, O Lord, in thy loving kindness to pour thy holy light into our souls, that we may ever be devoted to thee, by whose wisdom we were created, and by whose providence we are governed; through Jesus Christ our Lord. Amen.

Reveal thyself unto us, O God, that we may know thy will, and delight in doing it, with the same spirit manifested by thy Son; to whom, with thee and the Holy Ghost, be dominion and glory forever and ever. Amen.

The Tenth Sunday after Trinity.

Let thy merciful ears, O Lord, be open to the prayers of thy humble servants; and that they may obtain their petitions, make them to ask such things as shall please thee; through Jesus Christ our Lord. Amen.

Lord, we beseech thee, let thy favor be present with thy people who call upon thee; That what by thy inspiration they faithfully ask, by thy speedy bounty they may obtain; through the mercy of thy Son Jesus Christ our Lord. Amen

We beseech thee, O Lord, vouchsafe us an unceasing perseverance in praying unto thee, that as thou dost not forsake us in our sorrow, so thou mayest cherish us with more abundant grace when we continually beseech thy Majesty; through Jesus Christ our Lord. Amen.

The Eleventh Sunday after Trinity.

O God, who declarest thy almighty power chiefly in showing mercy and pity; Mercifully grant unto us such a measure of thy grace, that we, running the way of thy commandments, may obtain thy gracious promises, and be made partakers of thy heavenly treasure; through Jesus Christ our Lord. Amen.

Almighty and everlasting God, glorify thyself, we beseech thee, in all that we do and suffer, and lead us in that way in which we shall best escape the pollutions that are in the world, and attain at last to the unspeakable joys of the life to come; through Jesus Christ our Lord. Amen.

O Lord Almighty, the only-begotten Son of the Father; Loose us from the bonds of our sins, and fill us with all spiritual gifts, that so, thy grace preventing and following us, we may be thy faithful servants here, and be numbered with thy saints in glory hereafter; through thy mercy, O blessed Saviour. Amen.

The Twelfth Sunday after Trinity.

Almighty and everlasting God, who art always more ready to hear than we to pray, and art wont to give more than either we desire or deserve; Pour down upon us the abundance of thy mercy; forgiving us those things whereof our conscience is afraid, and giving us those good things which we are not worthy to ask, but through the merits and mediation of Jesus Christ, thy Son, our Lord. Amen.

Almighty God, to whom mercy belongeth, and whose delight it is at all times to spare and save; Accept, we beseech thee, our humble prayer, and set free thy servants that lie under the bondage of sin, according to thy merciful goodness; through Jesus Christ our Lord. Amen.

O God, the high and holy One, who inhabitest eternity, and dwellest with him also who is of a contrite and humble spirit, to revive the spirit of the humble, and to revive the heart of the contrite ones; Glorify thy grace, we beseech thee, in the midst of our manifold infirmities and sins, and through all temptation hold us up by thy mighty hand; that the trial of our faith, being much more precious than of gold that perisheth, though it be tried with fire, may be found unto praise, and honor, and glory, at the appearing of Jesus Christ; to whom, with thee and the Holy Ghost, be honor and glory, world without end. Amen.

The Thirteenth Sunday after Trinity.

Almighty and merciful God, of whose only gift it cometh that thy faithful people do unto thee true and laudable service; Grant, we beseech thee, that we may so faithfully serve thee in this life, that we fail not finally to attain thy heavenly promises; through the merits of Jesus Christ our Lord. Amen.

Grant us, O Lord, not to mind earthly things, but to love things heavenly; and even now, while we are placed among things that are passing away, to cleave to those that shall abide; through Jesus Christ our Lord. Amen.

Give us, heavenly Father, the spirit of faithfulness in the discharge of all the duties of life, that we may grow in spiritual things and attain holiness and everlasting bliss; through Jesus Christ our Lord. Amen.

The Fourteenth Sunday after Trinity.

Almighty and everlasting God, give unto us the increase of faith, hope and charity; and, that we may obtain that which thou dost promise, make us to love that which thou dost command; through Jesus Christ our Lord. Amen.

O heavenly Father, who hast taught us how great things were wrought, through faith, in times of old; Give, we beseech thee, to thy servants a strong and living faith; that, looking not at the things which are seen, but at the things which are not seen, we may win a like victory over the world, and finally behold with our eyes the things in which we have believed; through our Lord and Saviour Jesus Christ. Amen.

O Lord Jesus Christ, around whose throne is a rainbow like unto an emerald; Give us, we beseech thee, that hope which maketh not ashamed. Teach us to sow in hope, labor in hope, persevere in hope; that at the last we may joy before thee according to the joy in harvest, and our works may follow us, and heaven be attained; where we shall praise thee, with the Father and the Holy Ghost, world without end. Amen.

The Fifteenth Sunday after Trinity.

Keep, we beseech thee, O Lord, thy Church with thy perpetual mercy; and, because the frailty of man without thee cannot but fall, keep us ever by thy help from all things hurtful, and lead us to all things profitable to our salvation; through Jesus Christ our Lord. Amen.

Remember, O Lord, we pray thee, that we are but dust, and behold the contrition of our hearts, and grant that we, who through the weakness of the flesh cannot but fall, may by thy mighty power be lifted up; through Jesus Christ, thy Son, our Lord. Amen.

Let thy perpetual mercy, O Lord, accompany thy Church; that while it is placed among the storms of the world, it may both be refreshed with present gladness, and behold the brightness of eternal bliss; through Jesus Christ our Lord. Amen.

The Sixteenth Sunday after Trinity.

O Lord, we beseech thee, let thy continual pity cleanse and defend thy Church; and, because it cannot continue in safety without thy succor, preserve it evermore by thy help and goodness; through Jesus Christ our Lord. Amen.

Be present, O Lord, with the prayers of thy servants, we beseech thee, and let thy people created by thy power, and renewed by thy life, be ever saved by thy continual help; through Jesus Christ our Lord. Amen.

Almighty God, our heavenly Father, who hast promised to be with thy Church unto the end of the world, and that the gates of hell shall not prevail against it; Graciously make thy strength perfect in our weakness, and, according to thy promise, be present with us thine unworthy servants, and grant us thy merciful help; through Jesus Christ our Lord. Amen.

The Seventeenth Sunday after Trinity.

Lord, we pray thee that thy grace may always prevent and follow us, and make us continually to be given to all good works; through Jesus Christ our Lord. Amen.

Almighty God, our heavenly Father, who hast given us all things that pertain unto life and godliness through the glorious revelation of the gospel; Cause thy word to dwell in us richly, we beseech thee, and fill us with the knowledge of thy will in all wisdom and spiritual understanding, that we may walk worthy of the Lord unto all pleasing, being fruitful in every good work, and increasing in the knowledge of God; through Jesus Christ our Lord. Amen.

O Almighty God, we beseech thee, that as thou hast given unto us grace to receive thy Son, our Lord Jesus Christ, and to believe on his Name, so thou wilt grant us ever to abide stedfast in thy faith and in all good works, that when he shall come again to judge the world, we may stand before him with meekness of joy and confidence; through the merits of the same Jesus Christ our Lord. Amen.

The Eighteenth Sunday after Trinity.

Lord, we beseech thee, grant thy people grace to withstand the temptations of the world, the flesh, and the devil; and with pure hearts and minds to follow thee, the only God; through Jesus Christ our Lord. Amen.

O God, who willest not the death of a sinner, protect with thy heavenly aid those persons who are exposed to special temptations; and grant that in the fulfilment of thy commandments they may be strengthened by the assistance of thy grace; through Jesus Christ our Lord. Amen.

O God, who canst save by obedience of the spirit, men lost by the weakness of the flesh; Grant us so to have our inward sight quickened, and our better mind strengthened, that we may avoid that which destroys us, and lay hold on that which works perpetual peace; through Jesus Christ our Lord. Amen.

The Nineteenth Sunday after Trinity.

O God, forasmuch as without thee we are not able to please thee; Mercifully grant that thy Holy Spirit may in all things direct and rule our hearts; through Jesus Christ our Lord. Amen.

Almighty God, our heavenly Father, whose mercies are new unto us every morning, and who, though we have in no wise deserved thy goodness, dost abundantly provide for all our wants of body and soul; Give us, we pray thee, thy Holy Spirit, that we may heartily acknowledge thy merciful goodness toward us, give thanks for all thy benefits, and serve thee in willing obedience; through Jesus Christ thy Son, our Lord. Amen.

O Holy Ghost, the Comforter, Giver of life, Spirit of truth and holiness; Come, and dwell in the hearts of thy servants, quickening them into newness of life, guiding them into all truth, and sanctifying them wholly by thy power; that, being cleansed from every stain of sin, and delivered from all false doctrine and error, they may be living temples of thy holy presence; who, with the Father and the Son, livest and reignest one God for evermore. Amen.

The Twentieth Sunday after Trinity.

O Almighty and most merciful God, of thy bountiful goodness keep us, we beseech thee, from all things that may hurt us; that we, being ready both in body and soul, may cheerfully accomplish those things which thou commandest; through Jesus Christ our Lord. Amen.

O most loving Father, who willest us to give thanks for all things, to dread nothing but the loss of thee, and to cast all our care on thee who carest for us; Preserve us from faithless fears and worldly anxieties, and grant that no clouds of this mortal life may hide from us the light of that love which is immortal, and which thou hast manifested unto us in thy Son, Jesus Christ our Lord. Amen.

O God our Father, merciful and kind, long-suffering and of great goodness, whom the Angels and Archangels and all the host of heaven worship and adore, Look down upon us with compassion, and sanctify us throughout, that we may be to thee, as new-born sons, spiritual, pure and holy. Direct our steps in thy holy ways; preserve us from all temptations of body and soul; and cast down Satan under our feet. Pardon all our sins, backslidings and forgetfulness of thee; and grant us the rich mercy which is of thee in Christ Jesus our Lord, with whom and thy Holy Spirit, thou art blessed and praised by all thy creatures now and for ever. Amen.

The Twenty-first Sunday after Trinity.

Grant, we beseech thee, merciful Lord, to thy faithful people pardon and peace, that they may be cleansed from all their sins, and serve thee with a quiet mind; through Jesus Christ our Lord. Amen.

Almighty God, who hast given thine only Son to be a sacrifice and propitiation for the sins of the whole world; Grant unto us remission and forgiveness of all our sins, and continued growth in the blessedness of the spiritual life; through Jesus Christ our Lord, to whom, with thee and the Holy Spirit, be all dominion and glory, world without end. Amen.

Cleanse us, O Lord, from our secret faults, and mercifully absolve us from our presumptuous sins, that we may receive thy holy things with a pure mind; through Jesus Christ our Lord. Amen.

The Twenty-second Sunday after Trinity.

Lord, we beseech thee to keep thy household the Church in continual godliness; that through thy protection it may be free from all adversities, and devoutly given to serve thee in good works, to the glory of thy Name; through Jesus Christ our Lord. Amen.

We beseech thee, O Lord, to guide thy Church with thy perpetual governance; that it may walk watchfully in times of quiet, and boldly in times of trouble; through Jesus Christ our Lord. Amen

Mercifully regard, O God, the prayers of thy family, and while they submit themselves to thee with their whole heart, do thou prosper them with support, and encompass them with blessings, that, relying on thee as their guide, they may be entangled in no evils, but be filled with all good; through Jesus Christ our Lord. Amen.

The Twenty-third Sunday after Trinity.

O God, our refuge and strength, who art the author of all godliness; Be ready, we beseech thee, to hear the devout prayers of thy Church; and grant that those things which we ask faithfully we may obtain effectually; through Jesus Christ our Lord. Amen.

We beseech thee, Almighty God, to look upon thy servants, whom thou hast enabled to put their trust in thee; and grant them both to ask such things as shall please thee, and also to obtain what they ask; through the merits of thy Son, Jesus Christ our Lord. Amen.

O eternal God, who art great and wonderful in glory, the life of all, the help of those that flee unto thee, and the hope of those who cry unto thee; Cleanse us from sin, secret and open, and from every thought displeasing to thy goodness; cleanse our bodies and souls, our hearts and consciences, that with a pure heart and a clean soul, with perfect love and calm hope, we may venture fearlessly to pray unto thee; through him who hath taught us how to pray, thy blessed Son, Jesus Christ our Lord. Amen.

The Twenty-fourth Sunday after Trinity.

O Lord, we beseech thee, absolve thy people from their offences; that through thy bountiful goodness we may all be delivered from the bands of those sins, which by our frailty we have committed. Grant this, O heavenly Father, for Jesus Christ's sake, our blessed Lord and Saviour. Amen.

O Lord Jesus Christ; Be merciful unto us for thy Name's sake; wherein we have wandered from thee, bring us back; wash away the sins that we have committed; and set us, whom thou hast redeemed, at thy right hand, when thou comest to be our Judge; through thy mercy, O our God, who art blessed, and dost live, and govern all things, world without end. Amen.

O God, who hast given us the promise of thy heavenly rest, may we labor earnestly to enter into it. Quicken, we pray thee, our faith and hope. Teach us to mortify whatever in us is earthly, carnal and corrupt. Putting off the works of darkness, may we be clothed with truth, righteousness and purity, and walk as Christ walked, that we may have confidence and not be ashamed before him at his appearing. We ask it through the same Jesus Christ our Lord. Amen.

The Sunday next before Advent.

Stir up, we beseech thee, O Lord, the wills of thy faithful people; that they, plenteously bringing forth the fruit of good works, may by thee be plenteously rewarded; through Jesus Christ our Lord. Amen.

O God, so rule and govern our hearts and minds by thy Holy Spirit that being ever mindful of the end of all things, and the day of thy just judgment, we may be stirred up to holiness of living here, and dwell with thee forever hereafter; through Jesus Christ thy Son our Lord, who liveth and reigneth with thee and the Holy Ghost ever, one God, world without end. Amen.

Almighty God, we beseech thee, show thy mercy unto thy humble servants, that we who put no trust in our own merits may not be dealt with after the severity of thy judgment, but according to thy mercy; through Jesus Christ, thy Son our Lord, who liveth and reigneth with thee and the Holy Ghost ever, one God, world without end. Amen.

Saint Andrew's Day.

Almighty God, who didst give such grace unto thy holy Apostle Saint Andrew, that he readily obeyed the calling of thy Son Jesus Christ, and followed him without delay; Grant unto us all, that we, being called by thy holy Word, may forthwith give up ourselves obediently to fulfil thy holy commandments; through the same Jesus Christ our Lord. Amen.

Grant, heavenly Father, that in our services rendered to thee we may act with promptitude both in accepting salvation for ourselves and in leading others to a knowledge of thyself; through Jesus Christ our Lord. Amen.

Saint Thomas the Apostle.

Almighty and everliving God, who, for the greater confirmation of the faith, didst suffer thy holy Apostle Thomas to be doubtful in thy Son's resurrection; Grant us so perfectly, and without all doubt, to believe in thy Son Jesus Christ, that our faith in thy sight may never be reproved. Hear us, O Lord, through the same Jesus Christ, to whom, with thee and the Holy Ghost, be all honor and glory, now and forevermore Amen.

O Lord Jesus Christ, very God and very Man, who changest not, but art holy in all thy works; Take away from us, we humbly beseech thee, all unbelief, and fill us with the gifts of thy grace; through thy mercy, O our God, who art blessed, and dost live, and govern all things, world without end. Amen.

The Conversion of Saint Paul.

O God, who, through the preaching of the blessed Apostle Saint Paul, hast caused the light of the Gospel to shine throughout the world; Grant, we beseech thee, that we, having his wonderful conversion in remembrance, may show forth our thankfulness unto thee for the same, by following the holy doctrine which he taught; through Jesus Christ our Lord. Amen.

O Christ, the Son of God, who didst graciously choose Saint Paul to be thine Apostle, and didst enable him so to sow the good seed of thy Word throughout the world, that from it there has sprung up an abundant harvest unto thee; Grant that his teachings may sink deep into our hearts, and bring forth fruit to thy glory, who, with the Father and the Holy Ghost, livest and reignest ever, one God, world without end. Amen.

The Presentation of Christ in the Temple,
commonly called
The Purification of Saint Mary the Virgin.

Almighty and everliving God, we humbly beseech thy Majesty, that, as thine only-begotten Son was this day presented in the temple in substance of our flesh, so we may be presented unto thee with pure and clean hearts, by the same thy Son Jesus Christ our Lord. Amen.

Cleanse thou us, O good Lord, and so shall we be cleansed, and grant that as thy blessed Son was presented in the temple in the substance of our flesh, so with pure and clean hearts we may ever present ourselves before thee to offer up spiritual sacrifices to the honor of thy great Name; through the same Jesus Christ our Lord. Amen.

Saint Matthias's Day.

O Almighty God, who into the place of the traitor Judas didst choose thy faithful servant Matthias to be of the number of the twelve Apostles; Grant that thy Church, being always preserved from false Apostles, may be ordered and guided by faithful and true pastors; through Jesus Christ our Lord. Amen.

O God, the Light of the faithful and Shepherd of souls, who didst place thine holy Apostles in the Church that they might feed thy sheep by their words, and guide them by their examples; Grant us, we pray thee, to keep the faith which they taught, and to follow in their footsteps; through Jesus Christ our Lord. Amen.

The Annunciation of the blessed Virgin Mary.

We beseech thee, O Lord, pour thy grace into our hearts; that, as we have known the incarnation of thy Son Jesus Christ by the message of an Angel, so by his cross and passion we may be brought unto the glory of his resurrection; through the same Jesus Christ our Lord. Amen.

O God, who, regarding the humility of the blessed Virgin Mary, didst exalt her to such excellent grace that of her, according to the flesh, thine only-begotten Son should be born; Grant, we beseech thee, that we, humbling ourselves in all things after her example, may attain to be exalted; through the same Jesus Christ our Lord. Amen.

Saint Mark's Day.

O Almighty God, who hast instructed thy holy Church with the heavenly doctrine of thy Evangelist Saint Mark; Give us grace that, being not like children carried away with every blast of vain doctrine, we may be established in the truth of thy holy Gospel; through Jesus Christ our Lord. Amen.

O God, who didst bestow on blessed Saint Mark, the clear light of faith, and the might of holiness; Grant us the same firmness of faith in the truths he taught, and a fellowship with him in thine eternal glory; through Jesus Christ our Lord. Amen.

Saint Philip and Saint James's Day.

O Almighty God, whom truly to know is everlasting life; Grant us perfectly to know thy Son Jesus Christ to be the way, the truth and the life; that, following the steps of thy holy Apostles, Saint Philip and Saint James, we may stedfastly walk in the way that leadeth to eternal life; through the same thy Son Jesus Christ our Lord. Amen.

We beseech thee, O God, to grant us after the examples of Saint Philip and Saint James constancy in thy faith and truth; that, being grounded in divine love, we may be moved from its perfection by no temptations; through Jesus Christ our Lord. Amen.

Saint Barnabas the Apostle.

O Lord God Almighty, who didst endue thy holy Apostle Barnabas with singular gifts of the Holy Ghost; Leave us not, we beseech thee, destitute of thy manifold gifts, nor yet of grace to use them alway to thy honor and glory; through Jesus Christ our Lord. Amen.

O Father of mercies and God of all consolation; Fill us, we pray thee, with thy Holy Spirit, so that, after the example of thy blessed Apostle Saint Barnabas, the son of consolation, we, loving thee above all things, may delight in doing good to our fellow-men; through Jesus Christ our Lord. Amen.

Saint John Baptist's Day.

Almighty God, by whose providence thy servant John Baptist was wonderfully born, and sent to prepare the way of thy Son our Saviour by preaching repentance; Make us so to follow his doctrine and holy life, that we may truly repent according to his preaching; and after his example constantly speak the truth, boldly rebuke vice, and patiently suffer for the truth's sake; through Jesus Christ our Lord. Amen.

O Lord Jesus Christ, who didst make thy forerunner, Saint John Baptist, to be as a bright light in thy temple; Grant that we may ever shine in thy Church, with the ardor of faith, in works of charity, and in true humility; through thy mercy, O Christ our God, who, with the Father and the Holy Ghost, livest and reignest ever, one God, world without end. Amen.

Saint Peter's Day.

O Almighty God, who by thy Son Jesus Christ didst give to thy Apostle Saint Peter many excellent gifts, and commandedst him earnestly to feed thy flock; Make, we beseech thee, all Bishops and Pastors diligently to preach thy holy Word, and the people obediently to follow the same, that they may receive the crown of everlasting glory; through Jesus Christ our Lord. Amen.

O God, who didst cause blessed Saint Peter the Apostle to be loosed from his chains and to depart unhurt; Break, we beseech thee, the bands of our sins, and mercifully put away all evil things from us; through Jesus Christ our Lord. Amen.

Saint James the Apostle.

Grant, O merciful God, that, as thine holy Apostle Saint James, leaving his father and all that he had, without delay, was obedient unto the calling of thy Son Jesus Christ, and followed him; so we, forsaking all worldly and carnal affections, may be evermore ready to follow thy holy commandments; through Jesus Christ our Lord. Amen.

Grant, O Lord, that as thy holy Apostle Saint James, so soon as he was called, left the ship and his father, and followed thy Son Jesus Christ with all his heart, so we may ever with a glad will obey thy commandments; through the same Jesus Christ our Lord. Amen.

The Transfiguration of Christ.

O God, who on the mount didst reveal to chosen witnesses thine only-begotten Son wonderfully transfigured, in raiment white and glistering; Mercifully grant that we, being delivered from the disquietude of this world, may be permitted to behold the King in his beauty, who with thee, O Father, and thee, O Holy Ghost, liveth and reigneth, one God, world without end. Amen.

O God, who at the transfiguration of thine only-begotten Son didst confirm the mysteries of the faith by the testimony of the fathers, and didst wonderfully prefigure, by the voice from the bright cloud, the perfect adoption of sons; Grant, we beseech thee, that we may be co-heirs of the King of glory, and finally partakers of his glory; through the same Jesus Christ our Lord. Amen.

Saint Bartholomew the Apostle.

O Almighty and everlasting God, who didst give to thine Apostle Bartholomew, grace truly to believe and to preach thy Word; Grant, we beseech thee, unto thy Church, to love that Word which he believed, and both to preach and receive the same; through Jesus Christ our Lord. Amen.

O Christ, the power of God, and the wisdom of God, who didst give to thy holy Apostle Saint Bartholomew power to tread on serpents and scorpions; Strengthen us, we pray thee, by thy grace, that in thy might we may vanquish and overcome all our spiritual enemies, and with pure hearts serve thee, whom, with the Father and the Holy Ghost, we worship and glorify ever, one God, world without end. Amen.

Saint Matthew the Apostle.

O Almighty God, who by thy blessed Son didst call Matthew from the receipt of custom to be an Apostle and Evangelist; Grant us grace to forsake all covetous desires, and inordinate love of riches, and to follow the same thy Son Jesus Christ, who liveth and reigneth with thee and the Holy Ghost, one God, world without end. Amen.

O Lord Jesus Christ, who of thy great goodness, didst call Matthew the publican to be thine Apostle and Evangelist; Grant us, like him, to withstand temptation, and, turning from all the allurements of the world, to follow thee without delay; through thy mercy, O our God, who art blessed, and dost live, and govern all things, world without end. Amen.

Saint Michael and all Angels.

O everlasting God, who hast ordained and constituted the services of Angels and men in a wonderful order; Mercifully grant that, as thy holy Angels always do thee service in heaven, so, by thy appointment, they may succor and defend us on earth; through Jesus Christ our Lord. Amen.

O Lord, the King eternal; Send, we pray thee, thy holy Angels to defend us both in soul and body; and grant that as thou hast called us to share their blessedness in the world to come, so we may ever follow the example of their obedience, and delight to do thy pleasure; through Jesus Christ, thy Son, our Lord. Amen.

Saint Luke the Evangelist.

Almighty God, who calledst Luke the Physician, whose praise is in the Gospel, to be an Evangelist, and Physician of the soul; May it please thee that, by the wholesome medicines of the doctrine delivered by him, all the diseases of our souls may be healed; through the merits of thy Son Jesus Christ our Lord. Amen

Look mercifully, O God, on the prayers of thy supplicants and enlighten with thy health our bodies and souls, that no dark desires may have possession of those whom the light of heavenly grace daily renews. We ask it through Jesus Christ our Lord. Amen.

Saint Simon and Saint Jude, Apostles.

O Almighty God, who hast built thy Church upon the foundation of the Apostles and Prophets, Jesus Christ himself being the head corner-stone; Grant us so to be joined together in unity of spirit by their doctrine, that we may be made an holy temple acceptable unto thee; through Jesus Christ our Lord. Amen.

O Saviour, who didst send out thine Apostles to preach throughout the world, the gospel of thine everlasting kingdom; Grant that we who confess and adore in thy divine Person all the fulness of the Godhead, may so obey thee in a life of holiness and true charity that at the last we may come to thine eternal joys; through thy mercy, O Jesus Christ our Lord, who livest and reignest with the Father and Holy Ghost ever, one God, world without end. Amen.

All Saints' Day.

O Almighty God, who hast knit together thine elect in one communion and fellowship, in the mystical body of thy Son Christ our Lord; Grant us grace so to follow thy blessed Saints in all virtuous and godly living, that we may come to those unspeakable joys which thou hast prepared for those who unfeignedly love thee; through Jesus Christ our Lord. Amen.

O God, of whose gift thy blessed Saints, who are now at rest, overcame the world; Grant us now to follow in their footsteps, and after this life to be partakers with them of heavenly joys; through Jesus Christ, thy Son, our Lord. Amen.

Other Collects from the Book of Common Prayer.

✠

O God, from whom all holy desires, all good counsels, and all just works do proceed; Give unto thy servants that peace, which the world cannot give; that our hearts may be set to obey thy commandments, and also that by thee, we, being defended from the fear of our enemies, may pass our time in rest and quietness; through the merits of Jesus Christ our Saviour. Amen.

Almighty God, unto whom all hearts are open, all desires known, and from whom no secrets are hid; Cleanse the thoughts of our hearts by the inspiration of thy Holy Spirit, that we may perfectly love thee, and worthily magnify thy holy Name; through Christ our Lord. Amen.

O Almighty Lord, and everlasting God, vouchsafe, we beseech thee, to direct, sanctify and govern, both our hearts and bodies, in the ways of thy laws, and in the works of thy commandments; that, through thy most mighty protection, both here and ever, we may be preserved in body and soul; through our Lord and Saviour Jesus Christ. Amen.

Assist us mercifully, O Lord, in these our supplications and prayers, and dispose the way of thy servants toward the attainment of everlasting salvation; that, among all the changes and chances of this mortal life, they may ever be defended by thy most gracious and ready help; through Jesus Christ our Lord. Amen

Grant, we beseech thee, Almighty God, that the words which we have heard this day with our outward ears, may, through thy grace, be so grafted inwardly in our hearts, that they may bring forth in us the fruit of good living, to the honor and praise of thy Name; through Jesus Christ our Lord. Amen.

Direct us, O Lord, in all our doings, with thy most gracious favor, and further us with thy continual help; that in all our works begun, continued and ended in thee, we may glorify thy holy Name, and finally, by thy mercy, obtain everlasting life; through Jesus Christ our Lord. Amen.

Almighty God, the fountain of all wisdom, who knowest our necessities before we ask, and our ignorance in asking; we beseech thee to have compassion upon our infirmities; and those things, which for our unworthiness we dare not, and for our blindness we cannot ask, vouchsafe to give us, for the worthiness of thy Son Christ our Lord Amen.

Almighty God, who hast promised to hear the petitions of those who ask in thy Son's Name; We beseech thee mercifully to incline thine ears to us who have now made our prayers and supplications unto thee; and grant, that those things which we have faithfully asked according to thy will, may effectually be obtained, to the relief of our necessity, and to the setting forth of thy glory; through Jesus Christ our Lord. Amen.

O God, who art the author of peace and lover of concord, in knowledge of whom standeth our eternal life, whose service is perfect freedom; Defend us thy humble servants in all assaults of our enemies; that we, surely trusting in thy defence, may not fear the power of any adversaries, through the might of Jesus Christ our Lord. Amen.

Almighty God, who hast given us grace at this time with one accord to make our common supplications unto thee; and dost promise that when two or three are gathered together in thy Name thou wilt grant their requests; Fulfil now, O Lord, the desires and petitions of thy servants, as may be most expedient for them; granting us in this world knowledge of thy truth, and in the world to come life everlasting. Amen.

Most gracious God, the giver of all good and perfect gifts, who of thy wise providence hast appointed divers Orders in thy Church; Give thy grace, we beseech thee, to thy servant, to whom the charge of this Congregation is now committed; and so replenish him with the truth of thy doctrine, and endue him with innocency of life, that he may faithfully serve before thee, to the glory of thy great Name, and the benefit of thy holy Church; through Jesus Christ, our only Mediator and Redeemer. Amen.

O holy Jesus, who hast purchased to thyself an universal Church, and hast promised to be with the Ministers of Apostolic Succession to the end of the world; Be graciously pleased to bless the ministry and service of him who is now appointed to offer the sacrifices of prayer and praise to thee in this house, which is called by thy Name. May the words of his mouth, and the meditation of his heart, be alway acceptable in thy sight, O Lord, our strength and our Redeemer. Amen.

O God, Holy Ghost, Sanctifier of the faithful, visit, we pray thee, this Congregation with thy love and favor; enlighten their minds more and more with the light of the everlasting Gospel; graft in their hearts a love of the truth; increase in them true religion; nourish them with all goodness; and of thy great mercy keep them in the same, O blessed Spirit, whom, with the Father and the Son together, we worship and glorify as one God, world without end. Amen.

Lenten Prayers.

✠

O God the Father, who knowest our necessities, hear us, thy servants.

O God the Son, who was tempted like as we are, hear us, thy servants.

O God the Holy Ghost, who knowest how to deliver the ungodly out of temptation, hear us, thy servants.

O Lord God, we pray thee during these forty days to make us know ourselves as thou knowest us and to see our sins as thou seest them.

Help us to set our minds more on thee and less on the world.

Help us to resist the devil, as good soldiers of Jesus Christ.

Help us to keep our bodies chaste, our words holy, our thoughts pure, as being temples of thy Holy Spirit.

Lead us to give up something for thee to-day.

Lead us to help some person in body or soul to-day.

Lead us to pray for thy holy Church to-day.

Make us to-day and every day to obey thee as the children of God.

Make us to-day and every day to love thee as members of Christ.

Make us to-day and every day to serve thee, as inheritors of the kingdom of heaven.

Grant us so to take up our cross daily here, that we may receive the crown of glory hereafter, through Jesus Christ our Lord. Amen.

Almighty God, whose blessed Son, for our sakes did fast forty days and forty nights; Give us grace to use such abstinence, during this season dedicated to the exercise of repentance, that our flesh may be subdued to the spirit, and our minds the better disposed to approach thee with ardor and fervency of affection. Inure us, by self-denial to bring our bodies into subjection, and to punish all those excesses we have been guilty of in the use of thy creatures. Let our retirement from the world make us see the vanity and emptiness of it, and teach us to relish the pleasures of spiritual enjoyments. Make us heartily to bewail our sins and do thou work in us a godly sorrow unto salvation not to be repented of, that, perceiving how bitter a thing it is to depart from the living God, we may no longer continue at a distance from the Fountain of joy and happiness, but, confessing and forsaking our sins, may be entirely converted unto thee; through Jesus Christ our Lord. Amen.

O Lord, who through ages past has trained thy Church, as at this season, in finding out and striving against the secret or the open sins which may be displeasing in thy sight; By the help of the Holy Spirit lay open to us our hearts and lives, that we may in humble penitence lay them at the foot of the cross of Christ for cleansing through his most precious blood; through the same Jesus Christ our Lord Amen

O most merciful Saviour, who healest the inward man by outward afflictions, and by troubles in this world dost prepare us for eternal joys in the world to come; By that cup of sorrow which thou drankest for us, and by that weary path which thou troddest, grant that we may willingly drink of thy cup, and cheerfully follow thee along the road where thou hast gone before; who with the Father and the Holy Ghost now reignest one God, world without end Amen.

O Christ, the Son of God, who, for our sakes, didst fast forty days, and didst suffer thyself to be tempted; Grant that we may not be led astray through any temptations; and, since man doth not live by bread alone, nourish our souls with heavenly food; through thy mercy, O our God, who art blessed, and dost live, and govern all things, world without end. Amen.

Various Prayers.

✠

For those who have forsaken the Catholic Faith.

Almighty and merciful Father, we beseech thee for all who have forsaken the Catholic faith, all who have wandered from any portion thereof, or are in doubt or temptation through the enemies of thy Word, that thou wouldest visit them as a Father, reveal unto them their error and bring them back from their wanderings, that they in loyalty to thy Church and thy holy Word, may be led unto everlasting life; through faith in Jesus Christ, thy Son, our Lord. Amen.

For those we have led into Sin.

O merciful God, we pray thee most humbly for all who have sinned against thee through our fault, and all to whom we have taught evil by word or action Forgive their sins, and the evil we have caused by our wickedness do thou put away in thy mercy, through Jesus Christ our Lord. Amen.

For Neglected Persons.

O Lord Jesus Christ, who wast forgotten as a dead man out of mind; Shew forth thy loving kindness, we entreat thee, to all persons who in this world feel themselves neglected, or little loved, or forgotten. Be thou their beloved Companion, and let communion with thee be to them more dear than tenderest earthly intercourse. Teach them to seek thee in prayer, and to find thee in thy blessed Sacrament; teach them to discern thee in all with whom they come in contact, and to love and serve thee in them. On earth grant them comfort by the repentance of any who have wronged them, and in heaven comfort in the communion of all saints with each other and with thee. Grant this, O our God, who art blessed, and livest and reignest for ever and ever. Amen

For those who live in Sin.

Have mercy, heavenly Father, on all who are hardened through the deceitfulness of sin; Vouchsafe them grace to come to themselves, the will and the power to return to thee, and the loving welcome of thy forgiveness; through Jesus Christ our Lord. Amen

For the Thoughtless.

O God and Father of all, who delightest in the happiness of thy creatures; Send down thy Holy Spirit upon those who are drawn away by the pleasures of youth, the opportunities of wealth, or the excitement of sin, to forget thee, and neglect their regenerate life. Enlighten them, calm them, control them, make them to see the vanity of earthly pleasures; and so subdue their natural energies by the power of thy supernatural love that they may spend them in thy service, to thy honor and glory; through Jesus Christ our Lord. Amen.

For the Censorious.

Have mercy, O God, upon those who are accustomed to speak harshly of their brethren, and grant that in all our judgments of others we may remember thy judgment, whereby we shall ourselves be judged, and may exercise that charity whereby we hope to be forgiven; for Jesus Christ's sake. Amen.

For the Worldly.

O God, whom truly to know is everlasting life; Pity the blindness of those who by the contemplation of thy creatures are drawn away from the faithful acknowledgment of thee their Creator. Make them to see the transitory character of all outward things and the beauty of thine eternal truth, that they may know thy love manifested by thine incarnate Son, and when the present age of their probation shall have passed away, may they be filled with thine own fulness; through the same Jesus Christ our Lord. Amen.

For Persons Unjustly Accused.

O Lord Jesus Christ, against whom false witnesses rose up; By thy most holy example of perfect patience and humility strengthen and support, we entreat thee, all persons unjustly accused or underrated. Comfort them by the ever-present thought that thou knowest the whole truth, and wilt in thine own good time make their righteousness as clear as the light. Give them grace to pray for such as do them wrong, and hear and bless them when they pray. Grant this through thy mercy, O our God, who art blessed, and livest and reignest forever and ever. Amen.

Against angry Passions.

O most meek and lowly Jesus, who didst suffer all insults and injuries in thy adorable person, and when struck in thy face by the soldier, didst but reply, Why smitest thou me? mortify in us all angry passions, that we may not return injuries with malice, nor ever meditate revenge, but bear all things patiently for thy sake, thou meek and silent Lamb of God, suffering Saviour of our souls; who, with the Father and the Holy Ghost, livest and reignest, one God, world without end. Amen.

Against Heresy.

Dissolve, O Christ, the schisms of heresy, which seek to subvert the faith, which strive to corrupt the truth; that as thou art acknowledged in heaven and in earth as one and the same Lord, so thy people, gathered from all nations, may serve thee in the unity of faith; to thy glory and honor, who, with the Father and the Holy Ghost, art one God, world without end. Amen.

Against Coldness in Prayer.

O God, pardon, we beseech thee, the wanderings and coldness of our prayers, and deal not with us according to our prayers or deserts, but according to our needs and thine own rich mercies in Christ Jesus our Lord. Amen.

Against Wandering Thoughts.

Heavenly Father, give us grace to fix our minds on thee, especially in times of prayer when we talk with thee. Stop the fancies of our wandering minds and the desires of our evil hearts. Destroy the power of the enemy of our souls, who tries at such times to draw our minds from heavenly thoughts. So shall we, with joy and gratitude, thank thee for all the evils we have escaped, and for all the good we have received; through Jesus Christ our Lord. Amen.

Against Sloth.

O Lord Jesus Christ, who hast said, My Father worketh hitherto, and I work; Grant us, we beseech thee, such zeal in thy service, that we may never be weary in well doing, but may labor stedfastly unto the end; through thy mercy, O our God, who art blessed, and livest and reignest forever and ever. Amen.

Against Self-deception.

O God, who hast warned us that the heart is deceitful above all things; Give us wisdom to know our shortcomings, errors and secret faults, and mercifully cleansing us therefrom, keep us from the temptations of spiritual pride; through Jesus Christ our Lord. Amen.

Against Sins of the Tongue.

We beseech thee, O Saviour, by those sacred words which in thy last agony thou didst utter upon the cross, that thou wouldest keep our tongues from evil, and our lips that they speak no guile, that as thy holy Angels ever sing thy praises in heaven, so with our tongues may we at all times glorify thee on earth; who livest and reignest with the Father and the Holy Ghost, one God, world without end. Amen.

Against Formalism.

O Lord Jesus Christ, whose ways are right, keep us in thy mercy from lip-service and empty forms, from having a name that we live, but being dead. Help us to worship thee by righteous deeds and lives of holiness; that our prayer also may be set forth in thy sight as the incense, and the lifting up of our hands be as an evening sacrifice; through thy mercy, O our God, who art blessed, and livest and reignest for ever and ever. Amen.

Against Insincerity.

O Lord Jesus Christ, who didst rebuke the barren fig-tree, bearing leaves but not fruit; Vouchsafe unto us perfect sincerity in thought and deed, and grant that we may carry out in our lives what we have learned in thy holy Word; through thy mercy, O our God, who art blessed, and livest and reignest forever and ever. Amen.

Against Presumption.

Almighty God, our heavenly Father, who didst suffer thine Apostle Saint Peter, presuming on his own power, miserably to fall, even so as to deny his Master; Grant to us, we beseech thee, that we may never presume on our own might and power, but being in our hearts humble and lowly, acknowledging our own infirmity, frailty and weakness, may ever, in all our doings, receive at thy mighty hand the strength and comfort which we need, to the due performance of thy holy will; through Jesus Christ our Lord. Amen.

Against Uncharitable Judgments.

O Lord Jesus Christ, to whom all things are possible; Inspire us, we entreat thee, with ardent faith in thy love and power when we supplicate thee for ourselves or for others. Keep us from judging uncharitably those for whom we pray, or from presumptuously estimating them as less acceptable than ourselves to thee; keep us from giving thanks with the Pharisee, but rend our hearts with the humble cry of the Publican. Hear us, O Lord, when we pray for all who need our prayers; and thy Name, with that of the Father and the Holy Ghost, shall have all the praise, world without end. Amen.

For Veneration of the Name of Jesus Christ.

Almighty God, who hast made the glorious Name of Jesus Christ thy Son our Lord most dear to thy faithful people, and most terrible to evil spirits; Grant that all who devoutly venerate this Name on earth may in this life receive holy consolation and comfort, and in the world to come, the joy of exaltation, and of eternal blessedness in heaven; through the same Jesus Christ our Lord. Amen.

For Truthfulness.

O God, the God of Truth, mercifully grant that the Holy Spirit of truth may rule our hearts, grafting therein the love of truth, and making us in all our thoughts, words and works to study, speak and follow truth, that we may be sincere before men and blameless before thee; for his sake who is the Truth, and in whose most blessed mouth was no deceit, Jesus Christ our Lord. Amen.

For Enlightenment.

O Lord Jesus Christ, who art the light of the blind, the way of the erring, and the resurrection of the dead; Enlighten the darkness of our hearts and minds, bring sinners to repentance, and make us to live in thee and for thee, whom, with the Father and the Holy Ghost, we worship and glorify ever, one God, world without end. Amen.

For Cleansing.

O Lord Jesus Christ, to whom glory in the highest is ever sung in heaven and on earth; Grant unto us and to all thy people thy good will, cleanse us from all our sins, and give us thy peace forever; through thy mercy, O our God, who art blessed, and dost live, and govern all things, world without end. Amen.

For Comfort.

O Almighty God, who art the author of everlasting felicity; Sustain and comfort us, we pray thee, in all the trials of this present life, and grant unto us at last, in thy presence, fulness of joy, and pleasures for evermore; through Jesus Christ our Lord. Amen.

For a Sense of Sin.

O God, who art of purer eyes than to behold iniquity; Mercifully grant unto us such a sense of sin, that we may receive cleansing, and such cleansing, that we may be made pure in heart, and may see thee for evermore; through Jesus Christ our Lord. Amen.

For the Spirit of Prayer.

O God of hope, the true Light of faithful souls, and perfect brightness of the blessed, who art verily the Light of the Church; Grant that our hearts may both render thee a worthy prayer, and always glorify thee with the offering of praises; through Jesus Christ our Lord. Amen.

For Rest.

O Lord Jesus Christ, the rest of the Angels and of all the Saints; Grant unto thy people to find in thee deliverance from all sin, and rest from every burden, so that, joining with Angels and Archangels in blessing thee, they may in all and through all things be blessed by thee; through thy mercy, O our God, who art blessed, and dost live, and govern all things, world without end. Amen.

For Peace.

O Christ our Lord, at whose coming peace returned to earth; Vouchsafe, we beseech thee, to keep ever in thy peace those whom thou didst reconcile unto thee by thy first coming, until, at thy coming again in glorious majesty, thou makest them to inherit eternal peace; through thy mercy, O our God, who art blessed, and dost live, and govern all things, world without end. Amen.

For Sanctified Learning.

O God, the Father Almighty; Grant us to have in thee the light of knowledge, and the fulness of all virtue, that, while we seek for the gifts of learning, we may never depart from thee, who art the Fountain of all wisdom; through Jesus Christ, thy Son, our Lord. Amen.

For Eternal Felicity.

O Lord, save us, we pray thee, who hope in thee, comfort us, according to thy Word, whom thou hast redeemed with thy most precious Blood, and grant us, with thee, perpetual joy and felicity, where sighing is at an end, and sorrow cannot come; through thy mercy, O our God, who art blessed, and dost live, and govern all things, world without end. Amen.

For Love of Friends and Enemies.

O God, who so lovedst the world that thou didst give thine only-begotten Son to reconcile the earthly with the heavenly; Grant that, loving thee above all things, we may love in thee our friends and our enemies; through the same thy Son Jesus Christ our Lord. Amen.

For a Child-like Spirit.

O Lord Jesus Christ, who, very God of very God, didst deign for us to become a little child, that the world which thou didst make might through thee be saved; Grant that, as unto us a Child is born, unto us a Son is given, we, born again through thee, may ever remain in the number of God's faithful children; through thy merits, O blessed Saviour, who, with the Father and the Holy Ghost, livest and reignest ever, one God, world without end. Amen.

For Confidence in the Judgment Day.

O God, who, by the mouth of thy holy prophets, didst promise that thine only-begotten Son should come in the flesh for us, and be born of a pure virgin, and hast in these last days fulfilled thy Word; Grant, we beseech thee, that when he who came once to redeem the world cometh to be our Judge, we may not be ashamed before him at his coming; through the merits of the same thy Son Jesus Christ our Lord. Amen.

For Humility.

O merciful God, who didst justify the publican, who, standing afar off, and beating his breast, confessed his sin unto thee; Grant unto us thy servants, meekly acknowledging our unworthiness, and supplicating thy favor, the forgiveness of all our sins; through thy mercy, and for the love of Jesus Christ, thy Son, our Saviour. Amen.

For Wisdom.

O Lord Jesus Christ, who art the Redeemer of all those who put their trust in thee; Loose thy people, we pray thee, from the bonds of their sins, fill their hearts and minds with true wisdom, and let thy peace and heavenly benediction, ever be with them; through thy mercy, O our God, who art blessed, and dost live and govern all things, world without end. Amen.

For Obedience.

O Lord Jesus Christ, make us to live soberly, righteously and godly, in this present world, looking for the blessed hope and thy glorious appearing, so that, running in the way of thy commandments, we may attain thy heavenly promises; through thy mercy, O our God, who art blessed, and dost live, and govern all things, world without end. Amen.

For Faithfulness.

O Christ, the Alpha and the Omega, the Beginning and the Ending, the Root and the Offspring of David; Mercifully grant unto us, our King and our Saviour, that we may serve thee faithfully here, and continue thine forever; through thy merits, O our God, who art blessed, and dost live, and govern all things, world without end. Amen.

For a Tender Conscience.

O God, save us from a blinded conscience, still more, from a hardened one. Make us to bring all our guilt at once to the fountain opened for uncleanness, the Blood of Christ. Endue our conscience with such holy tenderness, that the faintest approach of evil may awaken its testimony, and give us grace to obey its faintest remonstrance; for Christ our Saviour's sake. Amen.

For Self-examination.

O Almighty God, who dost love to dwell with the pure in heart, and hatest the least stain of sin; Help us to examine our souls. Give us thy Holy Spirit. Shew us our faults, O Lord, and help us to feel our sinfulness. Give us true sorrow for sin, and grace to overcome it, firm trust in thy mercy, and charity with all men, for the sake of Jesus Christ our Lord Amen.

For Cheerfulness.

O Lord Jesus Christ, the Lord that hath mercy on us; Teach our hearts to sing for joy when our lips sing praises unto thee for all thy mercies. Banish, we pray thee, from our souls, gloom, discontent and abject fear; and make thy love of us and our love of thee be in us joy, confidence and full satisfaction; hear us, O Saviour, who, with the Father and the Holy Ghost, livest and reignest, one God, world without end. Amen

For the Spirit of Praise.

O Lord Jesus Christ, worthy to be praised; Give us grace, we beseech thee, to attribute no good thing to ourselves; not desiring the praise of men, or puffing up our neighbor with vain flatteries, but ascribing all praise unto thee on whom praise waiteth; for thou alone, O Lord Jesus, with the Father and the Holy Spirit, art worthy of the blessing and thanksgiving, worship and magnifying, adoration and love, of Cherubim and Seraphim, Angels and Archangels, men and all creatures, world without end. Amen.

For Diligence.

O Almighty God, whose will it is that none should be idle; Give us, we pray thee, a diligent spirit, that whatever we find to do we may do with all our might, to thy honor and glory; for the sake of Jesus Christ our Lord. Amen.

For Gentleness.

O Christ, Son of God, who didst patiently endure the reproaches of thine adversaries when, like roaring lions, they gnashed upon thee with their teeth; Grant, we beseech thee, that we, following thine example, and the pattern of thy longsuffering, may become gentle to all; through thy mercy, O our God, who art blessed, and livest and reignest for ever and ever. Amen.

For Patience.

O God, who by the passion and death of thine only-begotten Son didst crush the pride of our enemy the devil; Grant to thy faithful servants, when they are in trouble, to bear in mind his sufferings, and cheerfully to endure all adversities; through the same Jesus Christ our Lord. Amen.

For Contentment.

O God, who hast taught us that our life is more than meat and our body than raiment; Teach us also to be content with such things as thou hast given us, and to seek in thee that godliness which, with contentment, is great gain; for the sake of Jesus Christ our Lord. Amen.

For Thankfulness.

O merciful God, who hast taught us by thy holy Word that it is a joyful and pleasant thing to be thankful; Give us grace, we beseech thee, to be truly and sincerely thankful for thy manifold mercies bestowed upon us, and grant that we may employ all thy gifts and mercies to the setting forth of thy glory, and the furthering of our own salvation; through Jesus Christ our Lord. Amen.

For a good use of Blessings.

Almighty and everlasting God, who healest us by chastening, and preservest us by pardoning; Grant unto thy suppliants, that we may both rejoice in the comfort of the tranquillity which we desired, and also use the gift of thy peace for the effectual amendment of our lives; through Jesus Christ our Lord. Amen.

For Love of God.

Most merciful God, we are conscious of grievous shortcoming in our love. Make us sensible of thy great love to us. In the gift of thy dear Son, in the communications of thy free grace, help us ever to trace thy goodness toward us. Enable us to show forth our love not only with our lips but in our lives; the love of a holy admiration, the love of a happy allegiance, the love of a respectful homage, the love of an entire devotion, the love of an instinctive desire and longing for thy presence, the love of an outspoken testimony to thy praise; these things we humbly ask for Jesus Christ's sake. Amen.

For Stability.

O Lord Jesus Christ, our Rock, give us wisdom, we beseech thee, to build our house upon the Rock and not upon the sand; that when floods of temptation, rain of affliction, winds of persecution, beat upon that house it may not fall, because it is founded upon a Rock; grant this through thy mercy, O our God, who art blessed, and livest and reignest for ever and ever. Amen.

For Holiness.

O Father of mercies, who hast foreordained thine elect to be conformed to the image of thy Son; So conform us, we beseech thee, unto him in holiness, that when he shall appear, we may be made like unto him in glory; through the same Jesus Christ our Lord. Amen.

For a Happy Death.

O Immortal Jesus, who when thou wast pleased to die, didst bow thine head and commend thy spirit into the hands of thy Father; Grant that when the hour of our departure shall come, we may be willing to leave this mortal life, and thou being present to our sight, and shining upon us with the light of thy countenance, we may joyfully commit our souls to thee, who art the Resurrection and the Life; who liveth and reigneth with the Father and the Holy Ghost, one God, world without end. Amen.

INDEX.

Accused, For persons unjustly, 211.
Adults, Funeral of, 84.
Afflicted, For the, 86.
Aged, For a Home for the, 159.
Alms Basin, Benediction of an, 100.
Altar, Benediction of an, 97.
Altar Cloth, Benediction of an, 103.
Altar Guild, For an, 132.
Altar Linen, Benediction of, 103.
Army and Navy, For the, 155.
Auxiliary, For the Woman's, 110.

Banner, Benediction of a, 103.
Baptism, Of Infants in Church, 1; in private, 8; of Adults, 14; Infant and Adult combined, 23.
Bell, Benediction of a, 101.
Blessings, For a good use of, 218.
Bible Class, For a, 130.
Blind, For the, 159.

Candles, Benediction of, 102.
Catholic Faith, For those who have forsaken the, 210.
Censorious, For the, 211.
Cheerfulness, For, 217.
Child-birth, After, 167.
Child, At birth of, 149; before baptism of, 150; funeral of a, 89.
Children, For Sunday School, 126; for neglected, 127; at School, 150; of a family, 150; sponsors for, 151.
Choir, With a, 122.
Choristers, Office with, 94.
Christians, For persecuted, 107.
Church, For restoration of a, 119; for an unfinished, 119; for Councils of the, 113; for unity of the, 116; for the Syrian, 108; throughout the world, 113.
Christ, For fellowship with, 70.
Cleansing, For, 214.
Collects, 170, 206.
Colleges and Schools, For, 156.
Comfort, For, 214.
Communicate, For one about to, 72.
Confirmation, Order of, 30; class, 130.
Conscience, For a tender, 216.
Contentment, For, 218.
Corner-stone Office, 95.
Cross, Benediction of a, 100.

Daughters of the King, For the, 110.
Deaconesses, For, 111.
Dead, Burial of the, 75.
Deaf and Dumb, For the, 159.
Death, For a happy, 219.
Despondent, For the, 71.
Departed, For the, 91.
Diligence, For, 217.
Diocese, For the, 114; for the Bishop of the, 115.
Discord, In times of, 155.
Divinity, For Students in, 157.
Dying, For the, 74.

Employer and the Employed, For the, 160.
Enemies, For love of friends and, 215.
Enlightenment, For, 214.
Eucharistic Prayers, 134.
Explorations, For, 161.

Family, Marriage in a, 151; at death in, 152; for absent members of, 151; prayers in the, 135; prayers for each day in the week in the, 141; special prayers of the, 148.
Faithfulness, For, 216.
Felicity, For eternal, 215.
Fellow-countrymen, For, 107.
Flag, At raising of a, 154.
Font, Benediction of a, 98.
Formalism, Against, 213.
Founders and Benefactors, For, 156.
Funeral Pall, Benediction of a, 103.

Gentleness, For, 217.
Gloria Christi, 73.
God, For love of, 218.
Guild Medals, Benediction of, 102.

Health, For recovery of, 70.
Heresy, Against, 212.
Home, For a new, 149; for an Orphan's, 158.
Holiness, For, 219.
Holy Communion Vessels, Benediction of, 97.
Holy Spirit, For the, 69.
Hospital, For an, 158.
Humility, For, 216.
Husband and Wife, For an, 149.

Illness, In a prolonged, 71.
Insincerity, Against, 213.
Jesus Christ, For Veneration of Name of, 213.
Judgment Day, For confidence in the, 216.
Judgments, Against uncharitable, 213.

Learning, For sanctified, 215.
Lenten Prayers, 208.
Love, For mutual, 148.

Marriage, Anniversary of a, 151.
Marriage Ring, Benediction of a, 102.
Matrimony, Solemnization of, 33.
Meeting, For a Vestry, 121.
Ministrations, For angelic, 70.
Ministry, For the increase of the, 109, 127.
Missions, Special prayers for, 106; for the Jews, 107; for fallen women, 108; for seamen, 108; for city, 109; for workers in city, 109; for colored people, 107; parochial, 122; for giving to, 111.
Missionary, For sending out a, 108; service, 104.
Mortality, For deliverance from sickness and, 167.

New Year's Day, Prayers for, 168.

Obedience, For, 216.
Organ, Benediction of an, 100.

Pain, For one in, 71.
Palms, Benediction of, 101.
Parish, For the, 118; for endowment of a, 119; in debt, 119; for anniversary of a, 120; for Guilds of, 131.
Passions, Against angry, 211.
Patience, For, 218.
Peace, For, 155, 166, 215.
Penitents, For confession of, 132.
Peril, For escape from, 167.
Persons, For neglected, 210.
Praise, For the spirit of, 217.
Prayer, Against coldness in, 212; for the spirit of, 214.
Presumption, Against, 213.
Pulpit, Benediction of a, 99.
Purity, For, 162.

Recovery, When there is no hope of, 72.
Rector, For a, 120; for a sick, 120; for a parish without a, 121.

Rectory, Benediction of a, 97.
Resignation, For, 152.
Rest, For, 215.
Retreat, For a clerical, 115.
Reverence for God's Name, 163; for the Lord's Day, 163.
Rood Screen, Benediction of a, 99.
Rulers and People, For, 153.

Saint Andrew, For Brotherhood of, 128.
Sanctuary Lamp, Benediction of a, 98.
Self-deception, Against, 212.
Self-examination, For, 217.
Service Books, Benediction of, 102.
School, For a, 157; for past members of, 157; for a reformatory, 158.
Sisterhoods, For, 111.
Sick, Visitation of the, 37; communion of the, 47; readings with, 57; special prayers for the, 69.
Sickness, For a minister's recovery from, 167.
Sin, For those we have led into, 210; for those who live in, 210; for a sense of, 214.
Sloth, Against, 212.
Sorrowing, For the, 90.
Spirit, For a child-like, 215.
Stability, For, 218.
State, For the, 153; for the Governor of, 153; for legislature of a, 153.
Students, For medical, 157.
Submission, For, 69.
Sunday School, For the, 124; for superintendent of, 124; for teachers of the, 125; for children of the, 126; for work of the, 127.
Surgical Operation, Before a, 71.

Temperance, For, 164.
Thankfulness, For, 218.
Thanksgiving, Harvest, 165; for recovery from sickness, 165; for a child's recovery from sickness, 166; for a safe return from Sea, 166; a general, 168.
Thoughts, Against wandering, 212.
Thoughtless, For the, 211.
Tongue, Against sins of the, 212.
Truthfulness, For, 214.

Vestments, Benediction of, 102.

Will, For one making a, 72.
Wisdom, For, 216.
Worldly, For the, 211.

Year, For the last day of the, 169.
Young Men, For, 128.

www.ingramcontent.com/pod-product-compliance
Lightning Source LLC
Chambersburg PA
CBHW021824230426

43669CB00008B/861